I0800461

POSTCARD HISTORY SERIES

# *Portland*

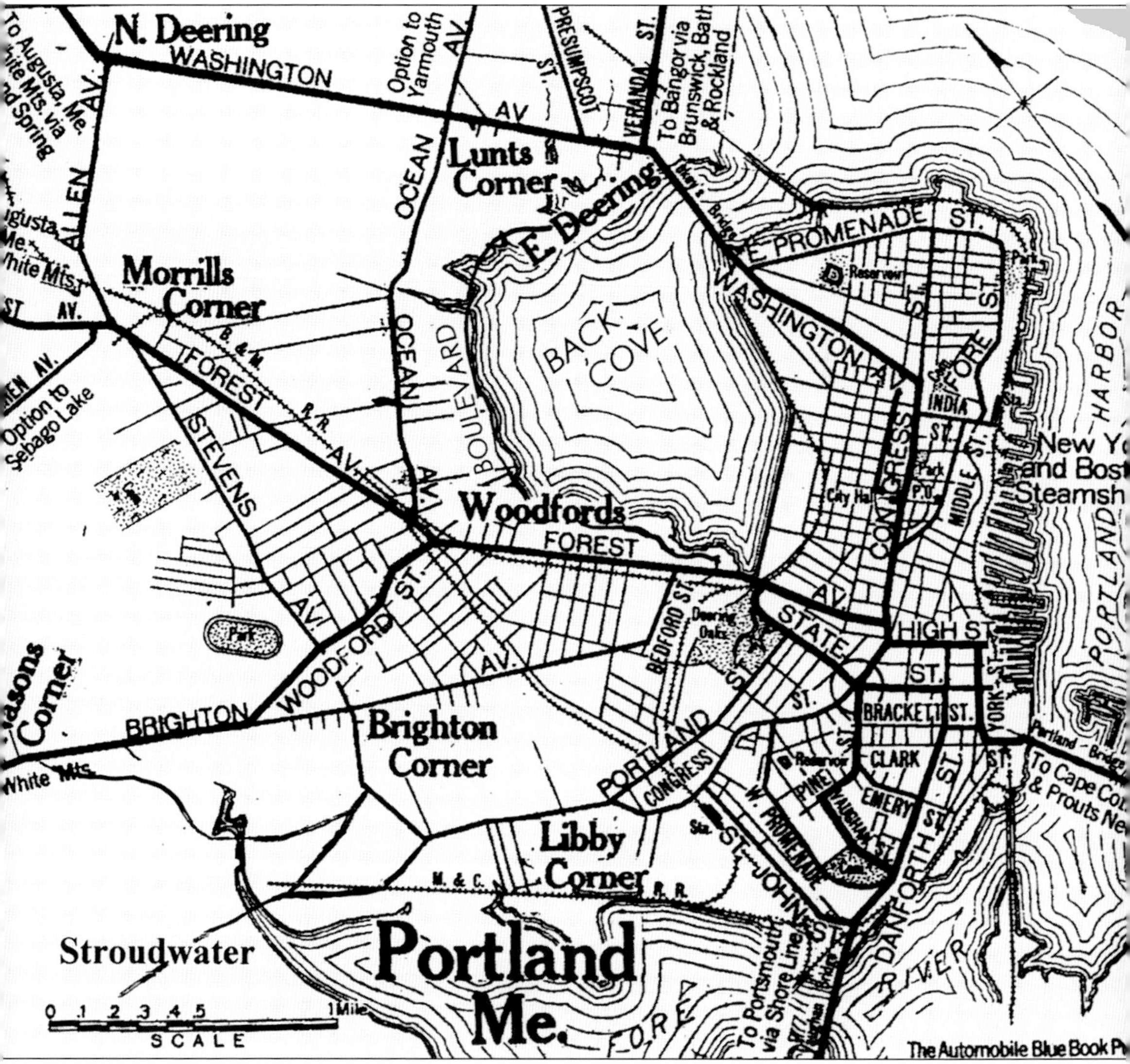


The city of Portland includes a number of islands; a peninsula; and adjacent territory, which was the city of Deering until its 1899 annexation. Publishers of the 1918 *Automobile Blue Book*, from which this map is adapted, had no interest in the islands and also omitted the northern and western limits of the city. However, most areas mentioned in the book are shown.

*On the front cover*: Please see page 10. (Courtesy of the Maine Historic Preservation Commission.)

*On the back cover*: A portion of Portland's bustling port appears in this *c.* 1900 view from the south side of the harbor. A great schooner, probably loaded with coal, heads toward its dock. Behind the vessel and to its left is the east end of the city waterfront, with a grain elevator and the wharves and loading chutes of the Grand Trunk Railway. On the skyline is mostly residential Munjoy Hill. (Courtesy of the Maine Historic Preservation Commission.)

POSTCARD HISTORY SERIES

# *Portland*

*Joyce K. Bibber and Earle G. Shettleworth Jr.*

ARCADIA
PUBLISHING

ISBN 978-0-7385-5033-6

Published by Arcadia Publishing
Charleston, South Carolina

Printed in the United States of America

Library of Congress Catalog Card Number: 2007923428

For all general information contact Arcadia Publishing at:
Telephone 843-853-2070
Fax 843-853-0044
E-mail sales@arcadiapublishing.com
For customer service and orders:
Toll-Free 1-888-313-2665

Visit us on the Internet at www.arcadiapublishing.com

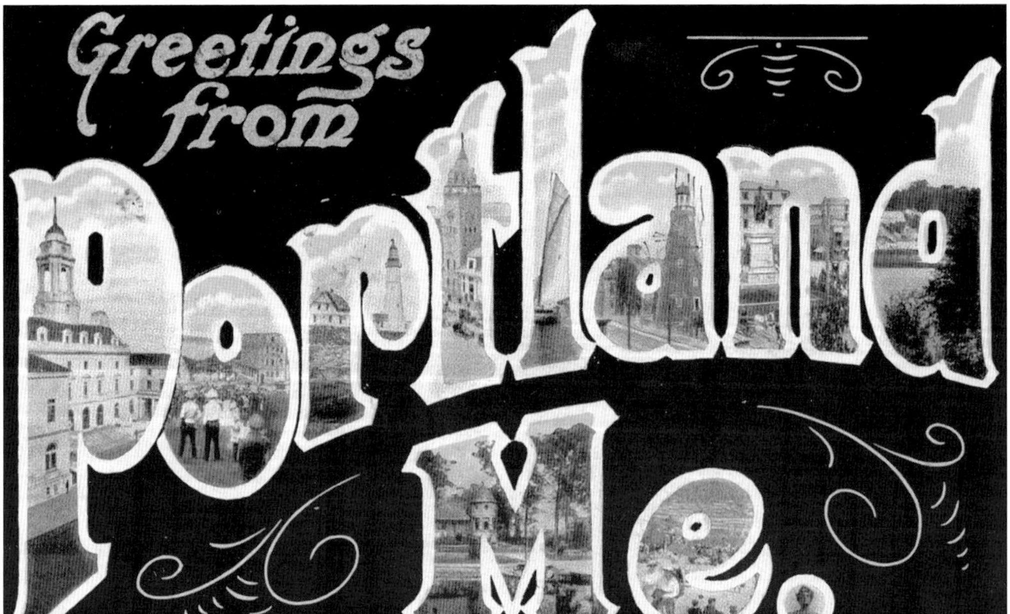

Novelty cards such as this one issued about 1912 by Chisholm Brothers were designed to highlight Portland's notable attractions, including Portland City Hall, Union Station, Portland Observatory, the Soldiers and Sailors Monument, and Deering Oaks.

# Contents

# ACKNOWLEDGMENTS

For help in preparing the introduction to this volume, the authors wish to acknowledge their debt to R. Brewster Harding and to his essay "Portland's Picture Post Card Pioneers," which appears in his book *Greetings from Maine*.

David Chaplin helped by providing information on the Portland Railroad Company, Riverton Park, and Cliff Island.

Most of the postcards that appear in this book are owned by the Maine Historic Preservation Commission in Augusta and are part of a large Portland collection that the commission acquired from Kenneth E. Thompson Jr. Thompson also furnished a few cards from his own collection (on pages 117, upper; 119, lower; and 121, upper), as did Greater Portland Landmarks (on pages 10, upper; 34, lower; 35, lower; and 114, lower).

Three previous Arcadia Publishing books that used Portland postcards, among other pictures, should be mentioned. Ruth S. Sargent's *The Casco Bay Islands* and Kimberly E. MacIsaac's *The Casco Bay Islands: 1850–2000* made it unnecessary to devote many pages to that area of Portland, while Frank H. Sleeper's *Portland* covered other aspects of the city from those found in this volume. In the few cases where duplication of images in those books may exist, the present authors have introduced these views to illustrate data that they see as vital to their story.

Finally, the authors dedicate this volume to the memory of Frances W. Peabody—historic preservationist, humanitarian, and good friend.

# Introduction

Portland's position as Maine's largest city is due to a combination of natural features, as well as to the drive of various leading men. Its peninsula is high and well drained and opens to a deepwater port, protected from the wildest ocean storms by a chain of islands. Farseeing citizens brought about a network of roads and railroads (also, briefly, a canal), which connected the port to the state's hinterland, as well as to other states and to Canada. They and others also developed a variety of manufacturing concerns, giving employment to new arrivals—from the nearby countryside, from elsewhere in the United States, and from abroad. A diverse population promoted a range of cultural activities. Moreover, the picturesque location encouraged other people to visit, making tourism another industry.

Picture postcards helped spread information about the area's beauty and points of interest, and it was a Portland man who first brought such postcards to the United States. Adam Leighton, a manager of the Chisholm Brothers firm, had long been involved with publicizing the local area through pictures, as the company specialized in view books illustrated first with lithographs and then with black-and-white photographs. Familiar with pictorial postcards used in Europe, Leighton purchased sheets of one-cent postals from the government and had single-color pictures put on the side not reserved for an address. The first were in 1888. He later had others printed in Germany. They bore the Chisholm company name.

Leighton's cards were not especially popular at first, but five years later, colored cards were used to advertise the World Columbian Exposition in Chicago, and Leighton recognized the potential. In a deal soon struck with the German House of Frey, Leighton arranged to have photographs taken in various New England scenic spots—to be applied to similar cards and colorized abroad, labeled as from Leighton and Frey. The colored cards had more appeal, and the postcard business grew. Soon Portland photographer George W. Morris had cards printed by a different German firm, and other companies followed suit.

Government regulations on mailed cards were eventually relaxed, under pressure from the growing number of businesses with an interest in the picture cards. After an act of Congress in May 1898, it was no longer necessary to use the preprinted postal cards, as the post office would allow 1¢ stamps to be applied to any postcard. Previously any card not on government-stamped stock—except for printed advertisements with no handwriting—had required higher postage. The lower postal rate encouraged the public to use them, even though the entire back had to be reserved for an address. Printers frequently left space for a short message next to the illustration (see page 9). In 1907, postcards were allowed to have divided backs, with half to be used for a message. Portland firms continued to do well.

The 1898 act had led to the issuing of more pictorial cards by a wider number of companies, and many were published in the United States, both in color and in black (or sepia) and white. American printers, including the newer firms working in Maine, were aided by the 1910 tariff, which raised prices of imported cards, so that even the Leighton firm, now directed by Hugh C. Leighton, changed tactics and joined with a New York company to print postcards in the United States. The quality of those pictures was lower, as were colorful cards from other American companies. Some were not even photographs but were drawings made from photographs.

Although colored postcards continue to be printed, aided by improvements in color photography, they are less valued today than they were when pictures of faraway (and nearby) places were a novelty. In the early years of the 20th century, many people collected the cards, and special albums were available, with slits arranged to hold the card corners. The era of the postcard craze ended sometime around World War I. By then, the color seemed less necessary. Even before that time, it was apparently possible for camera enthusiasts to print their own cards or to have them printed locally on card stock. (Comments on some of them, as well as the subject matter, suggest amateur work.)

Useful as they are, picture postcards have some limits as historical documents. Not only were few of their photographs made during the years before 1888, but they also tended not to be event oriented, with occasional exceptions (see page 62). Postcards took time to produce, and their manufacturers wanted long-term appeal. Thus, they usually left coverage of current events to newspapers.

The same desire for general appeal led their photographers away from most residential districts to the public areas frequented by local residents and visitors alike. Sometimes a bent toward showing the picturesque led to cleaning up images—or to enhancing them. Confusing backgrounds might be brushed out—although few went as far as the owners of the Roma Cafe (see page 10), which actually stands close by similar homes on either side. Street scenes were commonly touched up by erasing a few electric poles and wires so that trolley cars seemed to run without their power sources. The practice was so general as to make unusual a view of Middle Street with a web of wires overhead (see page 99). Some publishers wiped out advertising signs. Others may have added them—or at least have increased their legibility.

For example, compare the picture of Monument Square on page 10 with that on page 50. It is difficult to accept either of these views as wholly correct. Positions of individual people show that the same negative was used, but differently. The second card has been cleaned up. Edwards and Walker (in what was formerly the United States Hotel) did have advertising on the front of its building, and there was other advertising nearby. This view may well have been touched up, with the signs reinserted, even enhanced. One trolley car and a few nearby people have been erased from the neater version, along with many poles, but were all the poles in this version really there—and were they as tall as shown? A flagpole was actually on the building to the left but not protruding from a window—and the flag shown is too large.

Almost anything could be faked, of course. Flags were inserted as a touch of color or simply to fill in an empty sky; artists sometimes drew them to be much larger than would be suited to the site, just as novelty cards unabashedly offered examples of fish big enough to be ridden or of single potatoes filling a railroad car. Probably nobody accepted these last as fact, but what about an airplane hovering low over Union Station (see page 105)? Moreover, who, without a daylight version (see page 112) with which to compare the boat as well as the couple in the arbor, would doubt a lovely darkened moonlight view of the Presumpscot River? (See also page 77.)

Although not an issue in this volume, one should also remember that early photographs were taken in black and white and then sent elsewhere for printing and colorization. Unless the senders were very explicit, paint—or even brick—colors came back from abroad looking quite unlike the original. Henry Wadsworth Longfellow's birthplace can hardly have been repainted in the numbers of colors depicted in different cards, and Portland High School, built with a light tan-colored brick, was shown in red brick on one early card.

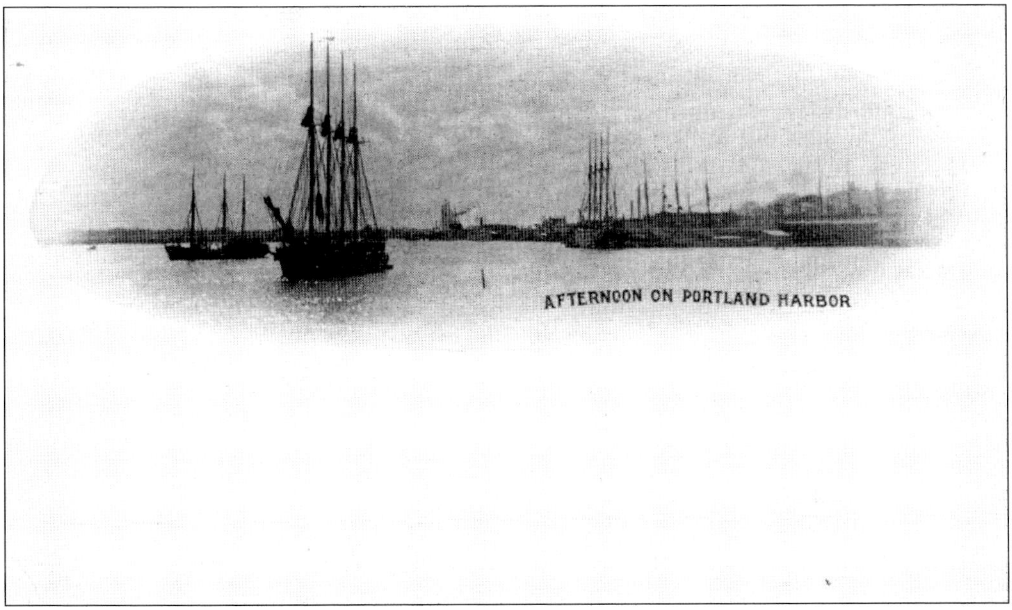


This early monochrome postcard (with space for writing) shows the harbor when masts from three- and four-masted schooners pierced the skyline. Even the address side, shown below, included scenes.

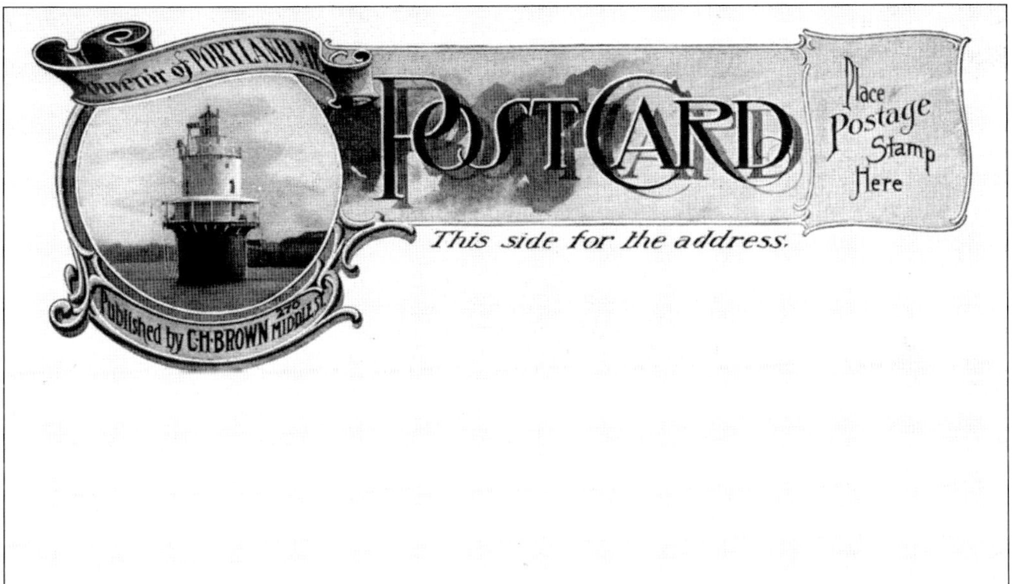

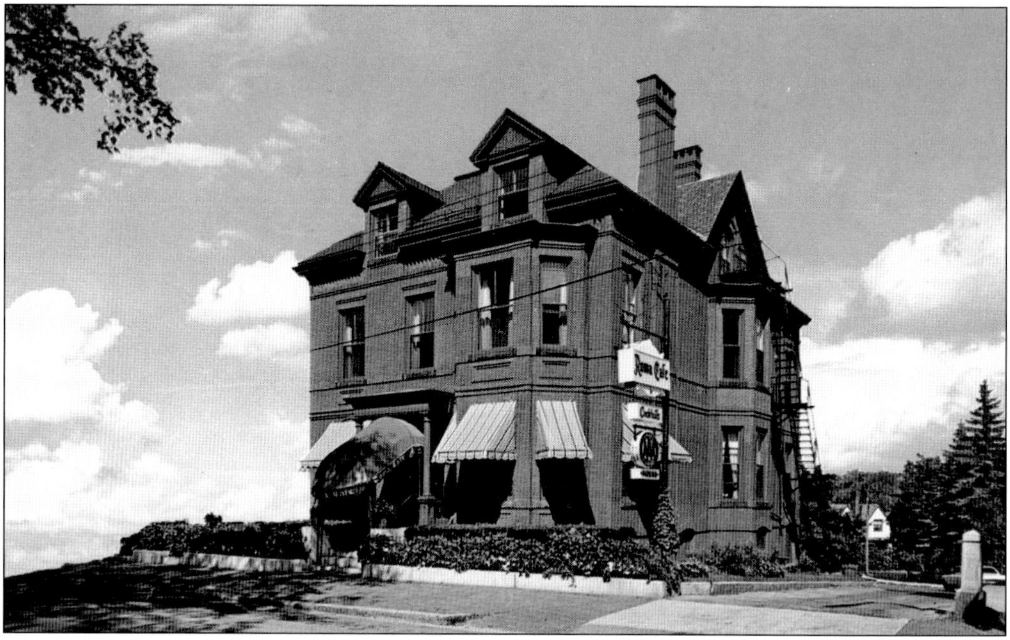

The Roma Cafe, built as the J. Henry Rines home in 1887 and turned into an upscale restaurant in the mid-1930s, is actually set among other buildings of about the same era, but the owner obviously wished to spotlight his business and not those next door.

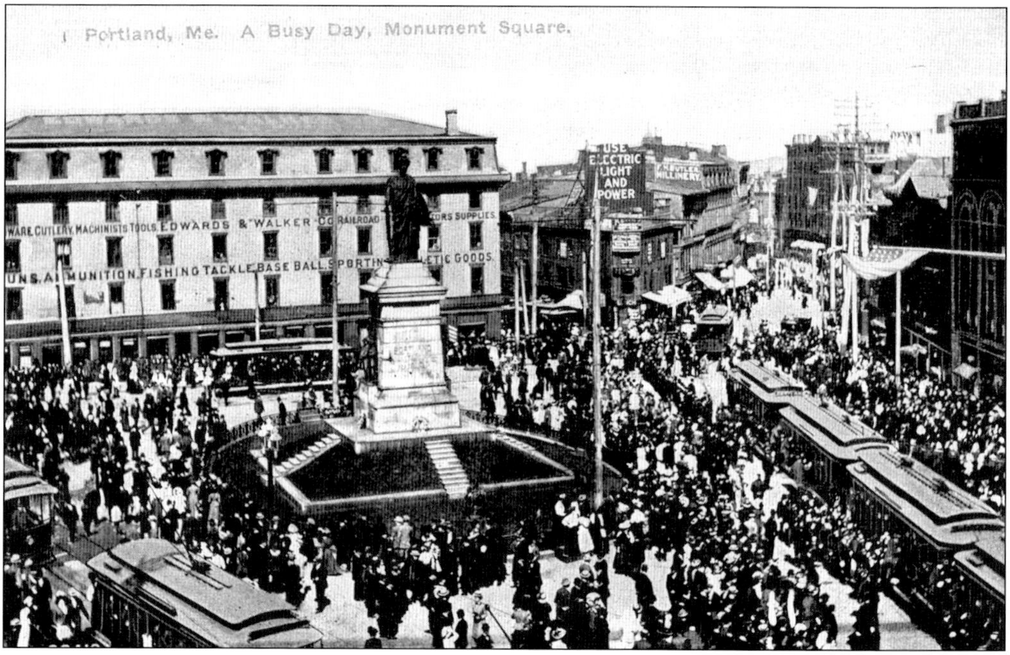


This scene of crowded Monument Square appears to have some of the writings on buildings enhanced and extra tall poles inserted. The flag on the right is oversize—and seems to extend from a window. Compare it with the cleaned-up version on page 50.

# *One*

# History

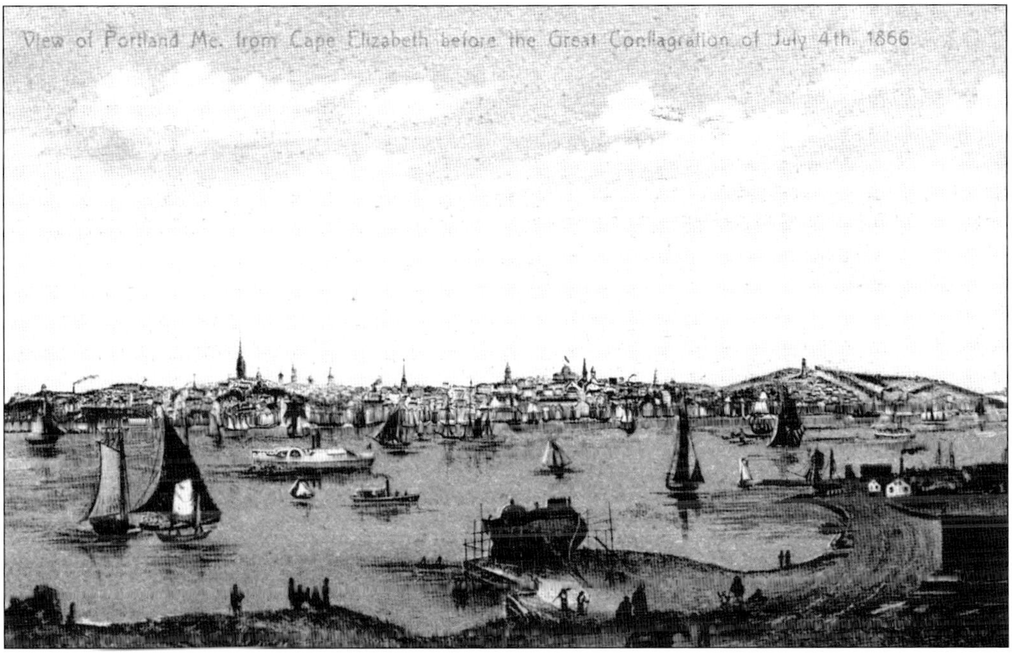


Although neither photographers nor postcards were around in the beginning, a city's history can be traced in cards showing paintings or drawings, monuments to early events, or remaining old buildings. More than 50 years after the great conflagration of July 4, 1866, this postcard was issued as a reminder of how Portland appeared shortly before the center of the city was laid waste by the worst urban fire up to its time in American history. The drawing was based on mid-19th-century prints. On the eve of its destruction, Portland boasted a population of 30,000, many of whom were engaged in the maritime activities symbolized by the busy harbor and the vessel under construction on the ways of a shipyard in Cape Elizabeth, now South Portland.

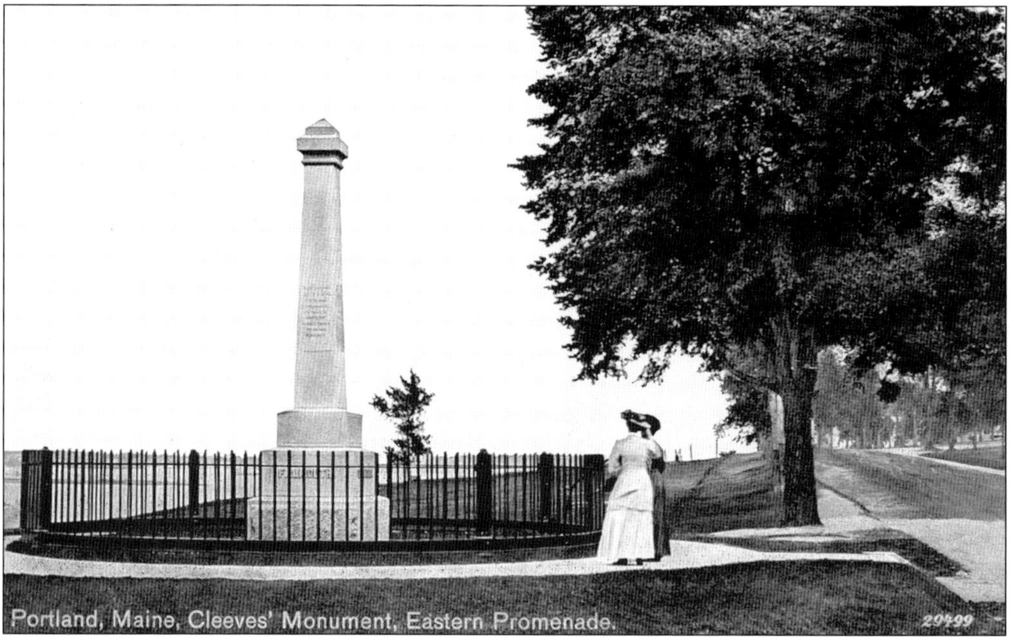


Located on the Eastern Promenade opposite the beginning of Congress Street, this granite monument was erected in 1883 to honor George Cleeve and Richard Tucker, who first settled the Portland peninsula in 1632. A recent statue of Cleeve overlooks the harbor on the property of the Portland Company on Fore Street, near his home site.

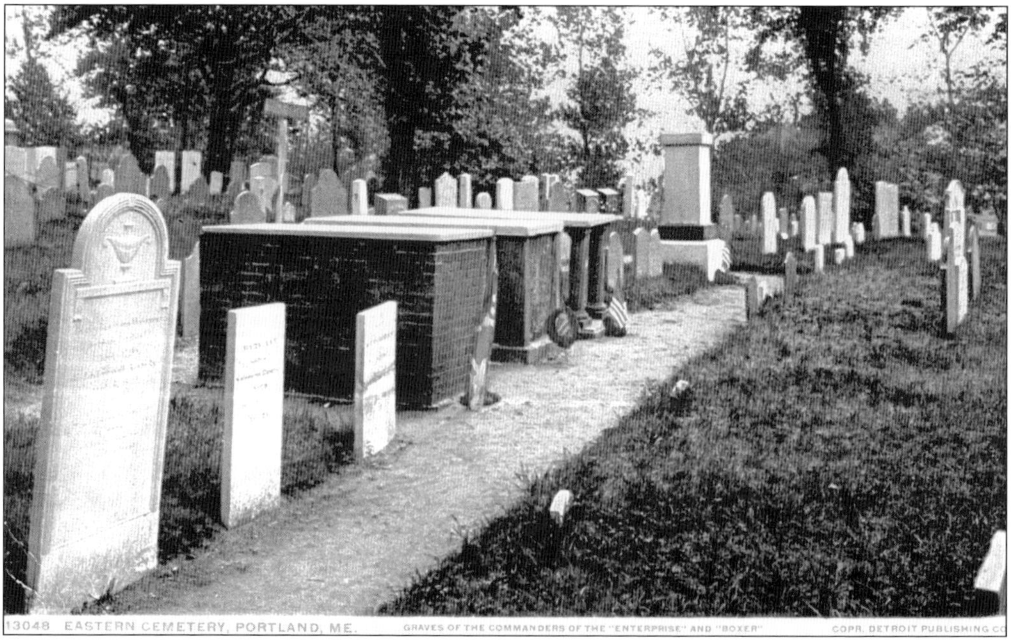


Located on Congress Street at the foot of Munjoy Hill, Eastern Cemetery dates back to the 17th century. In 1858, the city suspended most burials there. At the center of this view are the monuments of three naval officers killed in the battle between the British *Boxer* and the American *Enterprise* in September 1813. Both captains died and are buried side by side.

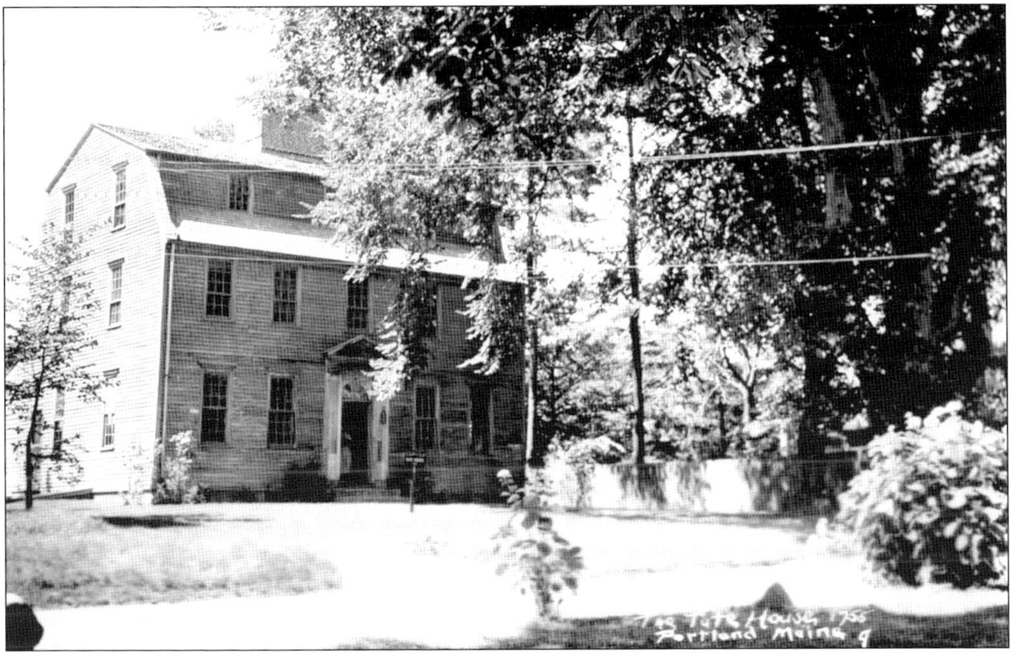


The 1755 George Tate House in Stroudwater is a rare example of a pre-Revolutionary home in the Portland area. It features fine woodwork on the interior. Tate came to Stroudwater from London about 1750 to direct procurement of pine masts for the Royal Navy. In 1931, the National Society of the Colonial Dames of America restored Tate's residence as a historic house museum.

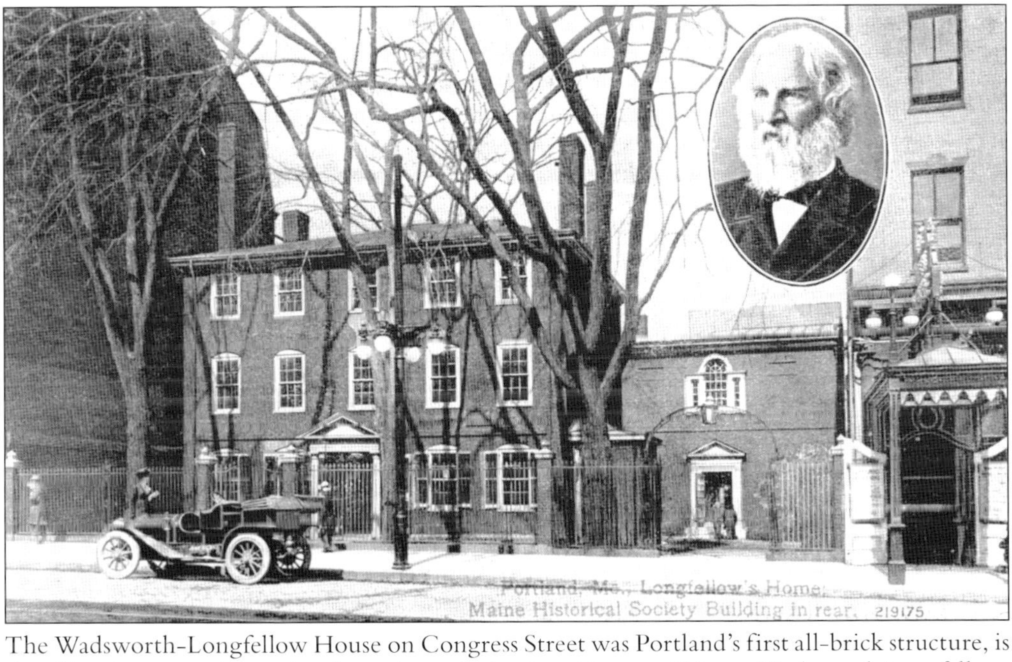


The Wadsworth-Longfellow House on Congress Street was Portland's first all-brick structure, is the oldest house on the peninsula, and was the boyhood home of Henry Wadsworth Longfellow. Built in 1785–1786 by Peleg Wadsworth, the poet's grandfather, the house was enlarged in 1815. In 1901, Anne Longfellow Pierce willed it to the Maine Historical Society, which maintains it as a museum.

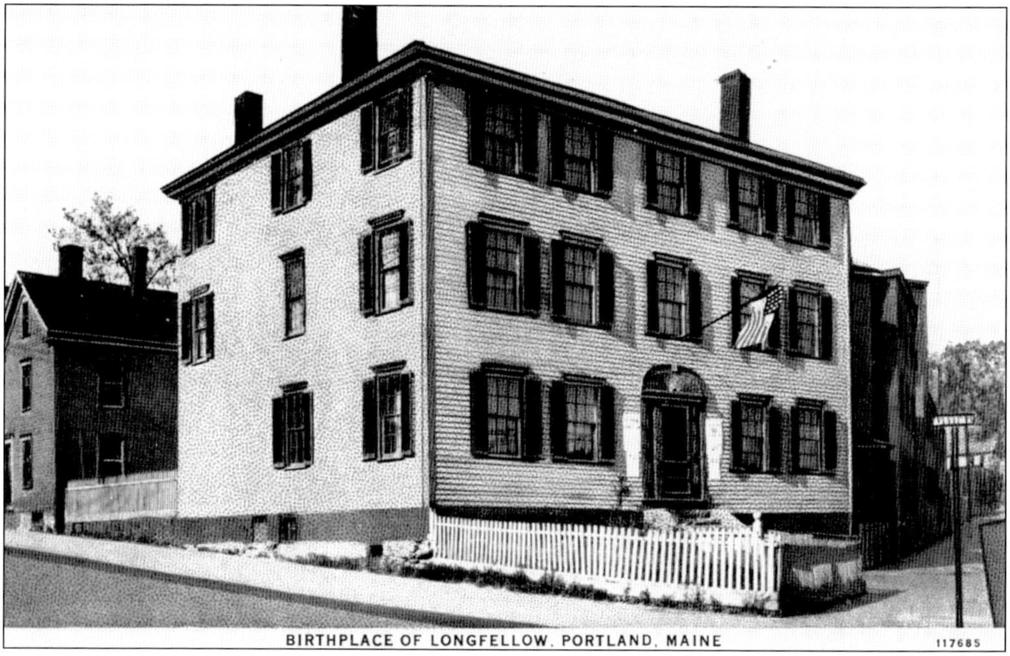


Henry Wadsworth Longfellow was born in this house at Fore and Hancock Streets in 1807 but soon moved to his grandfather's home. Reflecting the widespread enthusiasm for Longfellow's poetry, the International Longfellow Society acquired the property in 1914 and opened it as a literary shrine. Tastes in poetry changed, later efforts to preserve the house failed, and it was torn down in 1955.

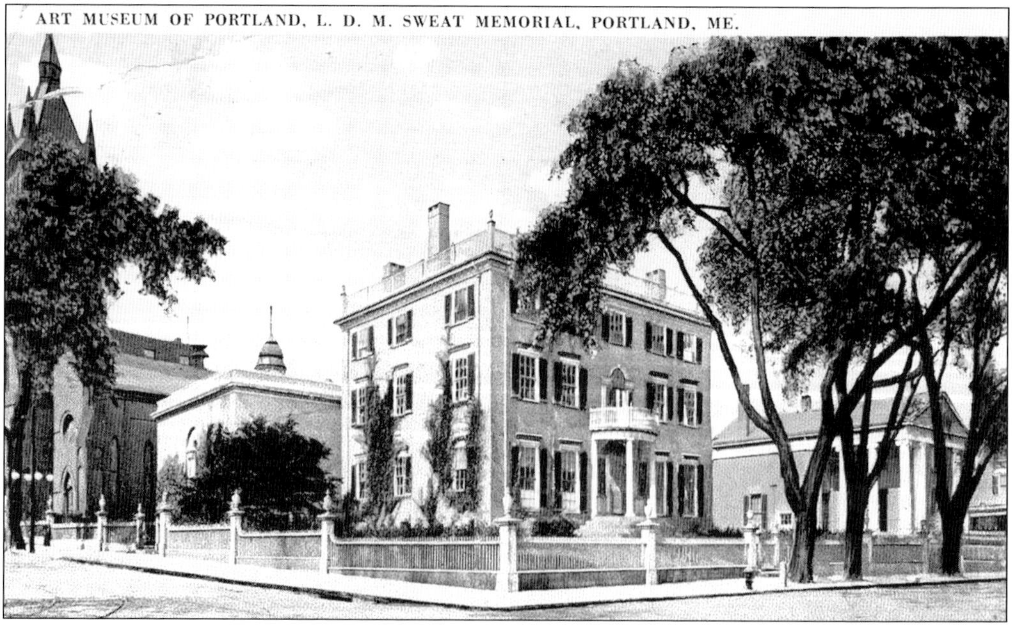


Portland's maritime prosperity between the Revolution and the 1807 embargo was reflected in the construction of numerous large Federal mansions. Hugh McLellan's home at the corner of Spring and High Streets was built by John Kimball Sr. in 1800. Since 1908, it has been part of the Portland Museum of Art, which added the Sweat Memorial Gallery, at the left, in 1911.

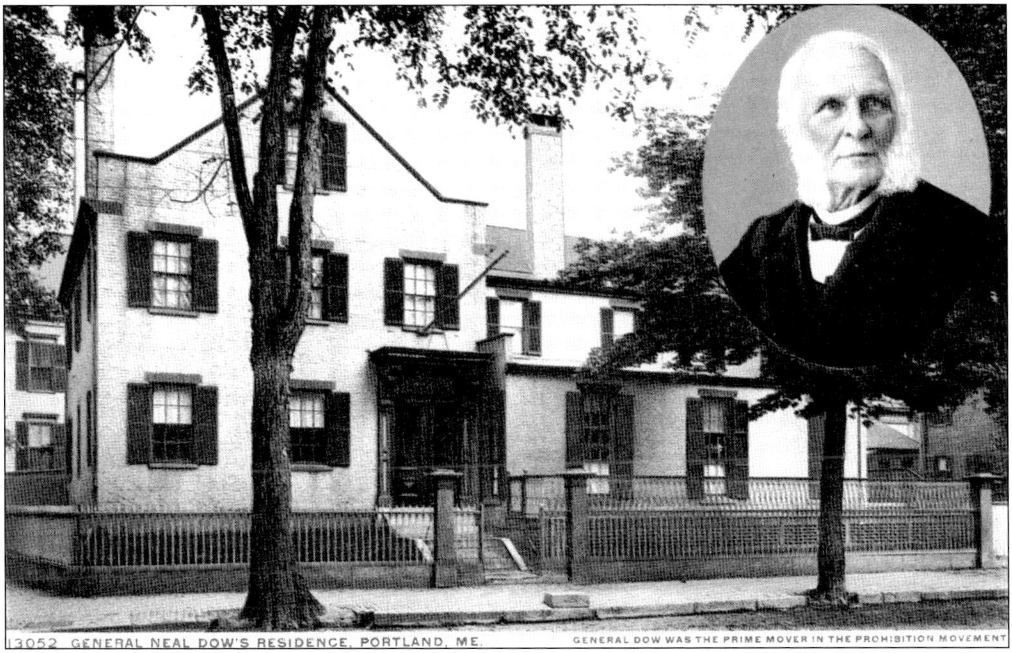


Neal Dow built his brick home on Congress Street in 1829 and died there in 1897 at the age of 93. Dow led the effort to adopt the nation's first state prohibition law in 1851 and was also active in antislavery and women's suffrage movements. He served twice as mayor of Portland, rose to brigadier general in the Civil War, and headed the Prohibition Party ticket in 1880.

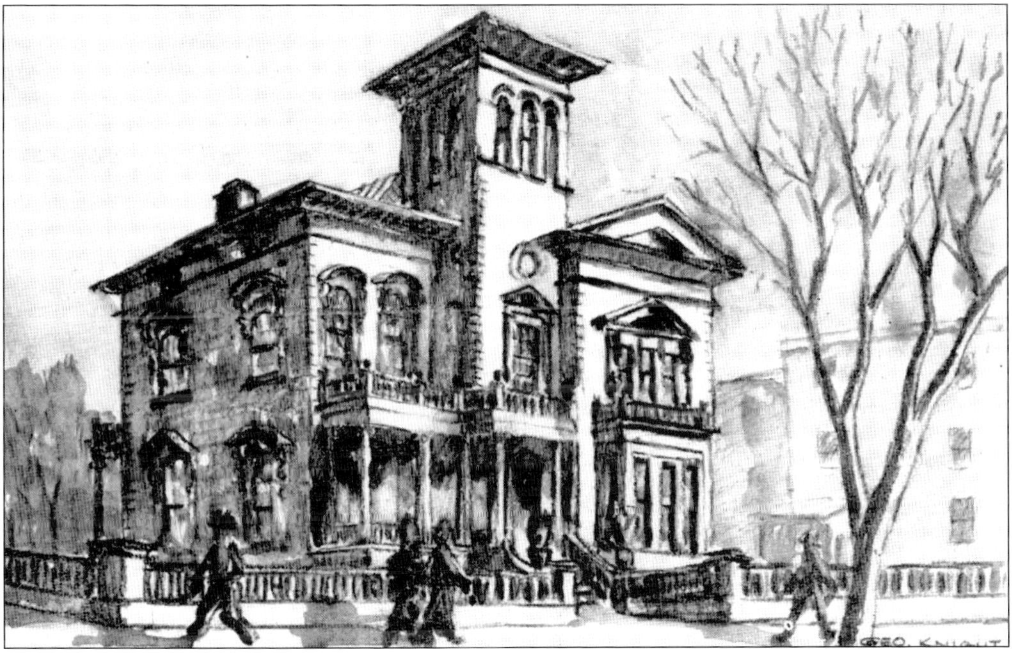

Maine-born Ruggles Sylvester Morse made a fortune as a hotelier in New Orleans, then built this brownstone villa at Danforth and Park Streets as a summer residence in 1858–1860. Henry Austin of New Haven was the architect. The Libby family, owners after 1893, preserved the elaborate interior decor and furnishings. Since 1941 the Victoria Mansion has been open to the public.

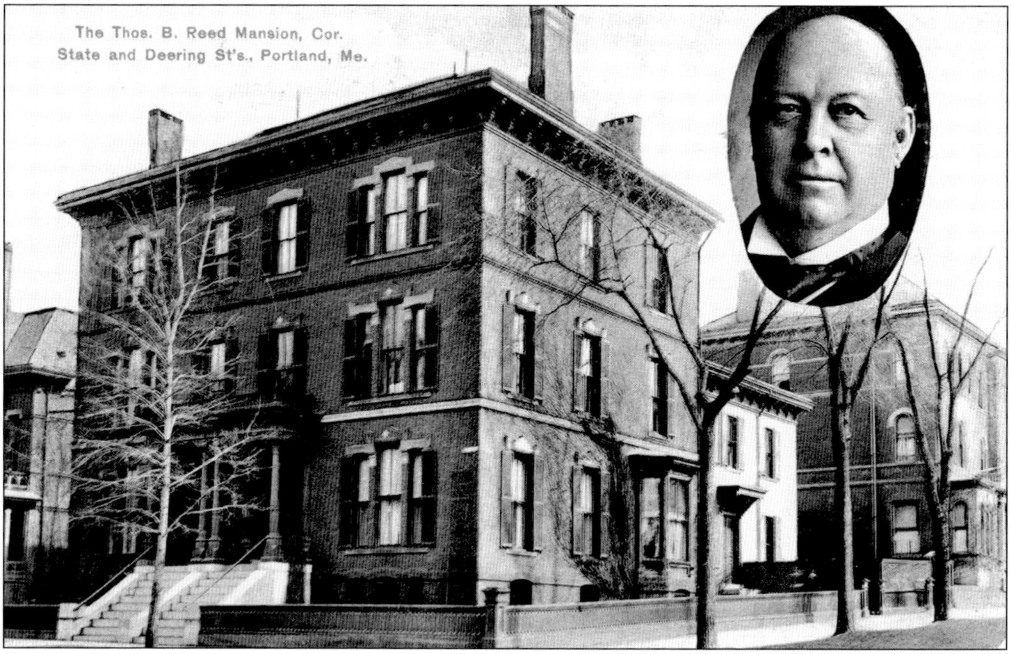


The right half of this brick double house at Deering and State Streets was the home of Thomas Brackett Reed from 1888 until his death in 1902. Born in Portland in 1839, Reed served as a congressman from Maine between 1876 and 1899. In 1889, he became Speaker of the House of Representatives and instituted major procedural changes, the effects of which are felt to this day.

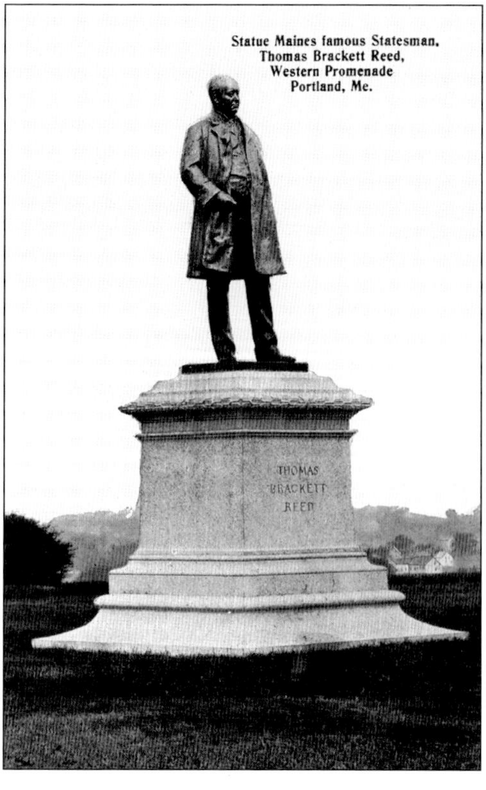


A bronze statue of Thomas Brackett Reed, standing at the head of West Street on the Western Promenade, was dedicated in 1910. Created by Burr C. Miller, it captures the imposing appearance of the six-foot two-inch, 275-pound congressman whose domination of the House earned him the title "Czar Reed." He was a figure to be reckoned with in the politics of his day.

Standing atop Munjoy Hill since 1807, the 82-foot octagonal tower known as the Portland Observatory was built under the direction of Capt. Lemuel Moody to observe and signalize shipping in the harbor. A system of flags told owners when a ship had been spotted so all could be readied for its arrival. In 1939, Moody's descendants gave this unique landmark to the city.

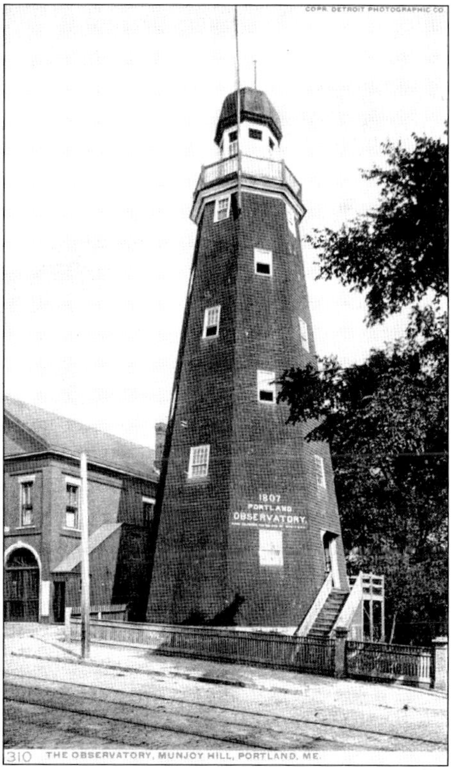


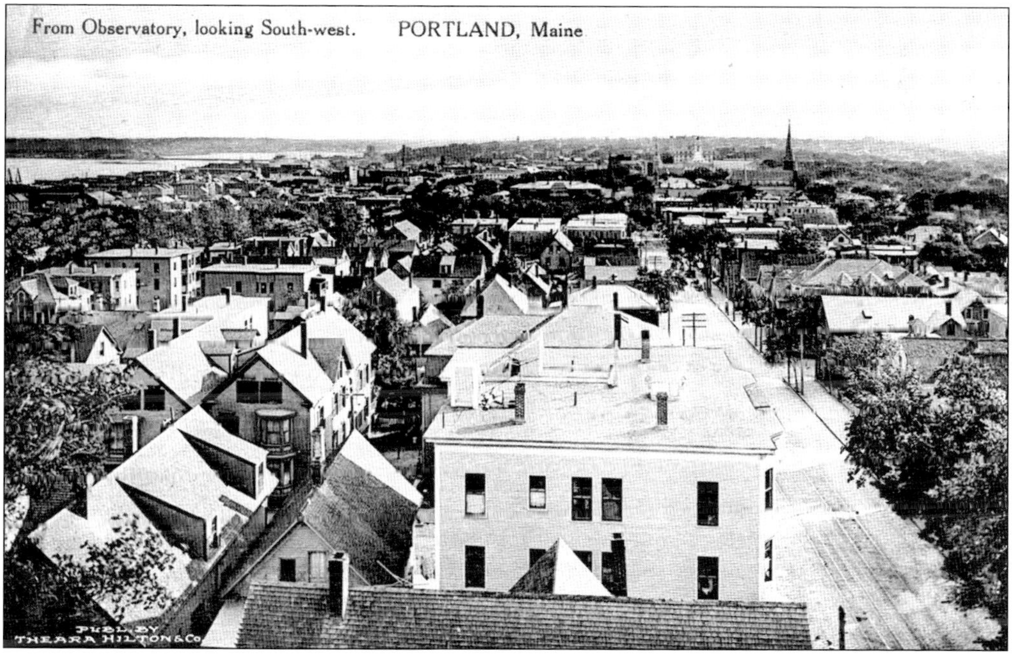


This view from the Portland Observatory shows how densely developed the slopes of Munjoy Hill had become by the early 20th century. Until the fire of 1866, the land between the Portland Observatory and Eastern Cemetery was used for grazing cattle, training militia, and public recreation. All this changed as the city's population expanded and multifamily dwellings were needed.

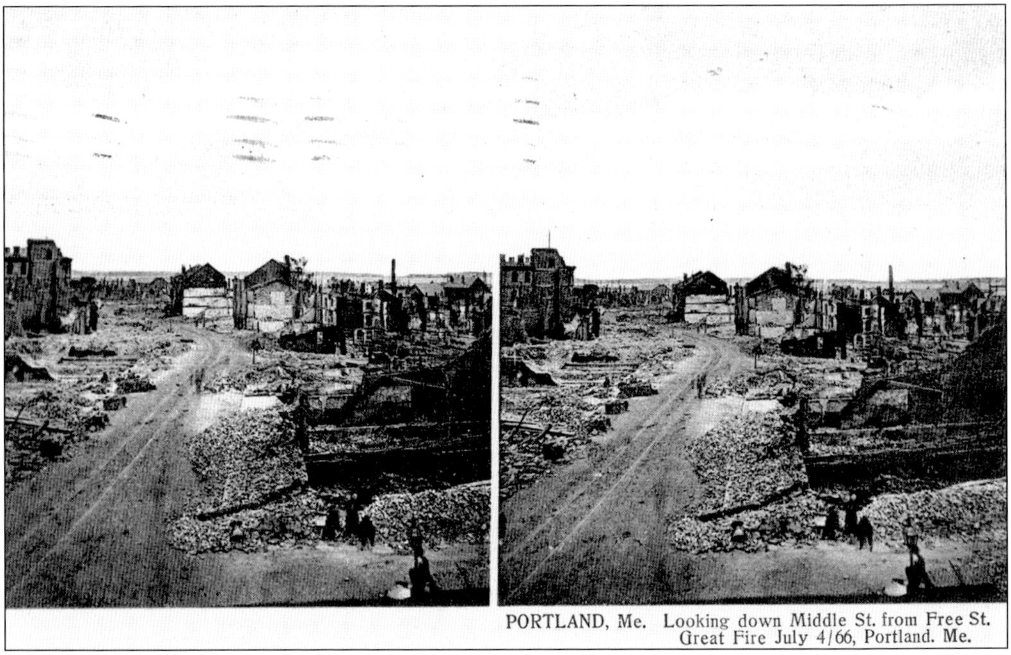


About four decades after the great fire of July 4, 1866, a few stereo views of the ruins made by Boston photographer John P. Soule were reproduced as postcards. Soule began recording the devastation of the city with his camera eight days after the event. This view looking east on Middle Street from Free Street has only a handful of burned-out shells of buildings left standing.

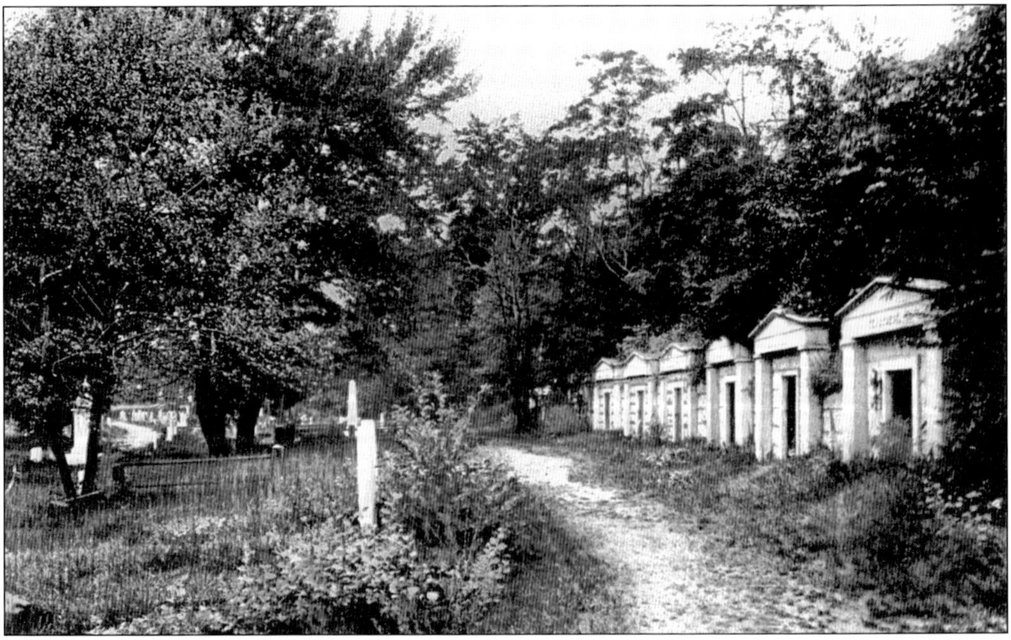

Needing a second cemetery on the peninsula, the city acquired 10 acres at Vaughan and Danforth Streets in 1829. It became Western Cemetery. Used mostly from 1830 to 1890, the cemetery accommodated 3,000 burials. This view shows the series of granite tombs built into the hill on the north side of the cemetery, including one owned by the Longfellow family.

# *Two*

# THE ISLANDS

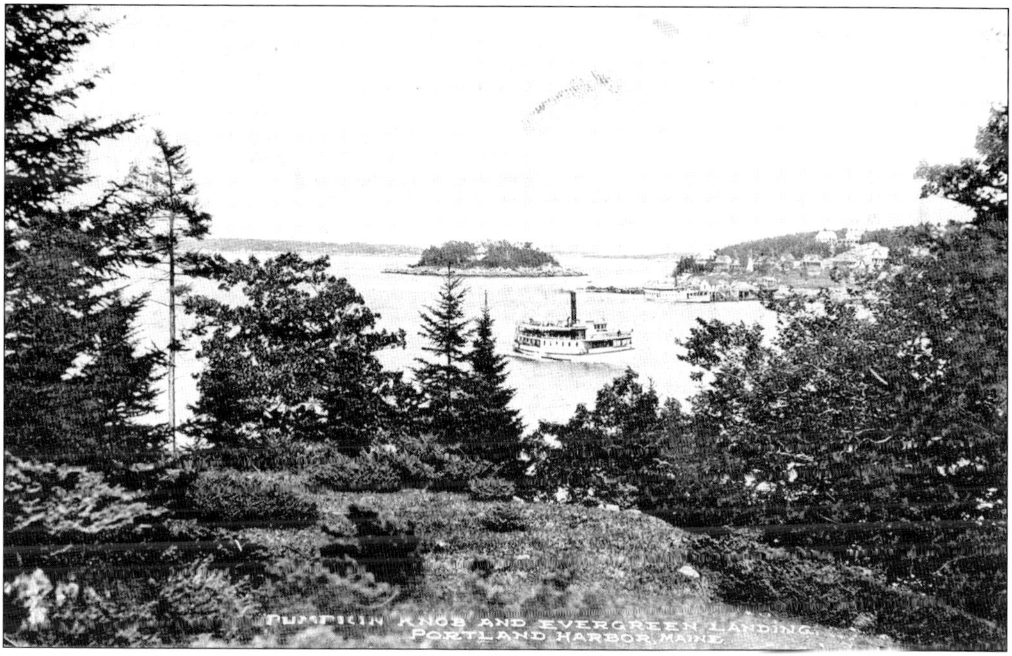


Most of the line of islands separating Portland's harbor from the outer ocean came within the boundaries of the city. Some were very small, but Peaks, Long, and Cliff Islands had numerous year-round residents early in the 20th century. Hope, Great Diamond, and Little Diamond Islands then had one resident family each, not counting military personnel. A few people maintained small farms, and many men fished. Various families supplemented other incomes by catering to visitors and summer residents, a large number of whom lived on the nearby mainland the rest of the year. With a good ferry service, summer residents could remain in close touch with city businesses. Above, a ferry passes between Diamond Island and the northernmost of the three landings on Peaks Island. Tiny Pumpkin Knob, in the center of the picture, held one summer residence.

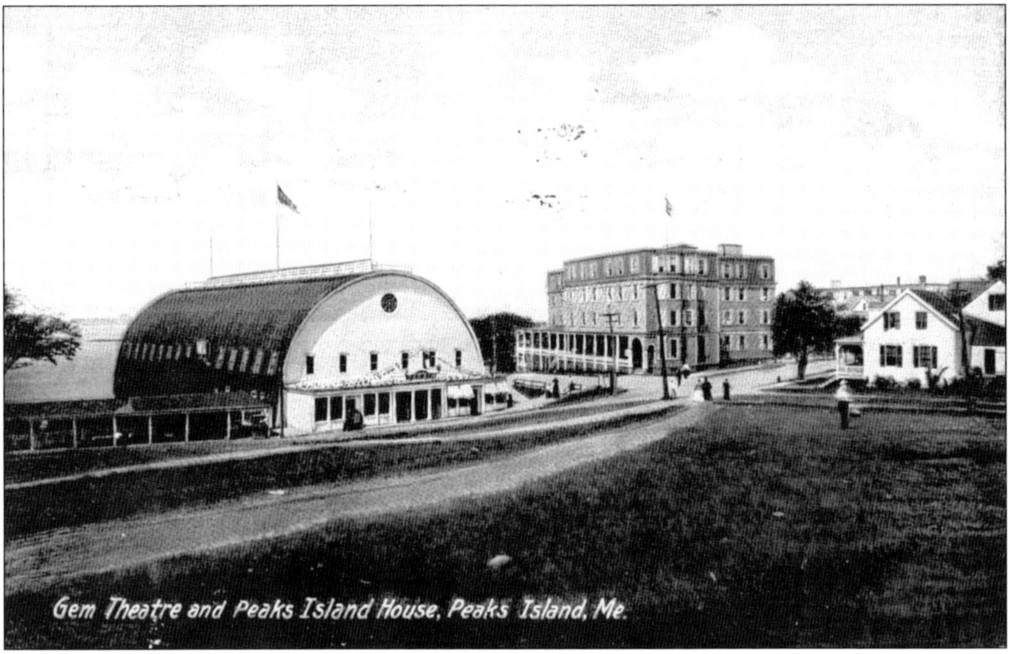


Peaks Island is the most populated and the closest to the downtown of the residential islands. Its people in the late 19th century erected summer hotels and attractions for day-trippers from the mainland. The Gem Theatre, constructed as a roller-skating rink in the 1880s, was turned into a summer theater in 1891. It sat among year-round homes at Forest City Landing.

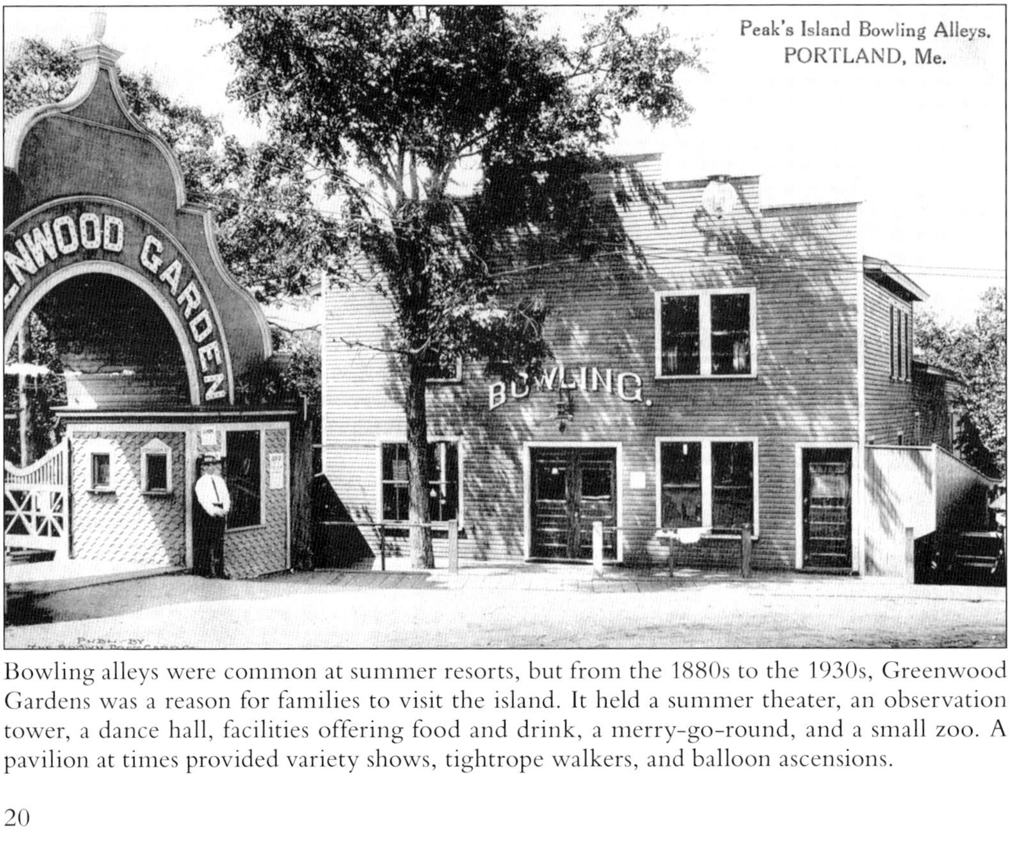


Bowling alleys were common at summer resorts, but from the 1880s to the 1930s, Greenwood Gardens was a reason for families to visit the island. It held a summer theater, an observation tower, a dance hall, facilities offering food and drink, a merry-go-round, and a small zoo. A pavilion at times provided variety shows, tightrope walkers, and balloon ascensions.

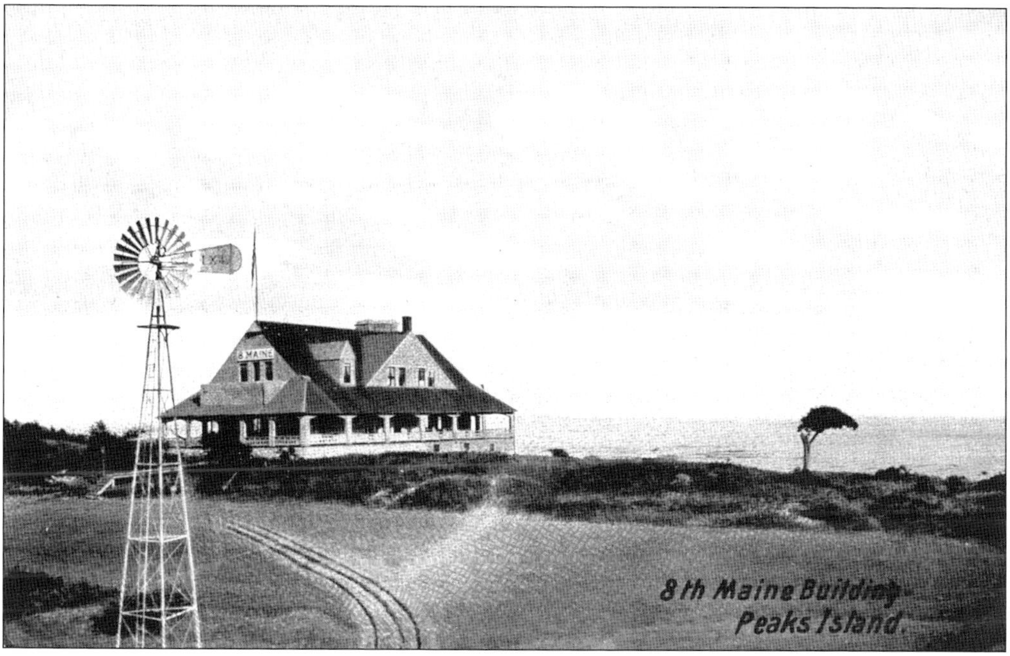


To the right is the much-photographed "Pair Tree." The building in the background is the 8th Maine Regiment Association Memorial Building, where regimental survivors and their families could take vacations. The 5th Maine had a similar building nearby, while veterans of four other Civil War regiments shared two cottages on nearby Long Island.

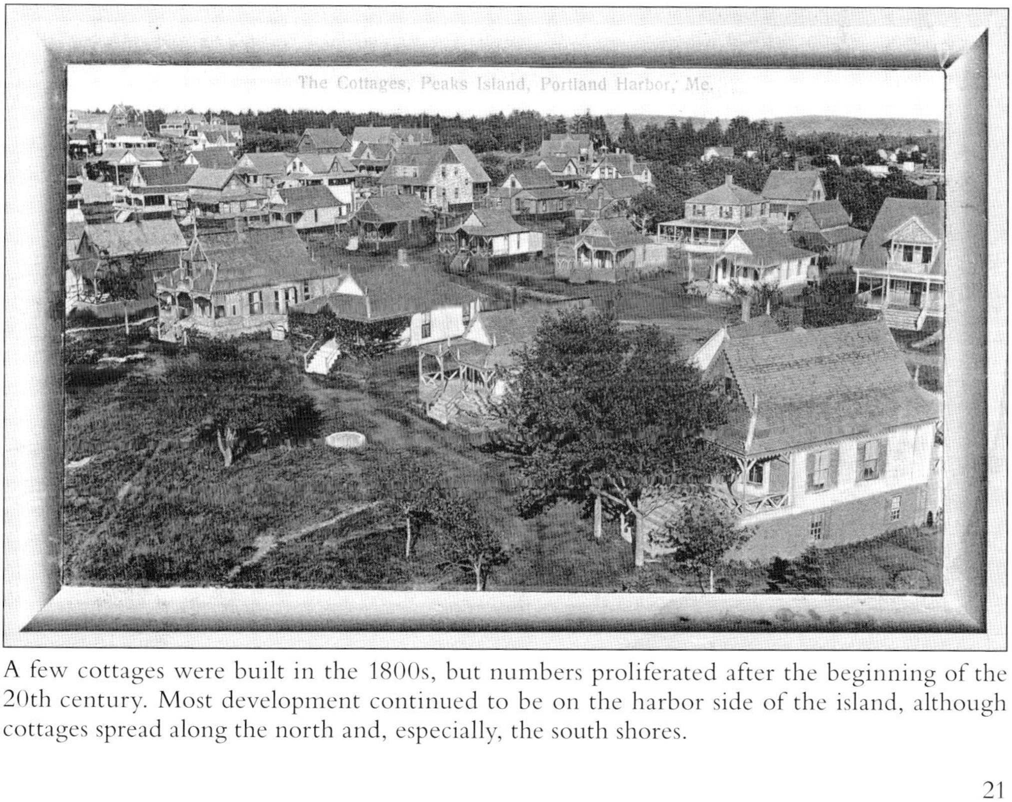


A few cottages were built in the 1800s, but numbers proliferated after the beginning of the 20th century. Most development continued to be on the harbor side of the island, although cottages spread along the north and, especially, the south shores.

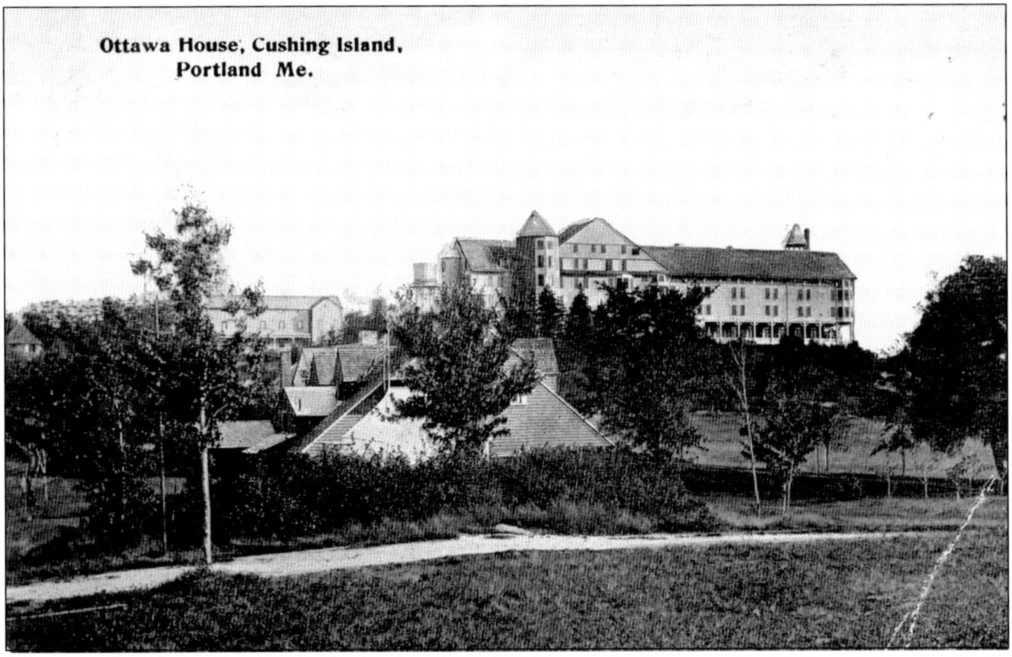


Cushing's Island was purchased by Lemuel Cushing, who built a large brick hotel there in 1862. He called it Ottawa House, hoping to attract a Canadian clientele. He and his sons increased the size of the structure and added small cottages around it. Large lots were sold for other summer homes. After the hotel burned in 1917, the island remained a colony of summer cottages.

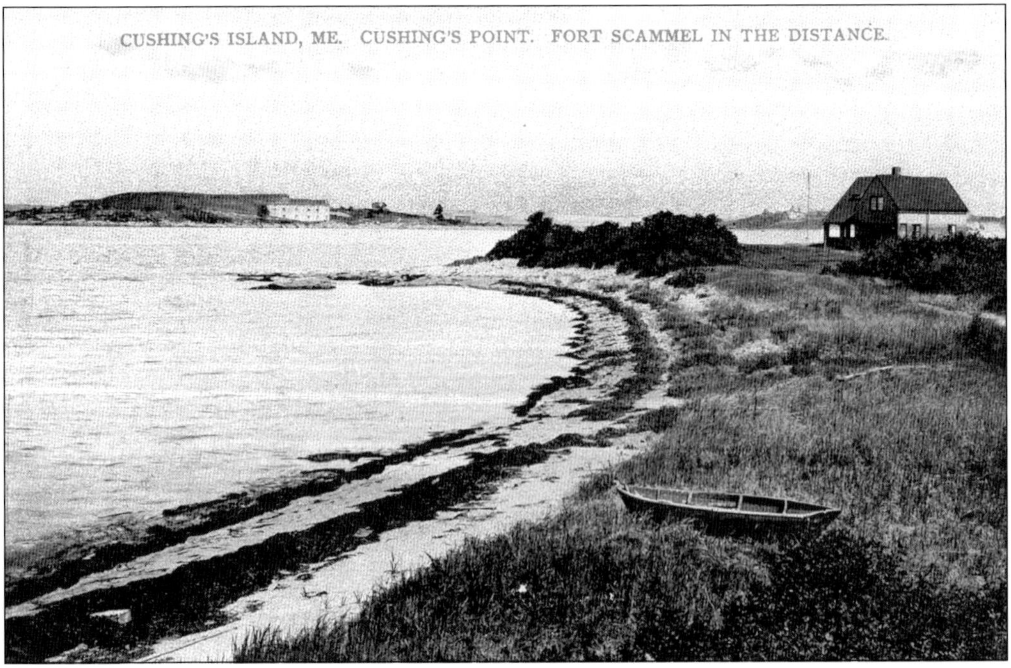


The William Bailey cottage on Cushing's Island is just one of many built in the late 1880s and designed by John Calvin Stevens. It is on the east shore, looking toward House Island, on the left, with its fort, and Peaks Island, on the right.

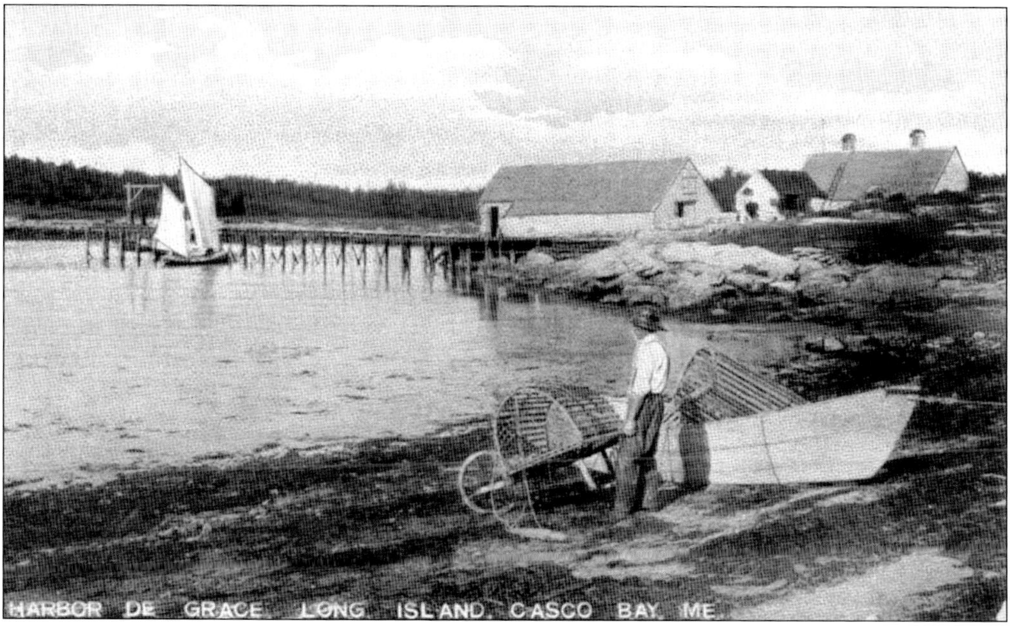


Long Island is larger than Peaks but has fewer inhabitants and is somewhat farther away from the city wharves. A picture of Harbor de Grace, a lovely cove on the outer (east) side of the island, suggests that fishing remained a more important occupation there than on islands with more frequent ferry service. A part of Portland at that time, the island became independent in 1993.

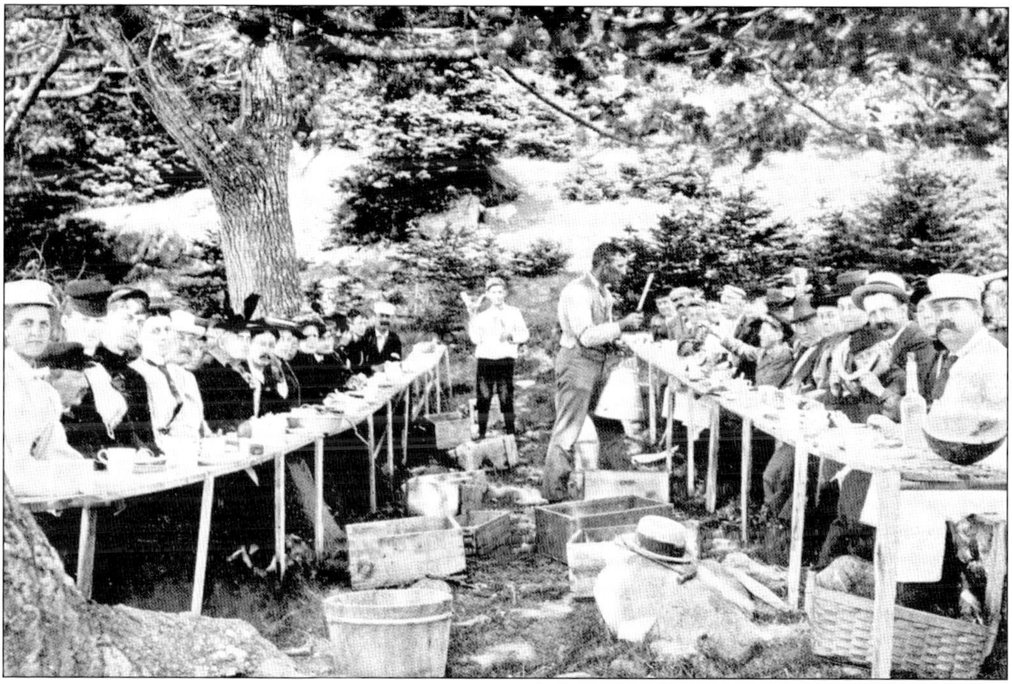

Fish—and shellfish—had their own attractions for tourists, and a favorite indulgence for many visitors was a clambake. This one took place on Long Island in 1896 and was photographed by George W. Morris. The narrow tables must have been erected for the purpose, designed to facilitate serving the crowd.

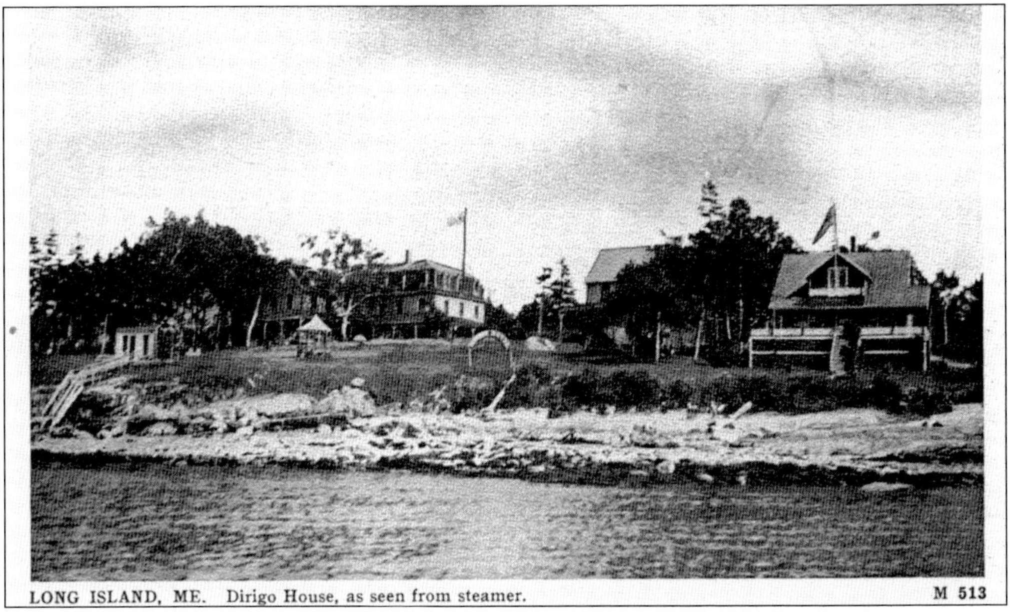


Long Island also had a range of boardinghouses, cottages, and summer hotels. The Dirigo House on Island Avenue was owned and operated from around 1880 through the 1920s by the Perry family, who lived elsewhere in non-summer months. Other hotels boasted pavilions for clambakes—or for dancing. Note how close to the northwest shore the steamer ran.

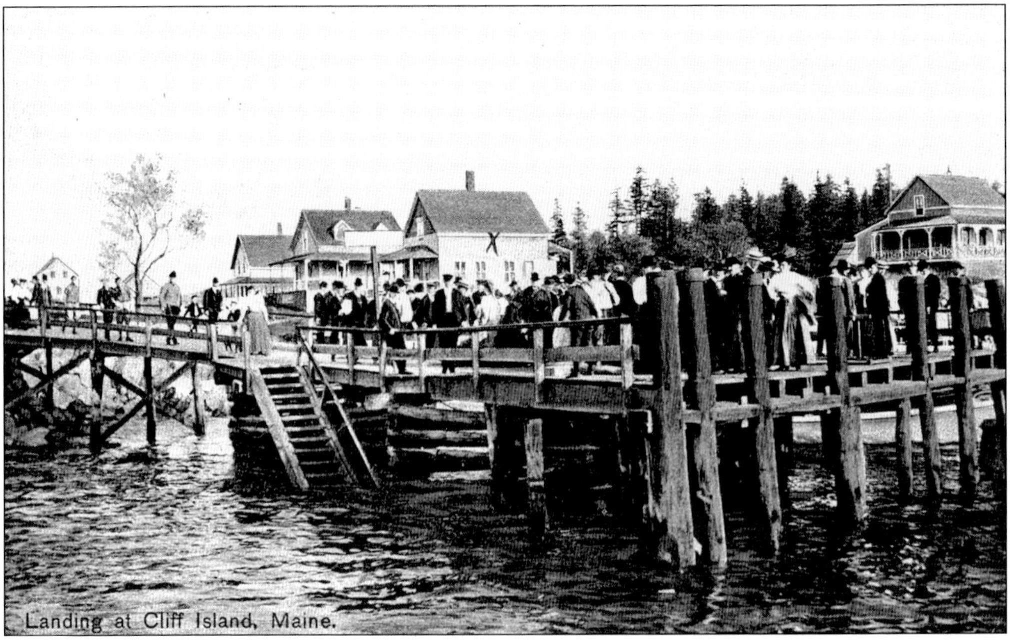


Cliff Island is even more removed from the city proper. With only one landing for steamboats (Peaks and Long Islands each had three or more at times), the dock might be expected to be busy at steamer time. The *X* marks a home visited by the card's sender. He was a representative of the Seventh-Day Adventist Church, the only church on the island.

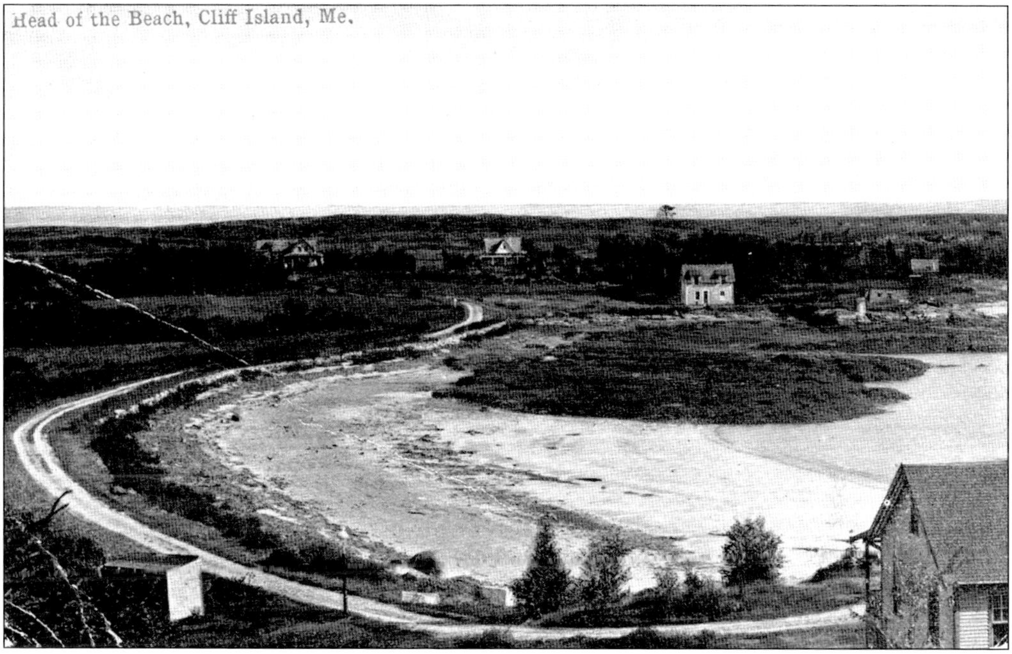


The island's unusual shape, rather like an *H*, with one side shorter than the other, forms bays and inlets, good harbors for the local fishermen. The view here is from the long western side over the crossbar and the shorter eastern section and out to the open ocean. Most development was on the west side.

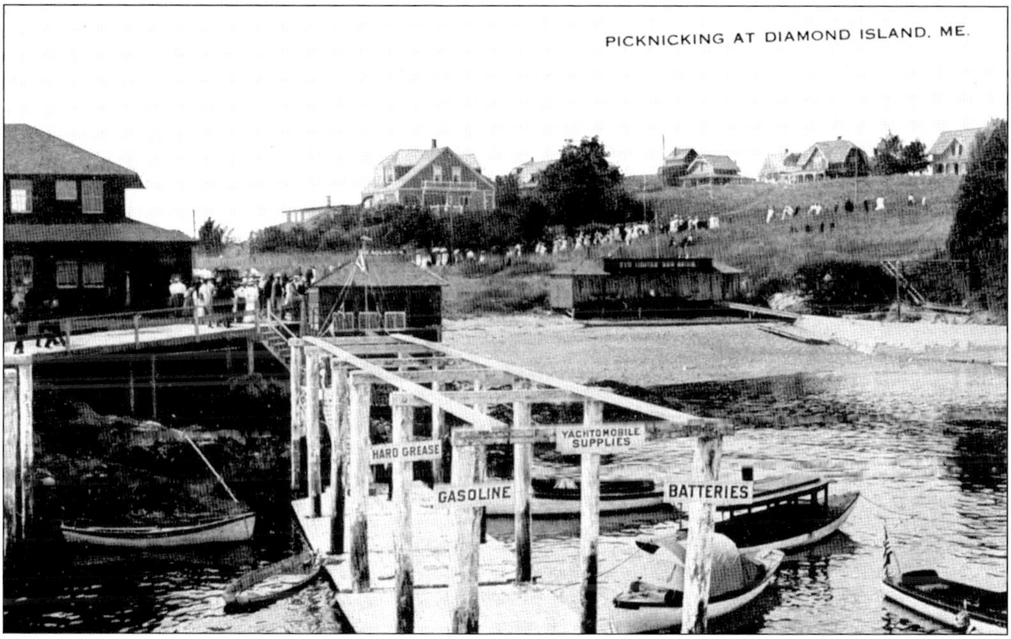


Both Great and Little Diamond Islands were, by the 20th century, essentially colonies of summer cottages. Near the dock of the latter was the casino (on the left). The casino was a community hall, owned and operated by an island association.

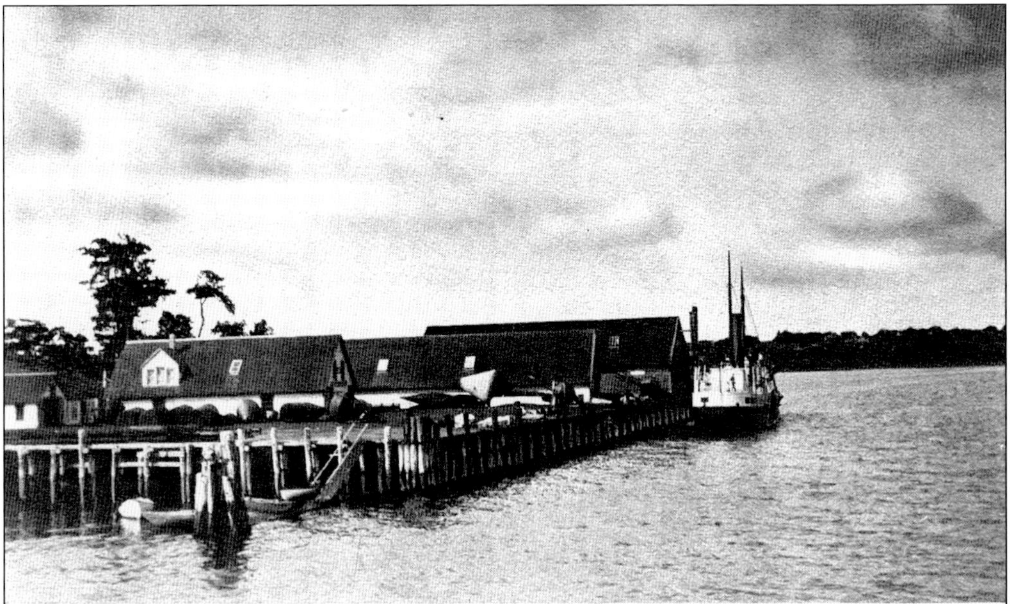

PORTLAND HARBOR, ME. Buoy Station of U. S. Gov't, Little Diamond Island M 432

On Little Diamond was a branch of the U.S. Lighthouse Service, which, among other duties, dispatched vessels to see that the many navigational buoys along the coast were in place and in good condition. The card is from 1909. In 1915, the U.S. Lighthouse Service and the U.S. Life Saving Service were made part of the U.S. Coast Guard.

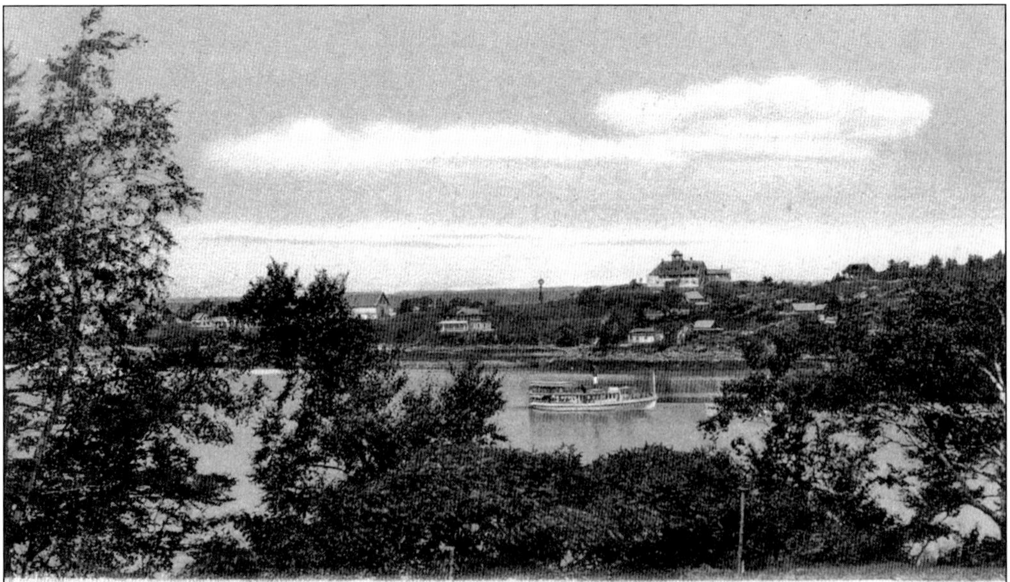

View of Great Diamond from Peaks Island.

Published in Germany for G. W. Morris, Portland, Maine.

Great Diamond Island was larger, with more cottages. The large building on the skyline is the clubhouse of the Portland Club. The island was also home to Fort McKinley and the 5th U.S. Infantry—and thus to a shifting group of army personnel and their families (see page 39).

# Three

# THE PORT

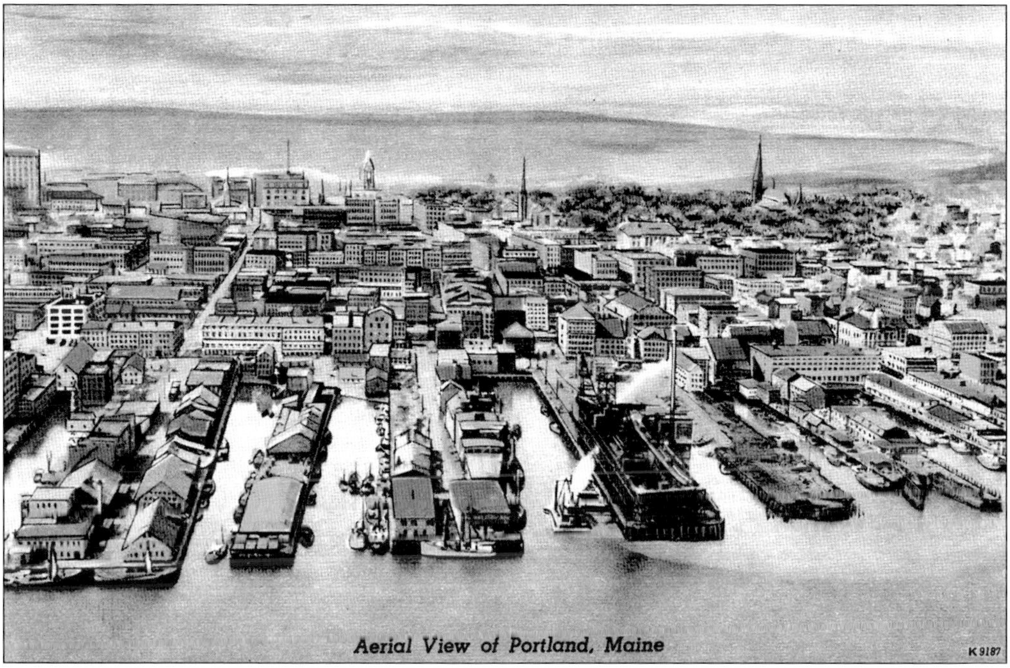


From the times of the early explorers, the deepwater harbor made what is now Portland noticed, and in later years, the port contributed immensely to the city's well-being. The numbers of wharves have changed over time, with new ones being developed and others being enlarged—or abandoned. Fill has shortened some and joined small piers into large open areas. A map of 1866 names 27 piers between those serving the railroad depots at either end. A modern map gives fewer than half that number. An early-20th-century view includes the middle area, where wharves have changed in lengths and ownership but have been most constant. From left to right are part of Richardson's, then Union, Widgery, Central, Long, and Commercial Wharves, Portland Pier, and part of Custom House Wharf. Across the peninsula is Back Cove.

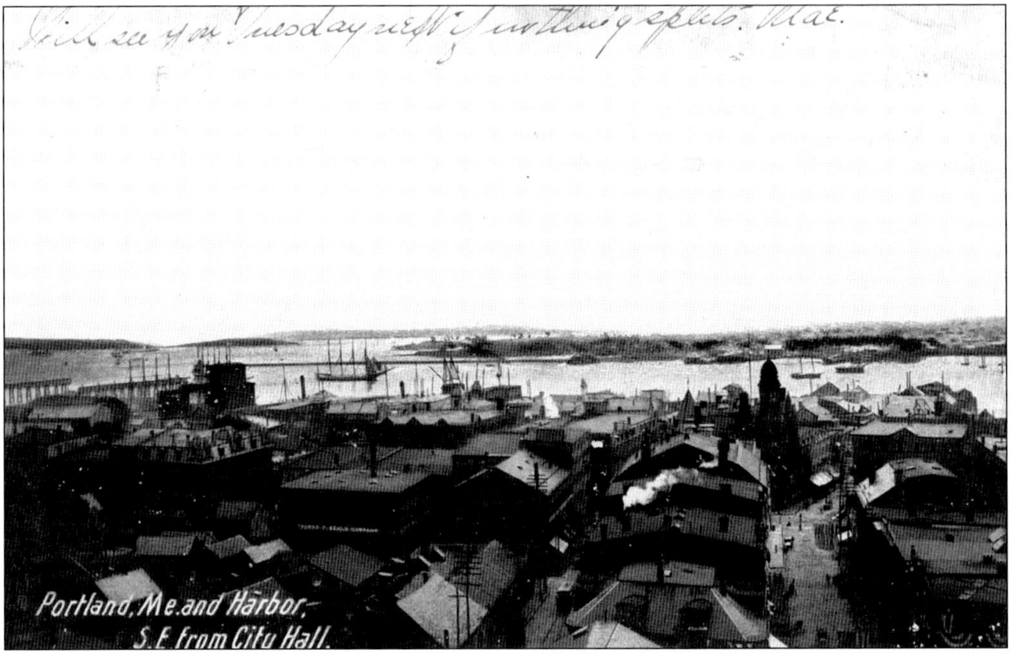


An early-20th-century view from the top of Portland City Hall shows the relationship between city, harbor, and harbor islands, with South Portland across Fore River. The trolley is on Market Street. The First National Bank building of 1884, on the corner of Middle and Exchange Streets, then sported a large clock tower with the weather vane from an early courthouse.

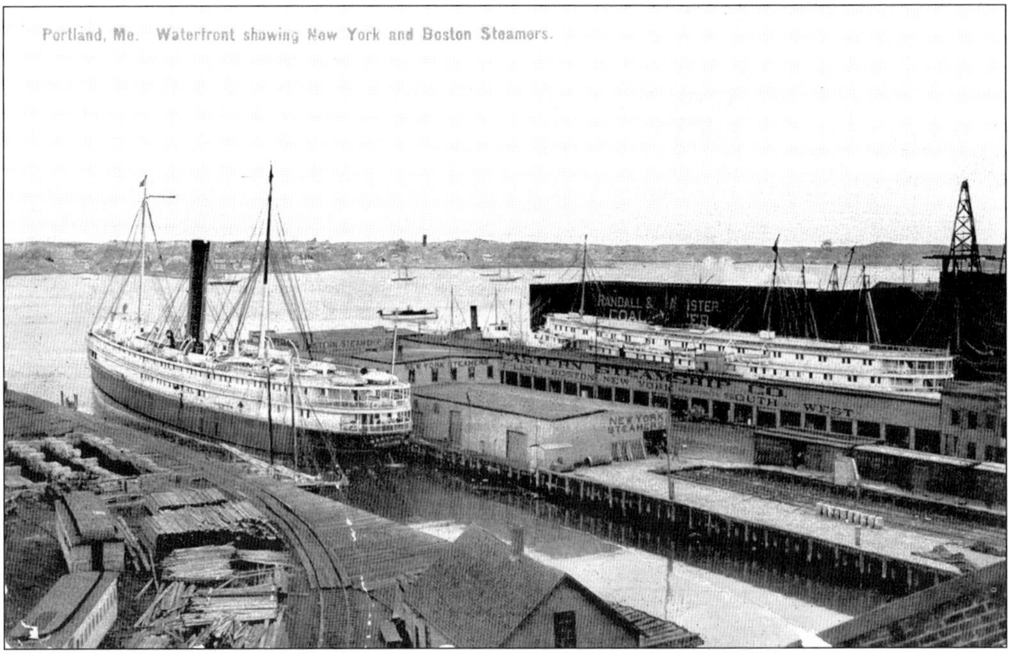


A steam-powered vessel operated between Portland docks and various Casco Bay locations as early as 1822. Well before the Civil War, oceangoing steamboats had established regular runs between Portland and other large cities along the East Coast. Traveling to Boston and to New York (or shipping products there) was, thus, a fairly simple undertaking.

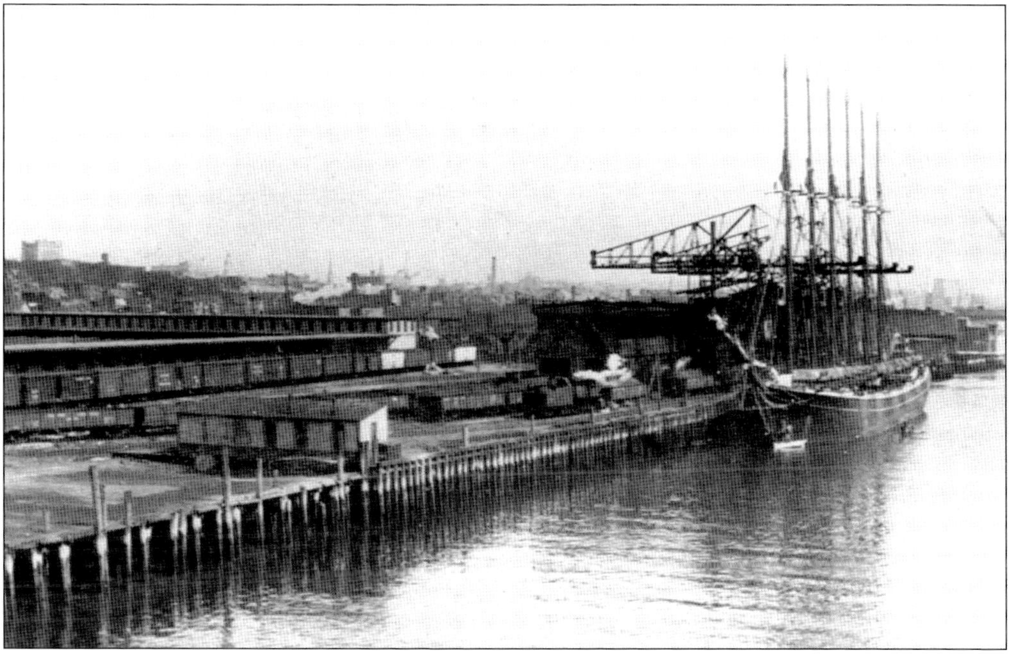

At the same time, large schooners sailed in and out of the port, carrying bulky goods like coal, ice, lumber, and salt. Portland's J. S. Winslow Company grew through the 1890s and 1900s to own, in the period between 1911 and World War I, the biggest fleet on the Atlantic coast. Schooners did a good business during the war, but most of the vessels were sold soon after.

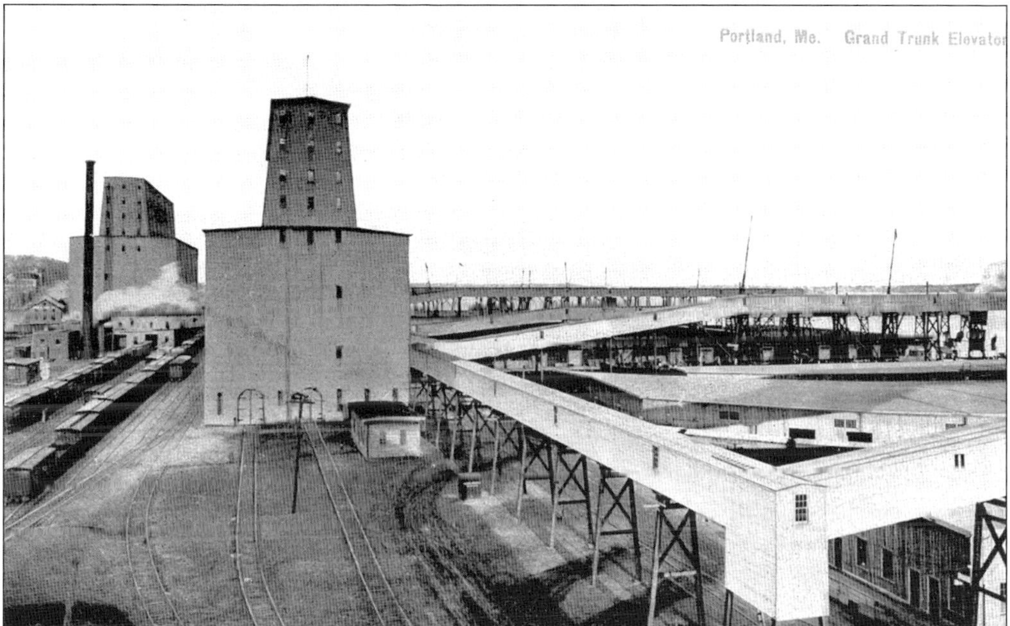


One major development of the 1840s and 1850s involved the building of a railroad (later leased to and operated as the Grand Trunk Railway) to Montreal so that goods, including grain from western Canada, could be shipped from Portland. From 1875 into the 1970s, the east end of the waterfront was marked by towering grain elevators and a system of loading docks.

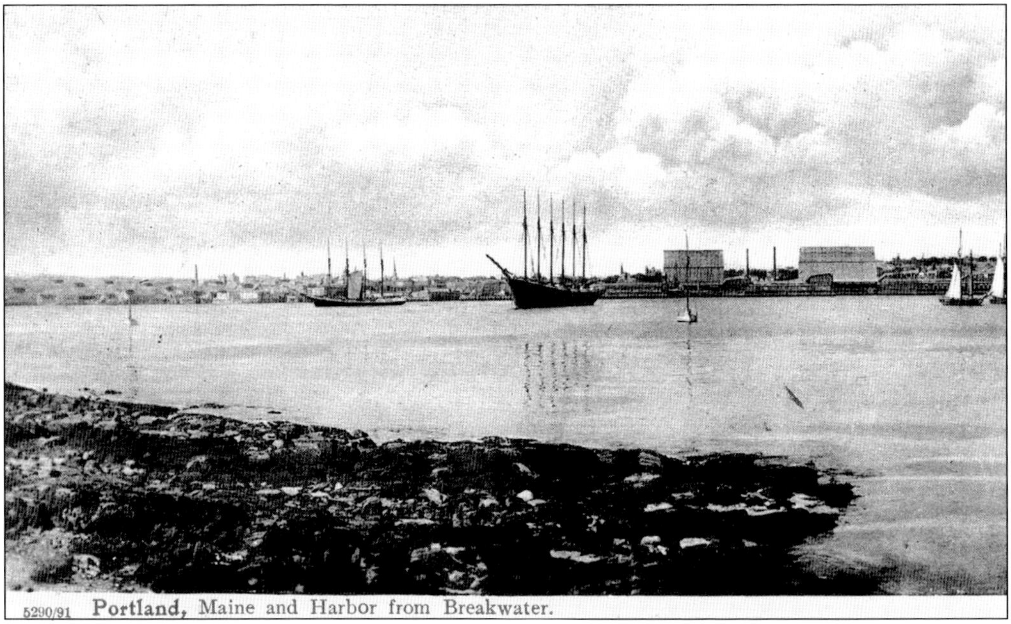


The elevators and Grand Trunk Railway loading docks were also impressive when viewed from the far side of the harbor. The huge structures dwarf the Portland Observatory on Munjoy Hill, seen just to the right of the second elevator.

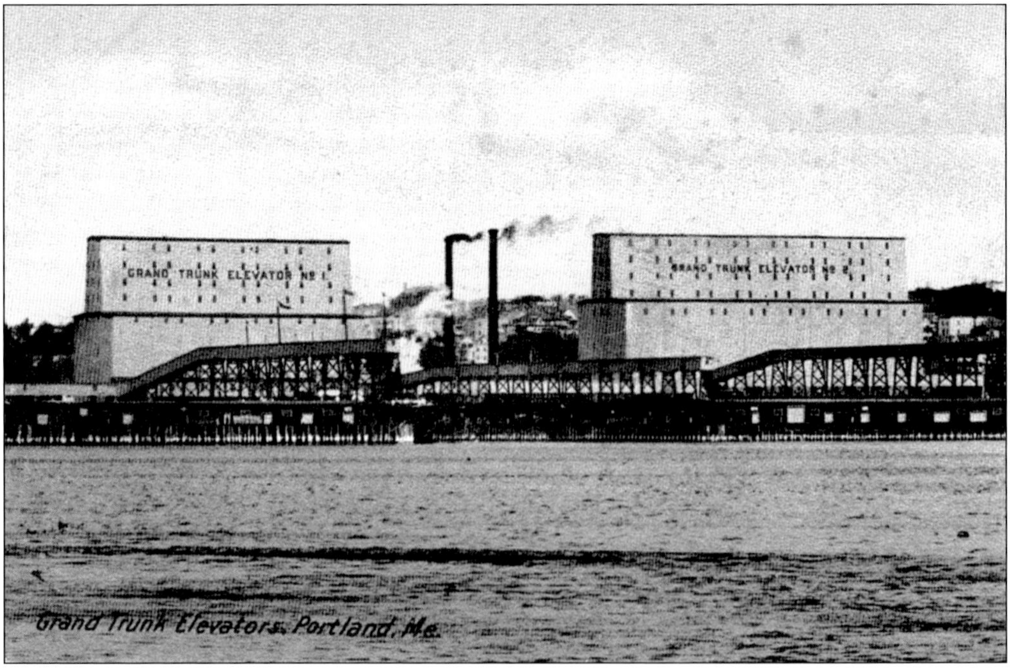


A closer view provides a better idea of the extent of the docks, which became less used after Canada subsidized rail lines to its eastern provinces and raised tariffs on goods shipped via the United States. In 1970, fire reduced the loading docks to ashes. The elevators were torn down a few years later.

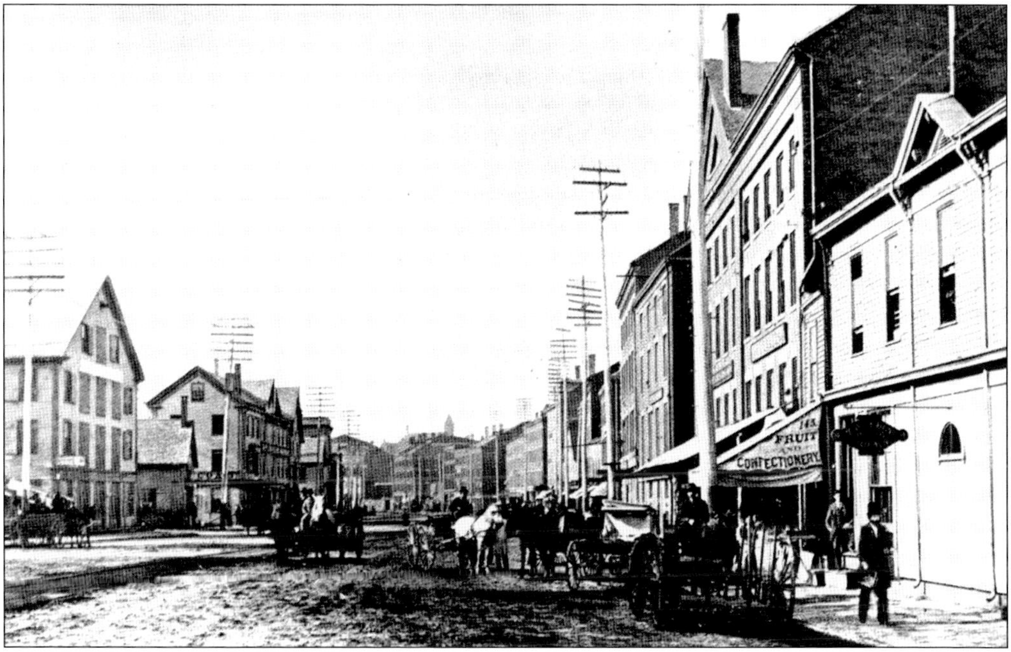


Commercial Street was built in the early 1850s, when the city filled in between the inner parts of early wharves, which were then lengthened to extend farther into the harbor. Railroad tracks down the street's center connected depots of different lines. When George W. Morris took this picture in 1895, the wharf side of the street, left, was almost as well built up as the inner side.

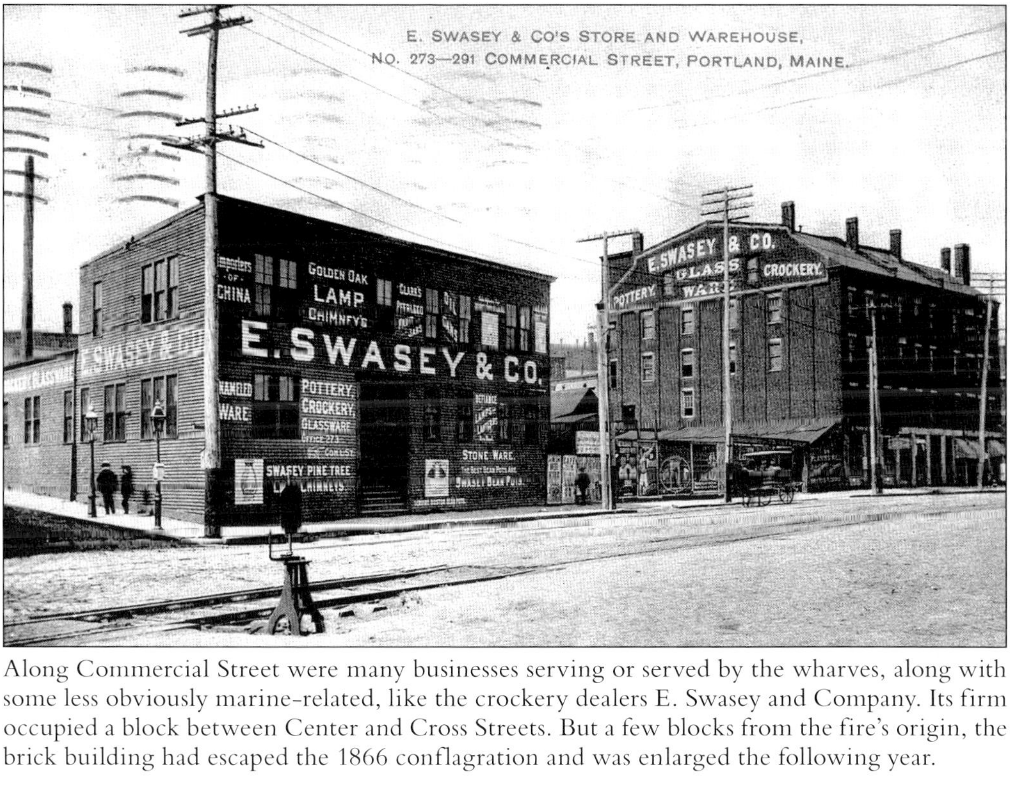


Along Commercial Street were many businesses serving or served by the wharves, along with some less obviously marine-related, like the crockery dealers E. Swasey and Company. Its firm occupied a block between Center and Cross Streets. But a few blocks from the fire's origin, the brick building had escaped the 1866 conflagration and was enlarged the following year.

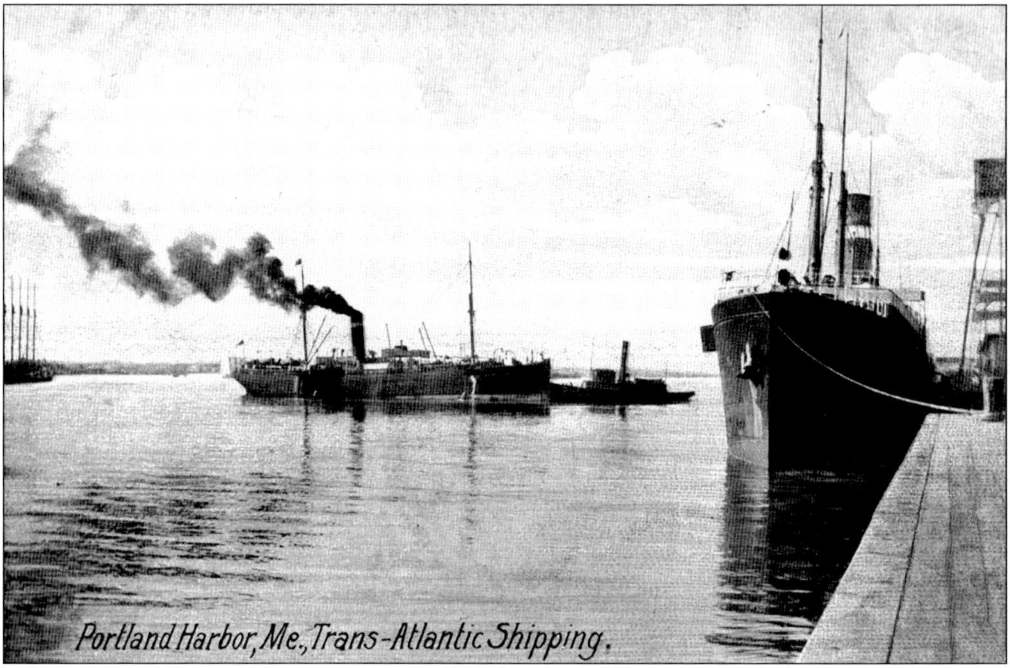


This photograph showing foreign shipping includes a big schooner, a couple of steam-powered cargo ships, and a harbor tug. A pier to the east of the grain-loading docks served steamers from Liverpool, bringing goods and passengers to take the train to Montreal in winter months when the St. Lawrence River was frozen.

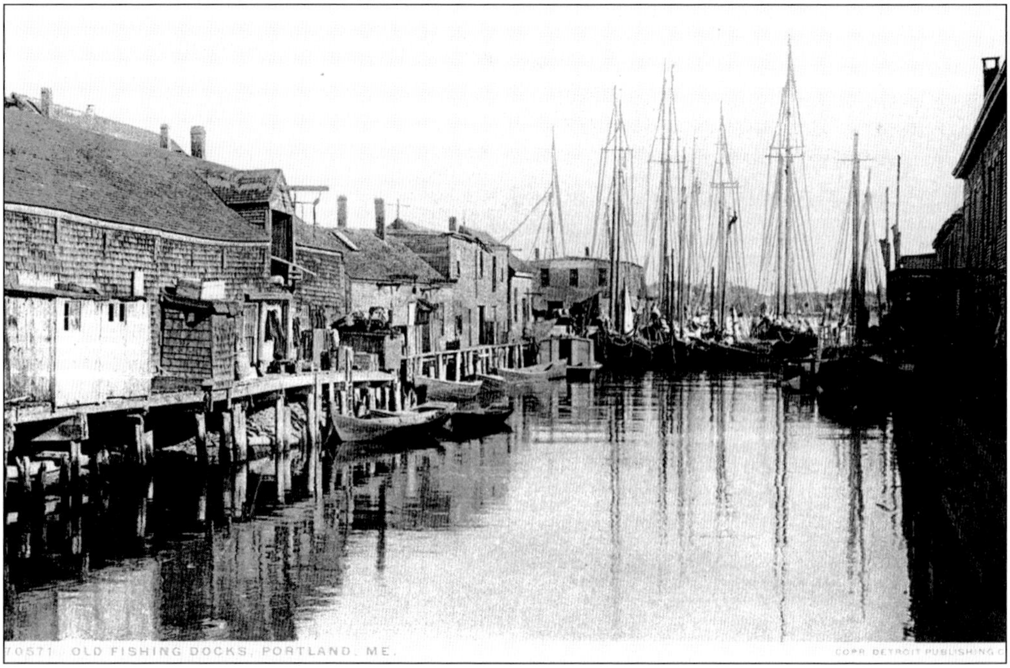


Also using the waterfront were fishing vessels—mostly sloops and schooners. Some had Portland as a home port; others came from smaller coastal towns, bringing their catches to the city market.

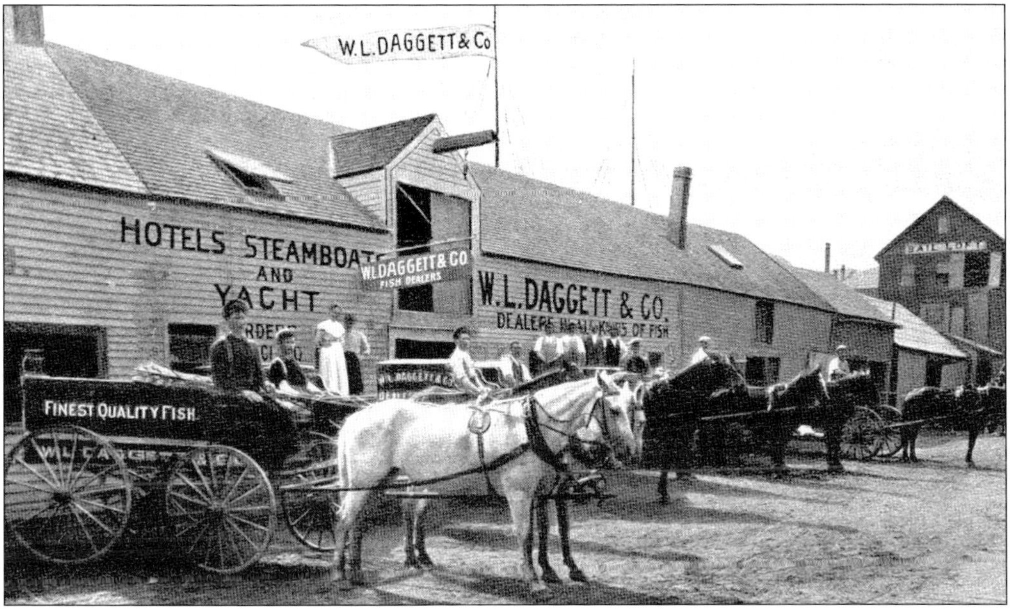


W. L. Daggett and Company, located on Portland Pier in the second decade of the 20th century, was one of the firms purchasing seafood. The signs explain the range of business. Fish were bought right off the fishing boats or from men who transported lobsters or clams for others. The wagons would be used for local deliveries. The Portland Sailmaking Company had the loft next door.

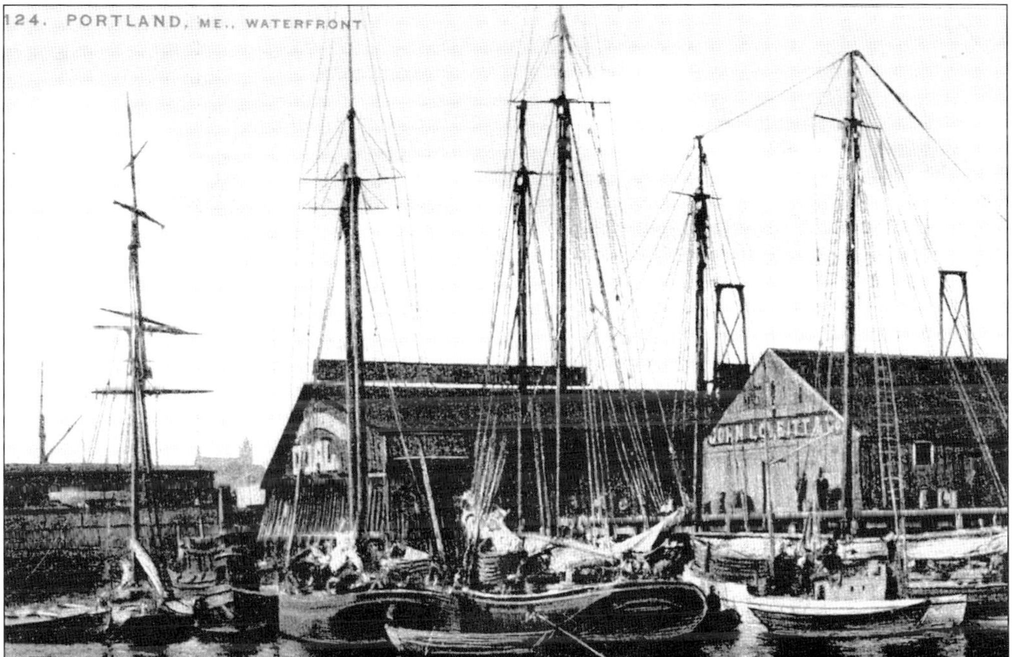


Another fish dealer of the period was John Loveitt, on the end of Commercial Wharf in 1913. He would also have bought locally, while Sargent-Dennison, the firm on the end of nearby Long Wharf, imported its coal—probably via big schooners.

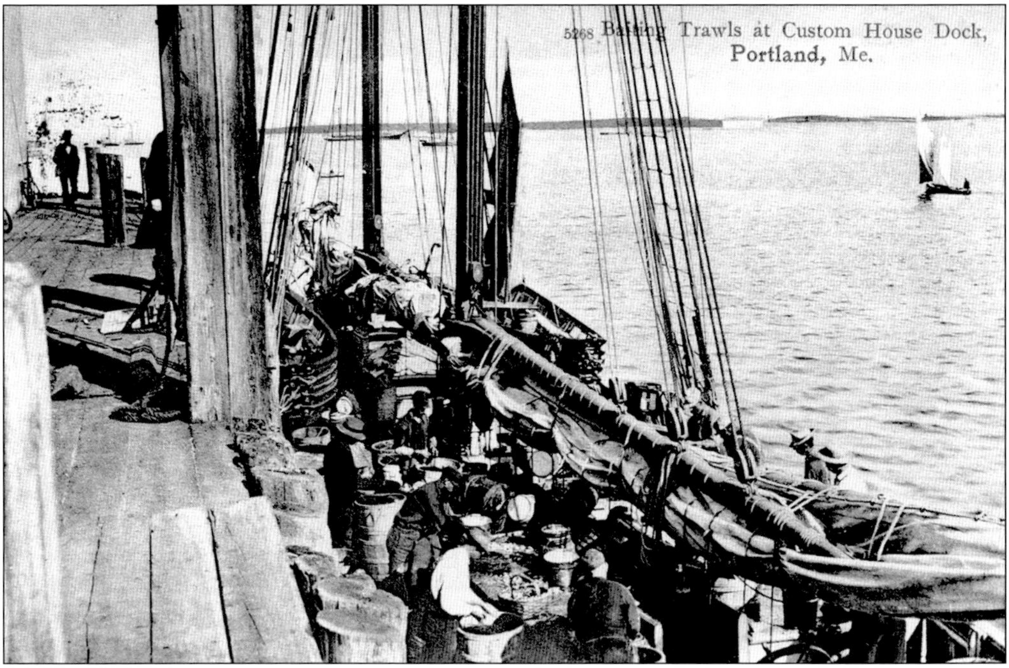


Bait could be purchased from dealers in port, and the hooks on long trawls were then baited before sailing. Note the nests of dories on either side toward the bow. Once on the fishing grounds, individual crew members would be "set off" in dories from the larger vessel, and each would handle his own trawl, returning to the bigger vessel when loaded or at the day's end.

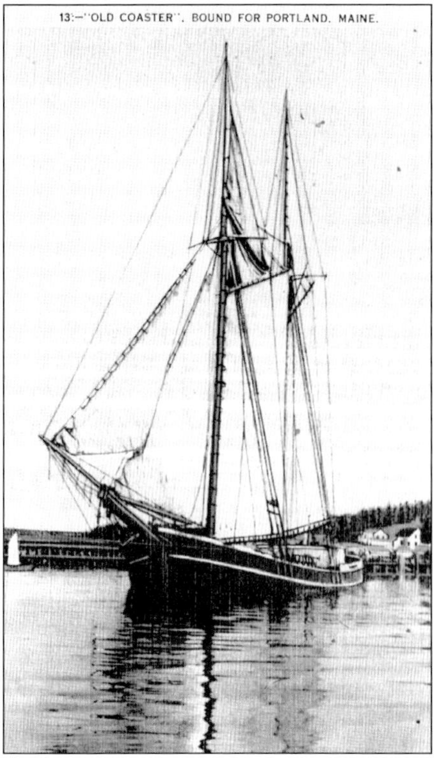


"Coasters" were sailing freighters that continued to move up and down the coast into the early decades of the 20th century, delivering a range of merchandise, from groceries and grain through building materials, to coastal communities. They also brought goods to the city, including clams, lobsters, farm produce, and hay (needed as long as city people kept horses).

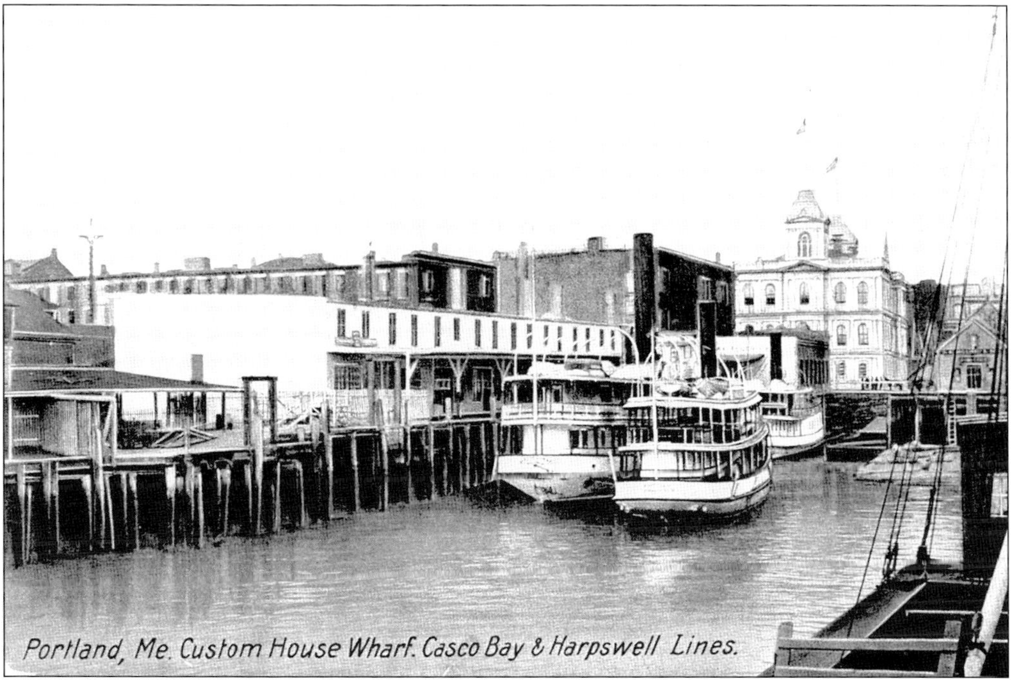


Various companies have run ferry services from Portland to its islands and beyond. The Casco Bay and Harpswell Lines operated from 1907 through 1919 and served the harbor islands on the way east to landings on Harpswell's peninsula and islands.

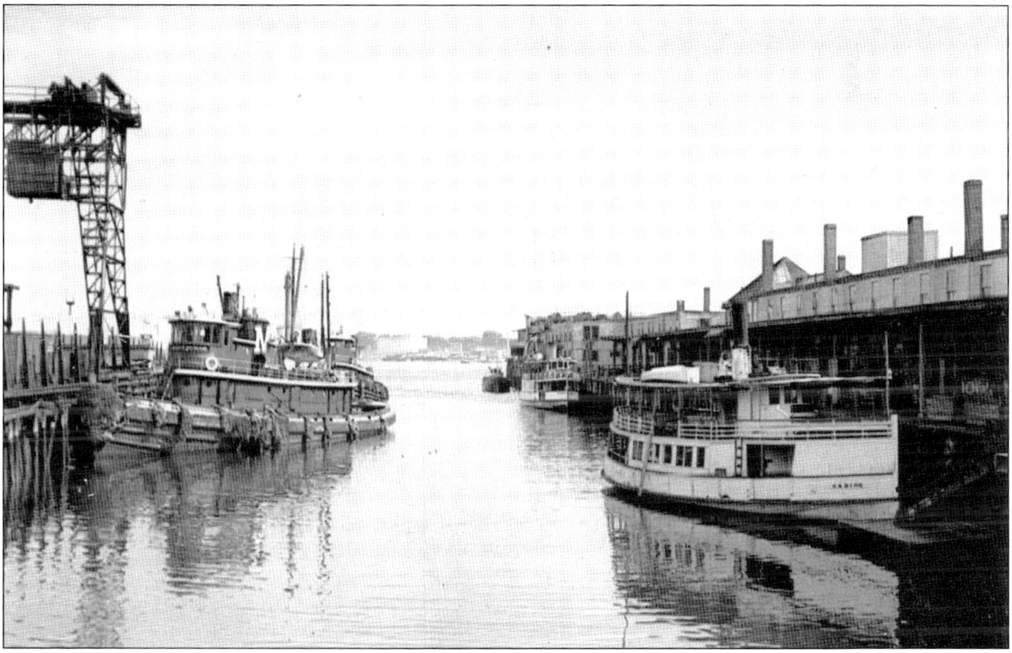

Beginning in 1920, the reorganized Casco Bay Lines ran local ferries, eventually moving from steamboats like the *Sabino*, shown here, to vessels with diesel motors. The *Sabino* operated from Portland between 1927 and 1961. In the 1980s, the private company became part of a transit district. Service continues, with fewer ports of call. The tug is at the Maine State Pier.

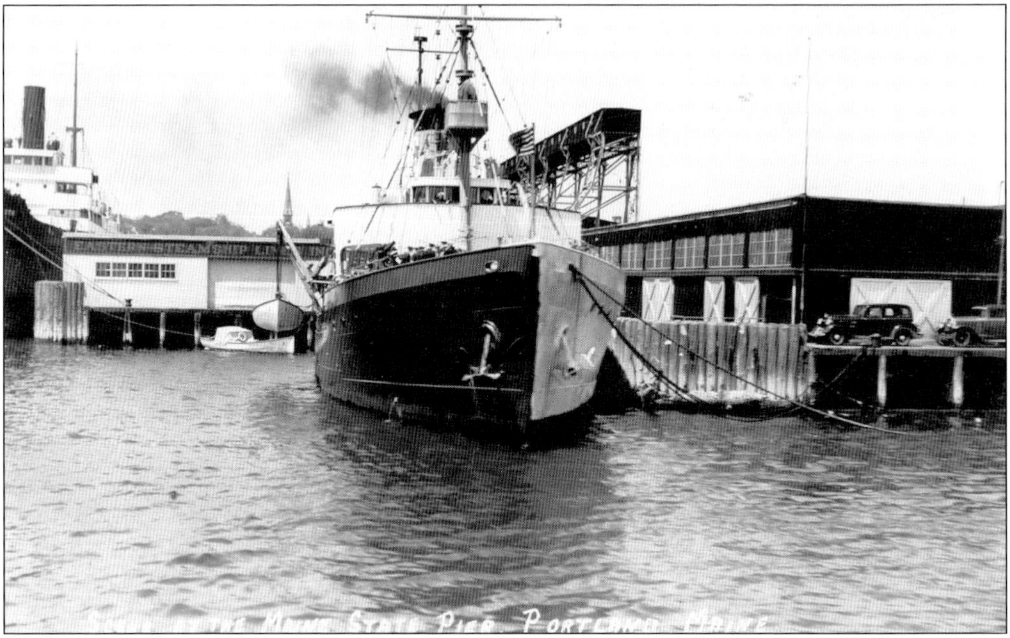

The Maine State Pier was built in 1923 with public money and was operated by a port authority. Eastern Steamship Lines soon took up residence, and the immigration service was also moved there. In the 1930s, it was home to a Coast Guard cutter and to a pilot boat. On its east side was a public boat landing.

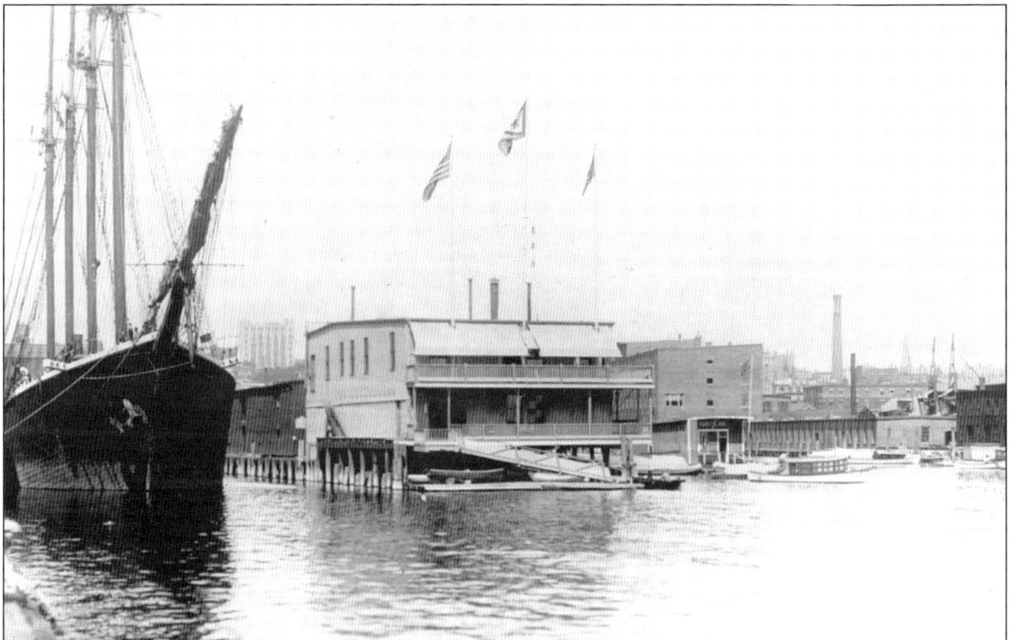

Pleasure vessels also used the harbor. In 1885, Portland Yacht Club built this clubhouse on the end of Central Wharf. It burned in 1926 and was replaced the following year by a lower building, designed by John Calvin Stevens, a yacht club member. Many of the boats at the dock are small powerboats. As early as 1914, they outnumbered sailboats among club members.

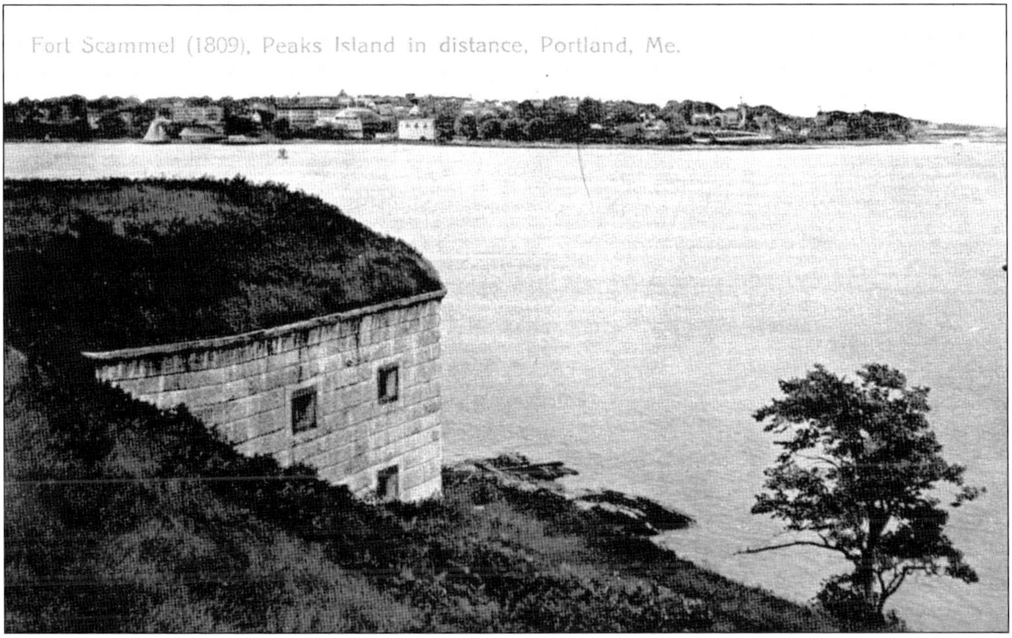


To protect the port, the U.S. government built a series of fortifications. Fort Scammel, on House Island, was named for a Revolutionary War officer. Begun in 1808, it was steadily enlarged into the 1890s, when it was manned for the Spanish-American War.

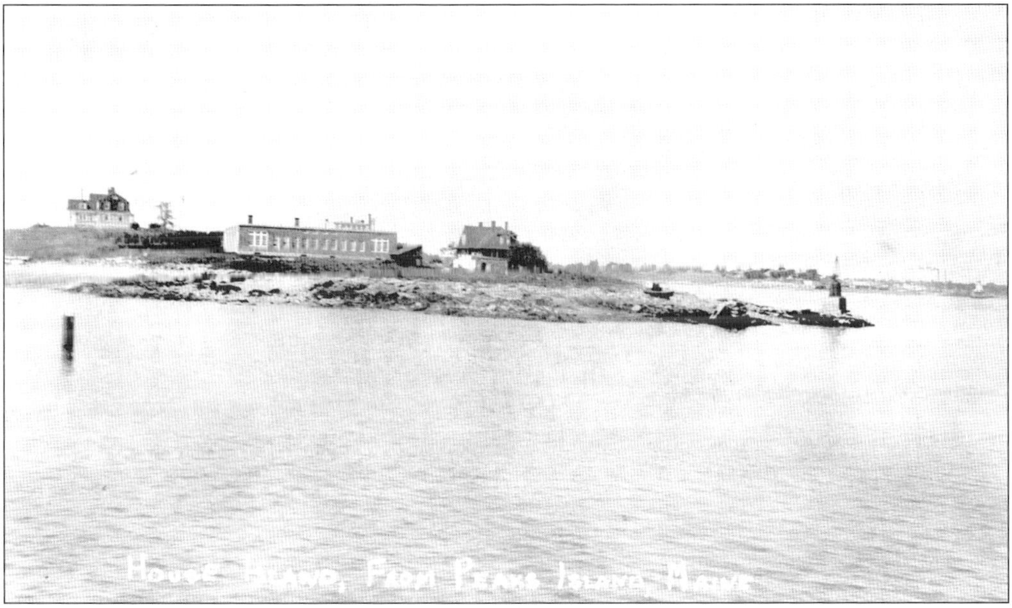


Even after the fort was placed on House Island's south end, the island held a small farm. For many years, until the Maine State Pier was constructed in 1923, House Island also served as a clearing place for immigrants entering the country via Portland Harbor.

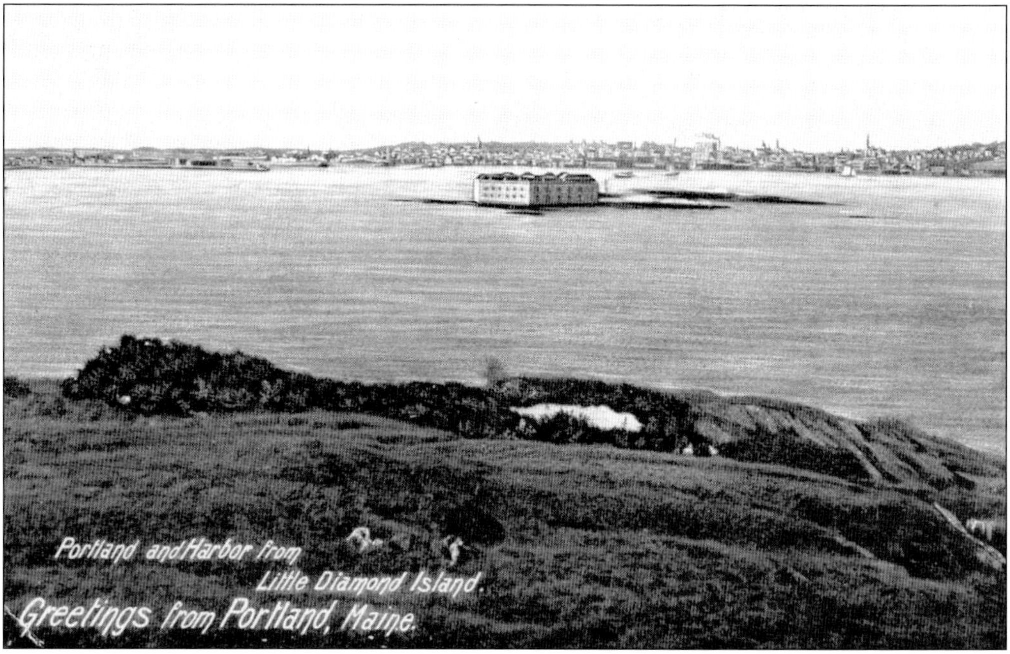


Another harbor fort was Fort Gorges, on Hog Island Ledge, begun in 1858 and completed after the Civil War. Like most of the stone forts along the Maine coast, it was never really tested. Ferdinando Gorges never visited Maine, but he spent half a lifetime, back in England, trying to encourage colonization of the area in the 17th century.

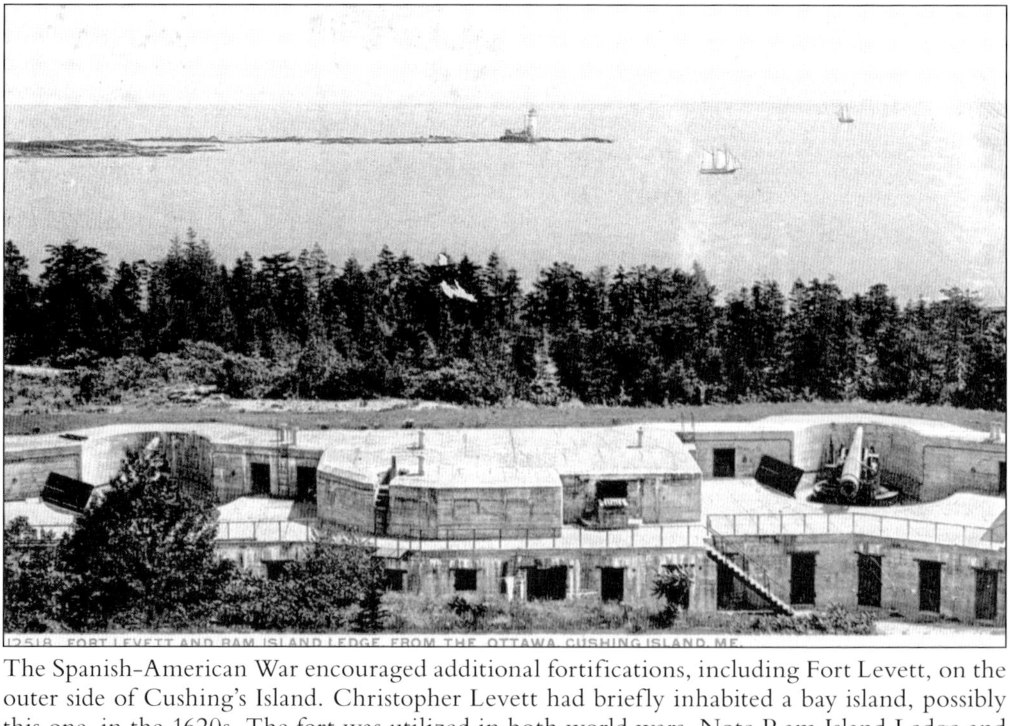


The Spanish-American War encouraged additional fortifications, including Fort Levett, on the outer side of Cushing's Island. Christopher Levett had briefly inhabited a bay island, possibly this one, in the 1620s. The fort was utilized in both world wars. Note Ram Island Ledge and its lighthouse.

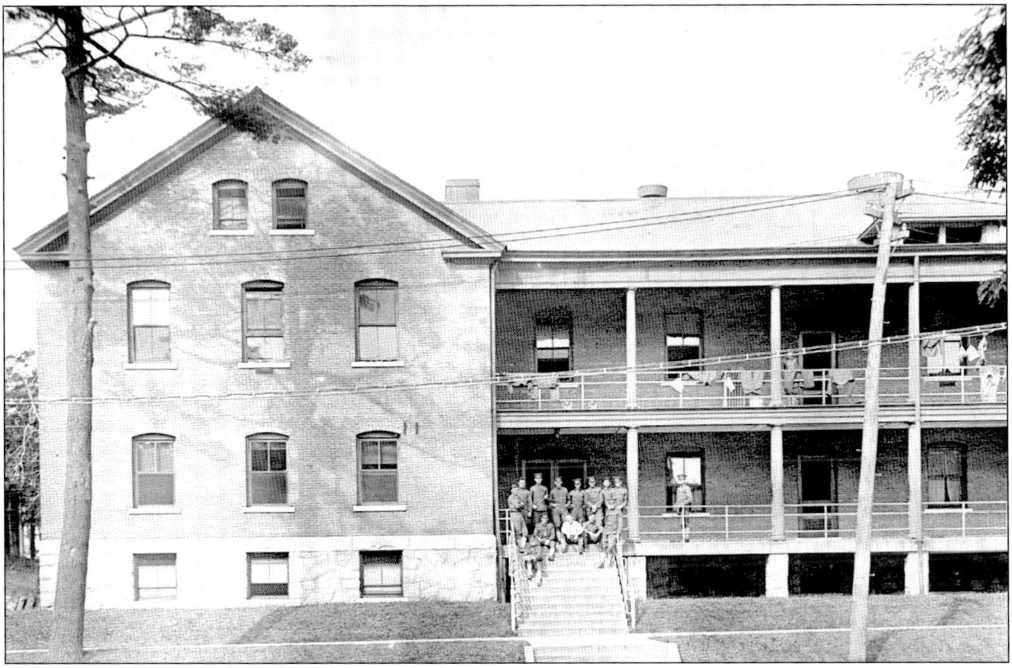

The brick buildings of Fort McKinley were erected on the northeast end of Great Diamond Island soon after the Spanish-American War and then manned in peacetime, as well as during wars. In August 1917, a soldier sent this card to an acquaintance, saying it was "the barracks we stay in."

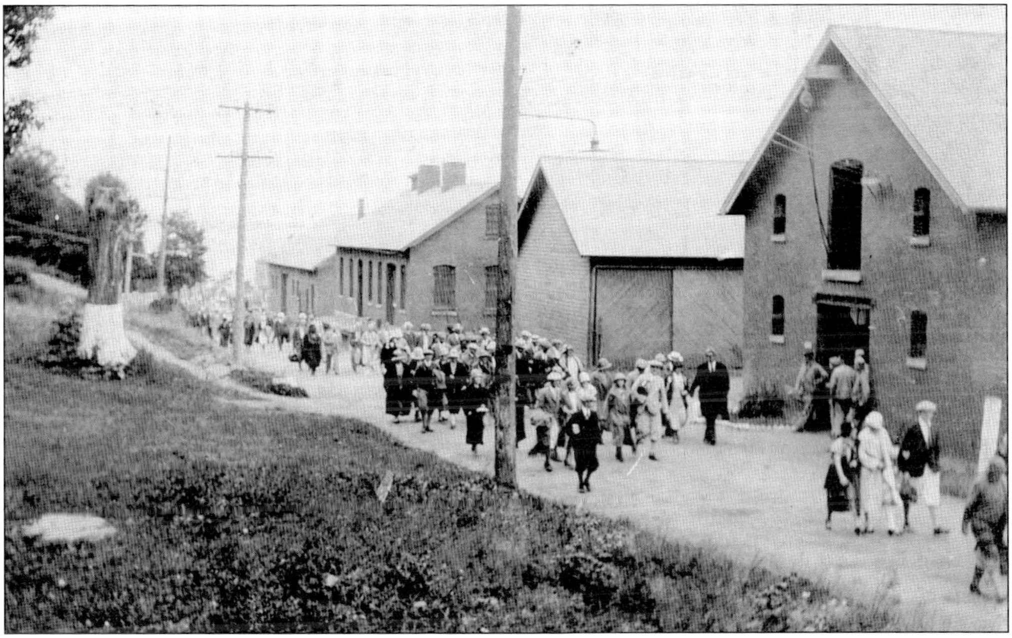

Civilians arriving for visitors' day in the late 1920s passed a row of supply sheds as they walked up from the dock. Fort McKinley was maintained through World War II, when the inner harbor was home to the Atlantic fleet, and most of the nearby islands were fortified in one way or another. It was deactivated in the late 1940s, and the property is now a residential community.

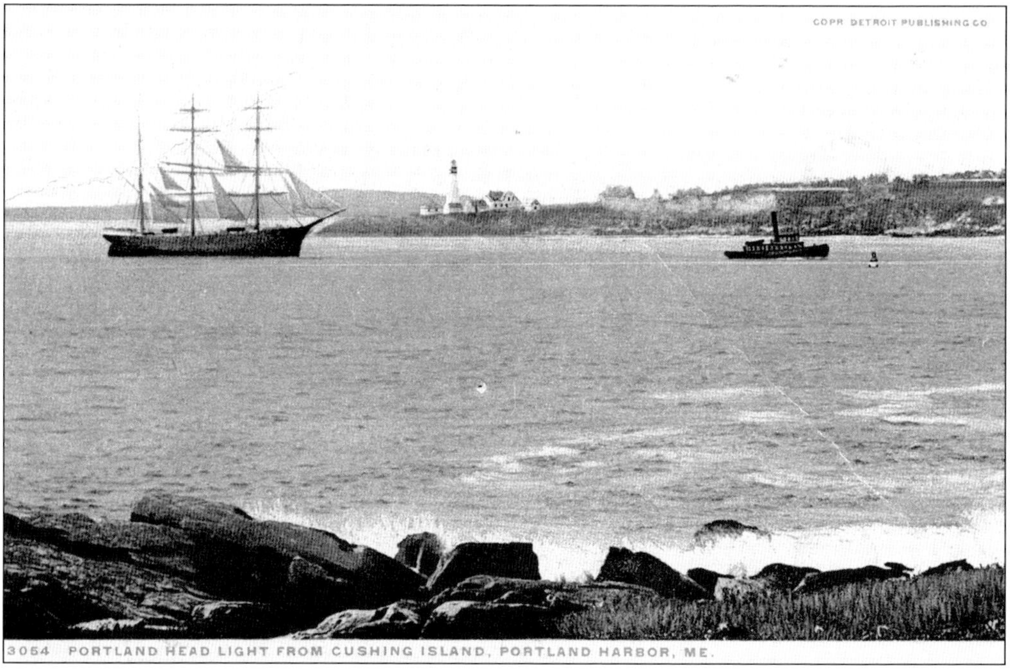


The harbor's lighthouses were mostly in neighboring towns. Here a tug tows a bark up the deepwater passage between Cushing's Island, in the foreground, and Cape Elizabeth. This passage was first marked by the lighthouse on Portland Head in 1791. Square-rigged vessels were rare by the 20th century. Note batteries of Fort Williams to the right of the lighthouse.

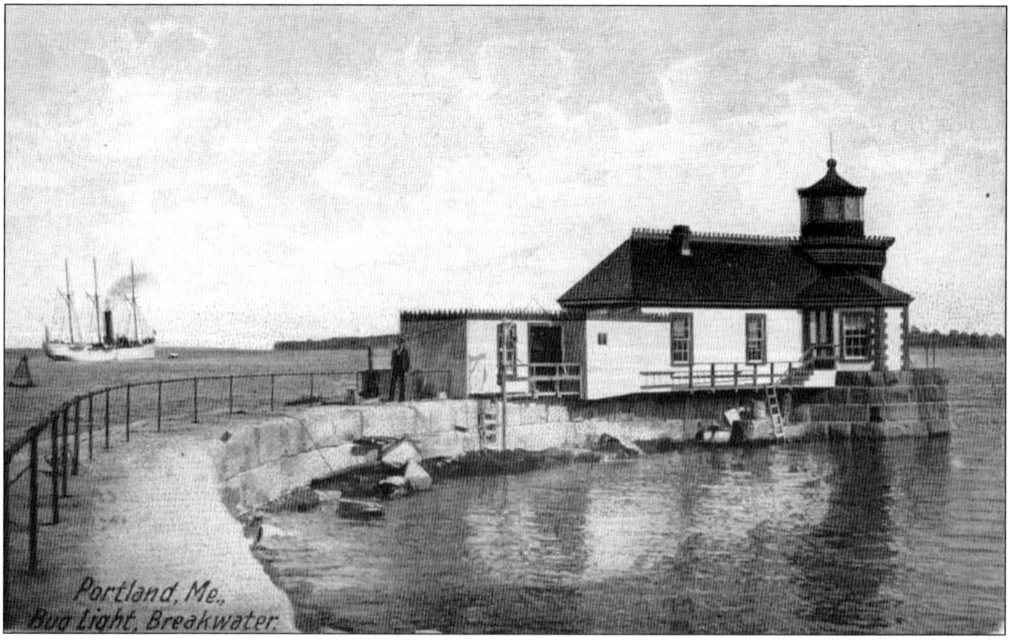


A breakwater to protect the harbor, begun in 1836, did not reach its planned length until 1872, when the iron tower, modeled after the Choregic Monument of Lysicrates (and cast by the Portland Company) was erected. The keeper's house was removed after the light was automated in 1935. The Breakwater Light, commonly called "Bug Light," is technically in South Portland.

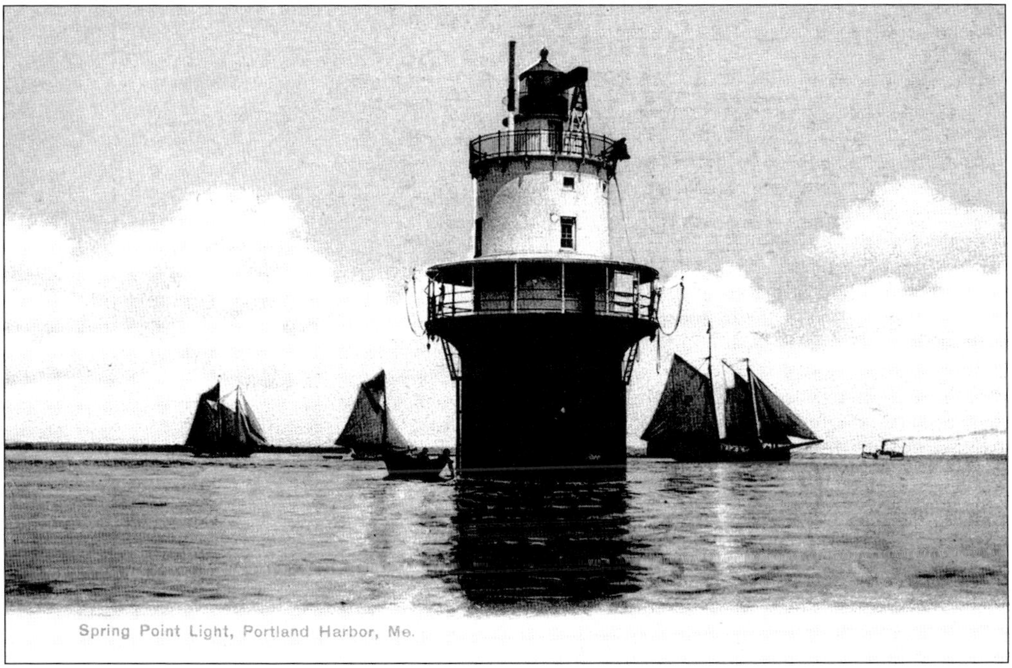


The Spring Point Light was built on an underwater ledge off Fort Preble in 1896–1897. For half a century, it stood as shown, surrounded by water. However, in the 1950s, another breakwater was built, connecting the lighthouse to the South Portland mainland at Spring Point.

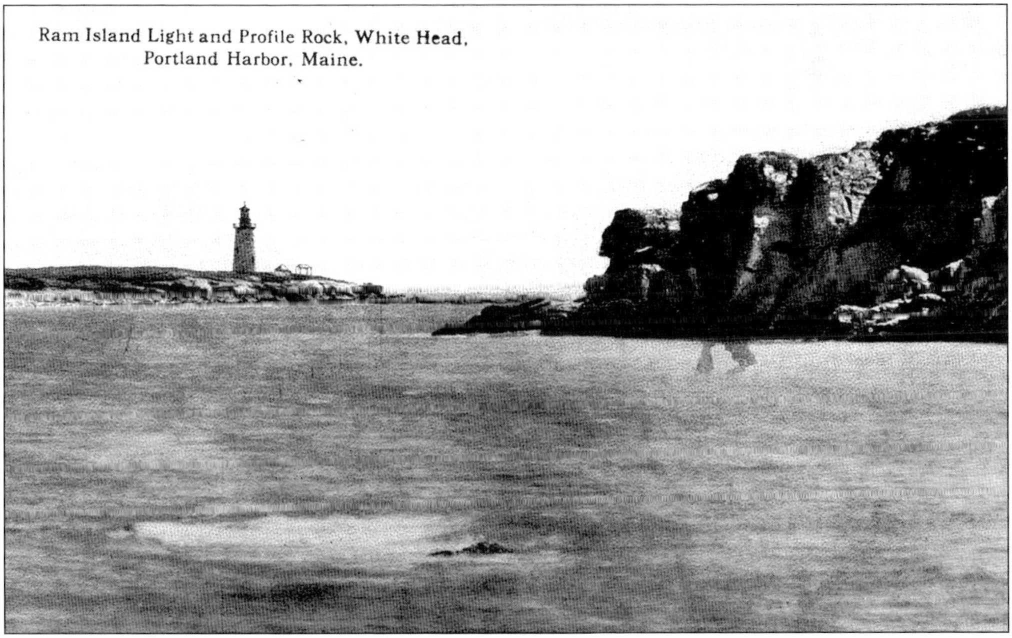


The newest lighthouse in the area was built on Ram Island Ledge and first lit in 1905. (Ram Island was between the ledge and the camera taking the picture. See page 38.) Island and ledge lie southeast of Portland's Cushing's Island, shown on the right. The southern route into the harbor thus passes between the light on Ram Island Ledge and that on Portland Head.

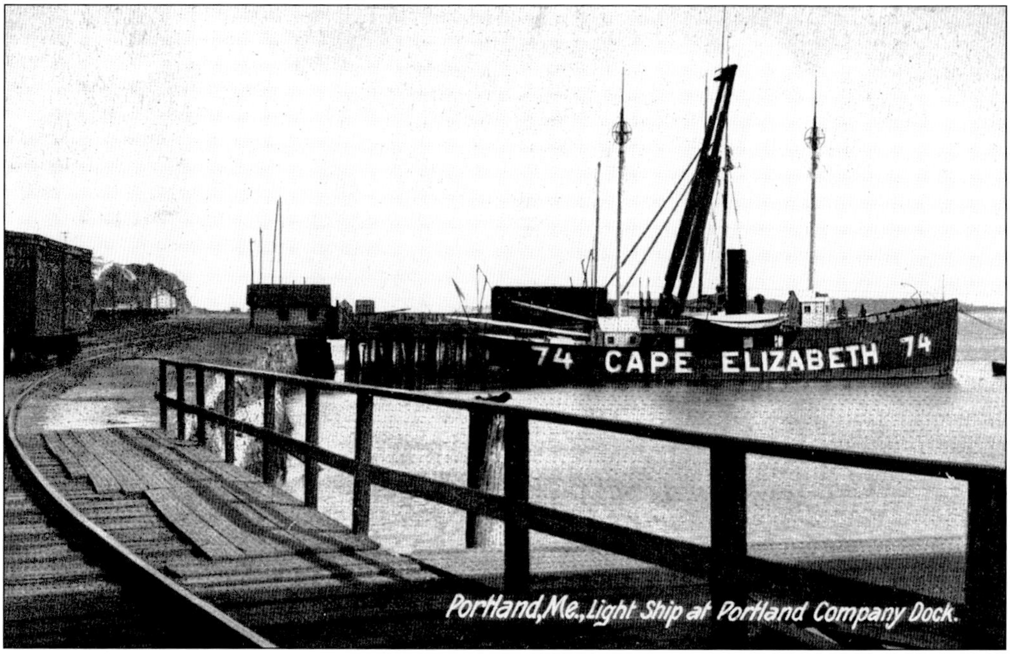


From 1903 to 1975 (except during World War II), a lightship, originally called the *Cape Elizabeth* but by 1910 renamed the *Portland*, was moored six miles south-southeast of Cape Elizabeth. The first wooden vessel was followed by a series of iron ones with the same name. A large navigational buoy replaced the ship in 1975.

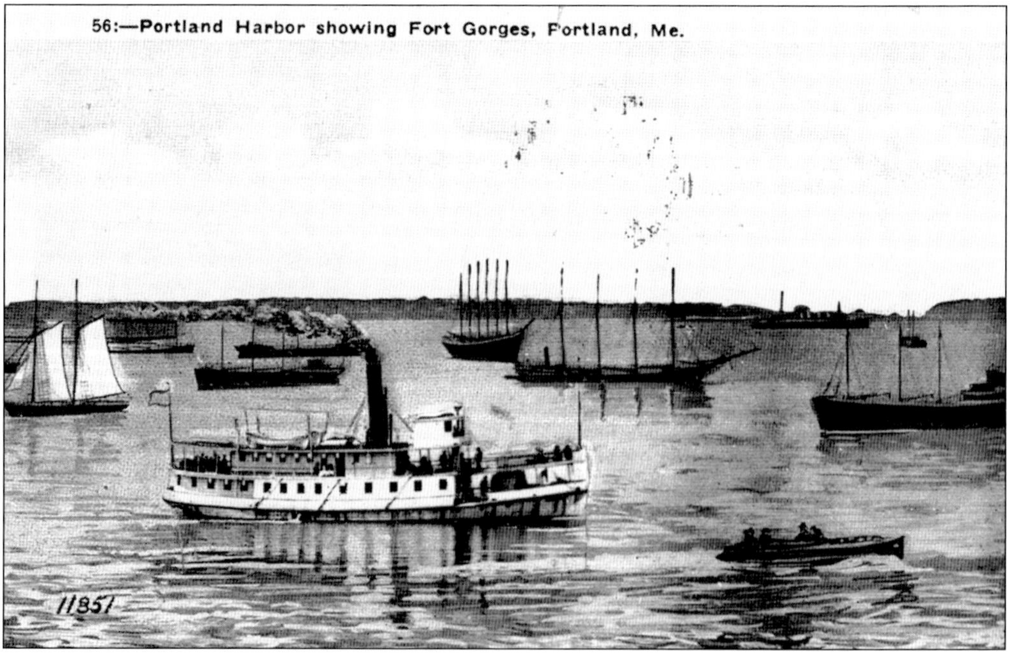


When illustrations were drawn from photographs, their content could easily be doctored. This all-inclusive example holds a small fishing or cargo schooner together with great schooners and larger powered vessels, with an island steamer near a pleasure powerboat—plus Fort Gorges. The steamer, the *Merryconeag*, was built in East Deering in 1888 and used until 1918.

*Four*

# Downtown

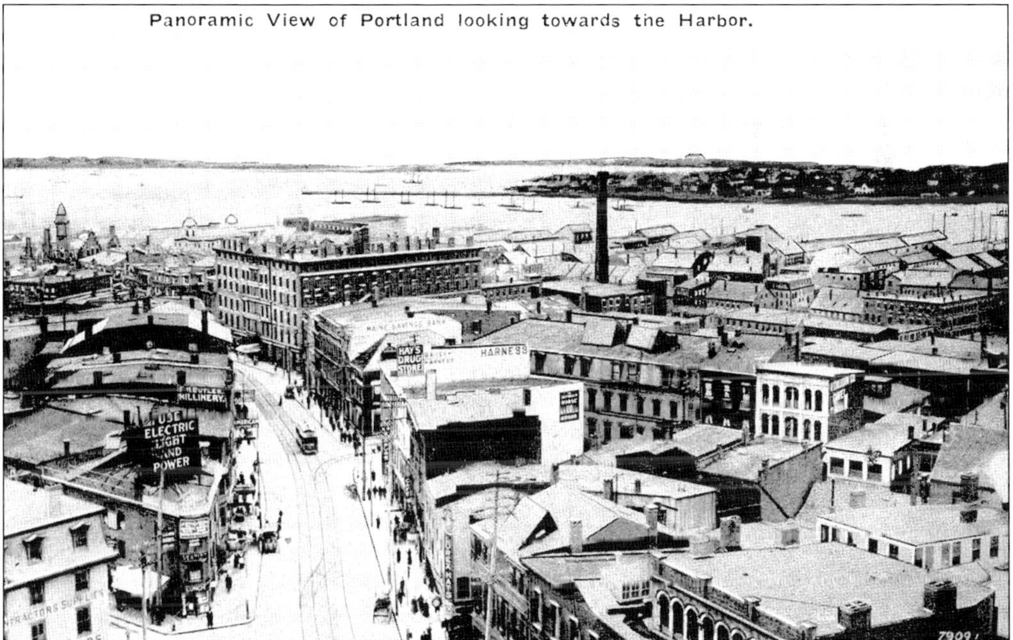


From the vantage point of the 10-story Fidelity Building (Portland's first skyscraper) in Monument Square, this view looking southeast down Middle Street to the Falmouth Hotel encompasses the Victorian business district that rose from the ashes of the Great Fire of 1866. In those years, retail and office development spread from its original location on Fore, Exchange, and Middle Streets to Congress Street between Monument Square and Longfellow Square. The harbor on the horizon is a reminder that Portland was built on a peninsula.

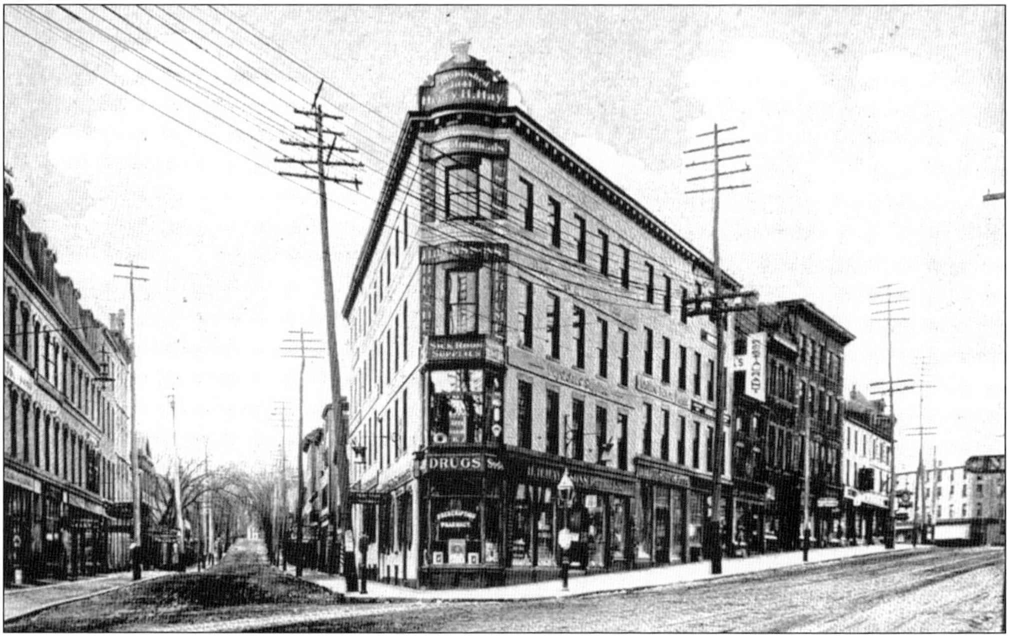


Hatmaker Byron Greenough built a three-story brick block at Free and Middle Streets in 1848. His hat and fur business was replaced in 1856 by H. H. Hay's drugstore, which barely escaped destruction in the great fire and operated at the location until 1964. In 1919, a fourth floor was added to this Lower Hay Block from designs by John Calvin Stevens and John Howard Stevens.

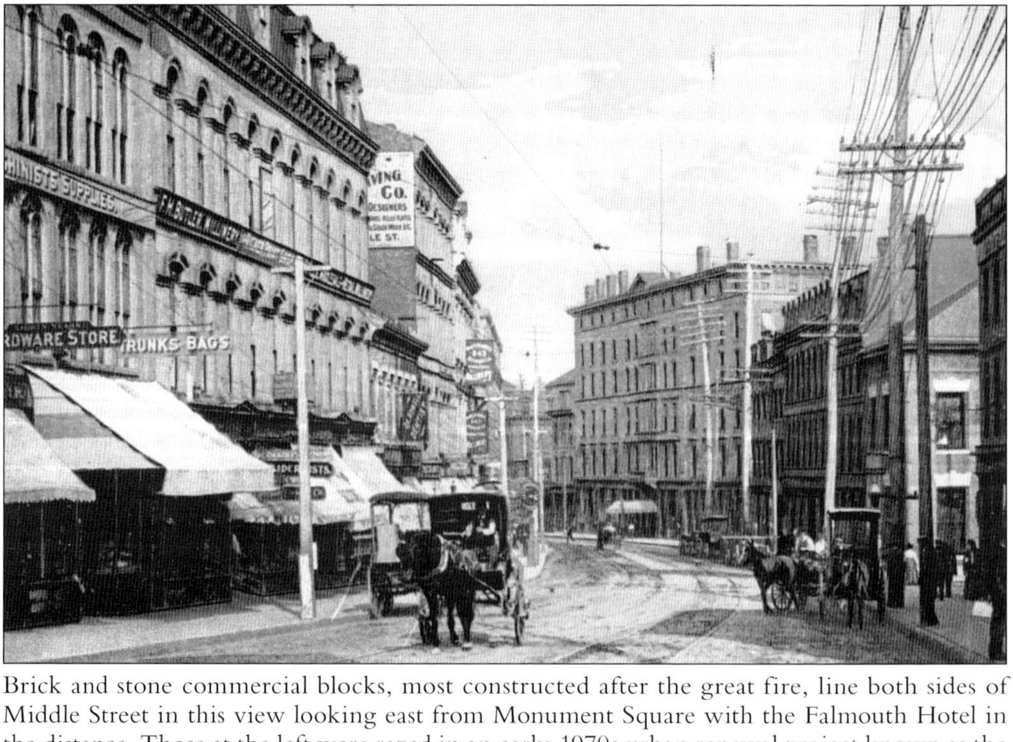


Brick and stone commercial blocks, most constructed after the great fire, line both sides of Middle Street in this view looking east from Monument Square with the Falmouth Hotel in the distance. Those at the left were razed in an early-1970s urban renewal project known as the Golden Triangle, which leveled the block now occupied by One City Center.

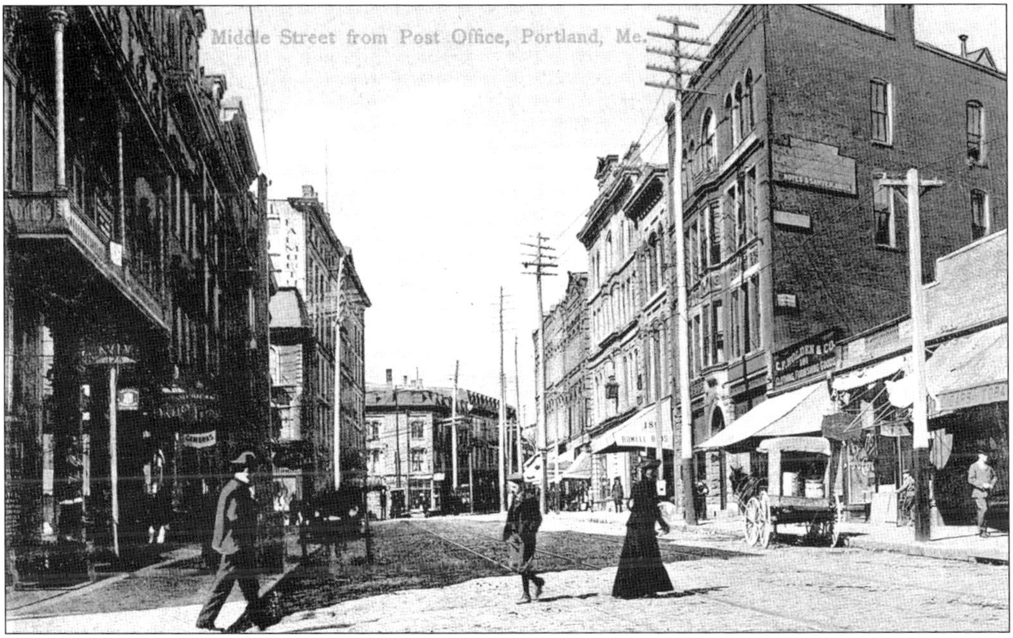


This view depicts the heart of what is now the Old Port area at Middle and Exchange Streets, looking west on Middle Street toward the intersection of Union Street. At center left can be seen the Falmouth Hotel, now gone, while at the immediate right is the Oxford Block, built in 1886–1887 from designs by John Calvin Stevens, who maintained his architectural office on the top floor.

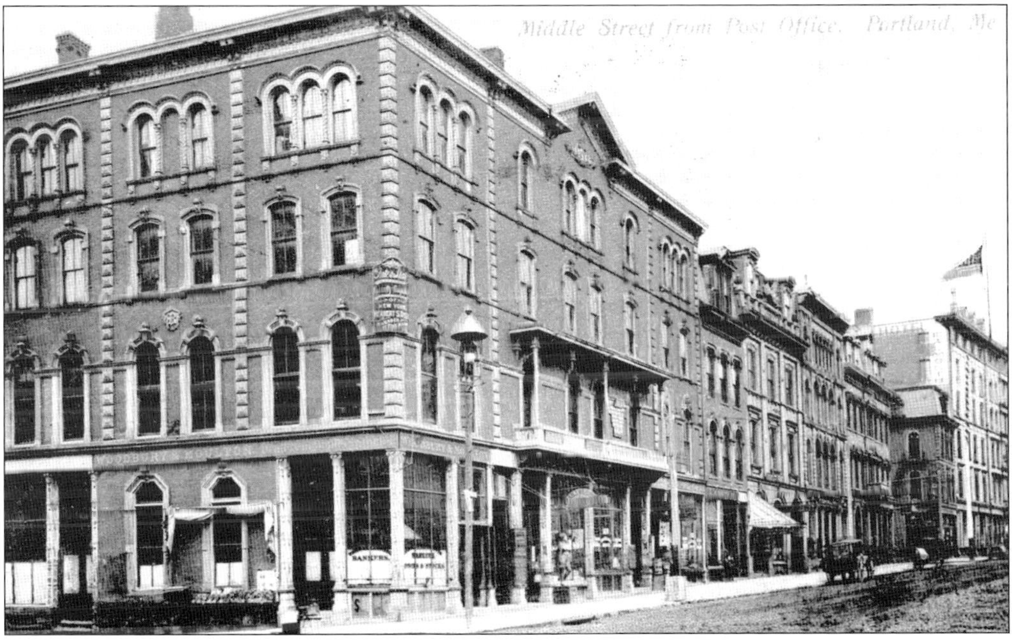


These commercial buildings lining the south side of Middle Street between Exchange and Union Streets were all constructed immediately after the 1866 fire. At the left is the Boyd Block of 1867, designed by George M. Harding, while at the right is the Falmouth Hotel of 1866–1868, the work of Charles A. Alexander. Only the Boyd Block and the small building next to it remain.

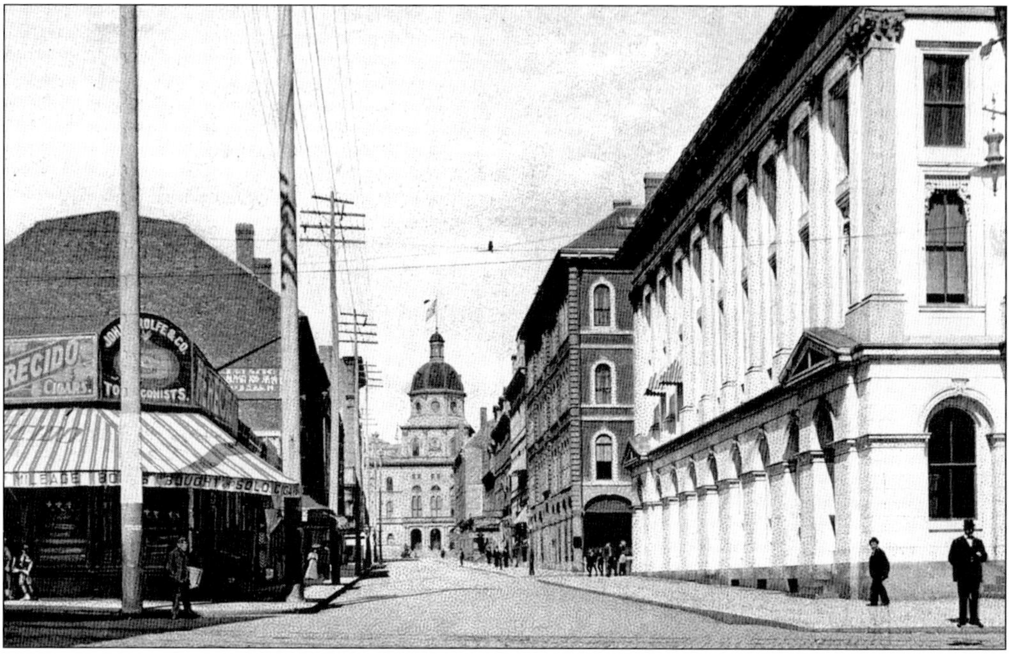


This postcard places the viewer at Middle and Exchange Streets, looking north up the latter to the Portland City Hall on Congress Street. The date is prior to 1908, when the domed city hall burned. At left, in the foreground, is the one-story wooden Fox Block, holding small shops, while the marble post office looms at the right. The sites of both of these buildings are now pocket parks.

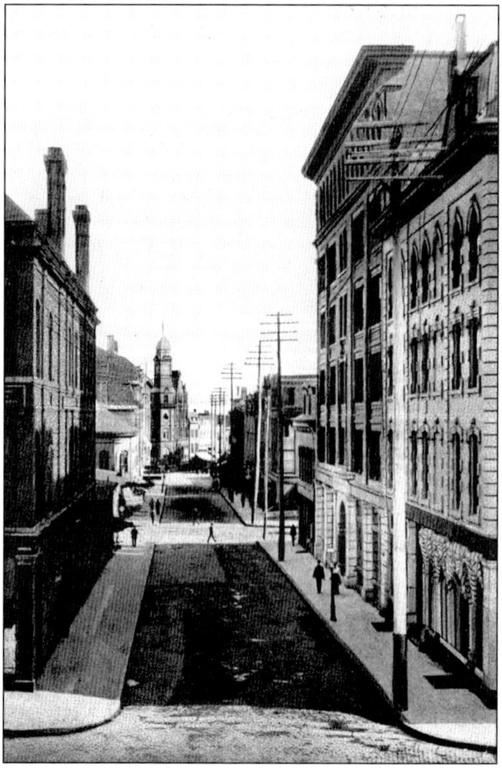

The vantage point of the previous card is reversed in this view from Congress Street down Exchange Street to the intersection of Middle Street. At the left is the Davis Block of 1885, replaced by a Gannett newspaper building, while the two blocks on the right housed the Union Mutual Life Insurance Company, later Unum. The tower is on the First National Bank.

Since its completion in 1884, the First National Bank has graced the southeast corner of Middle and Exchange Streets with its picturesque Queen Anne style of architecture in brick, stone, and terra-cotta. Designed by Boston's Henry Van Brunt, the block suffered a fire in 1947, which left its roofline altered and its tower reduced in height.

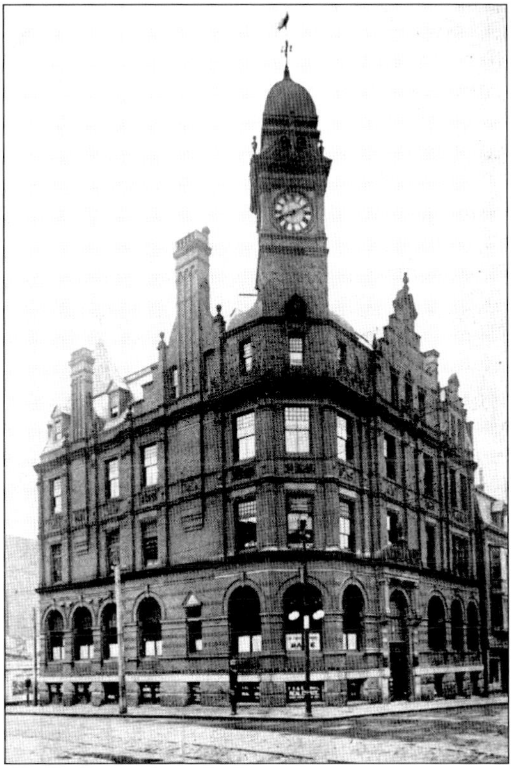

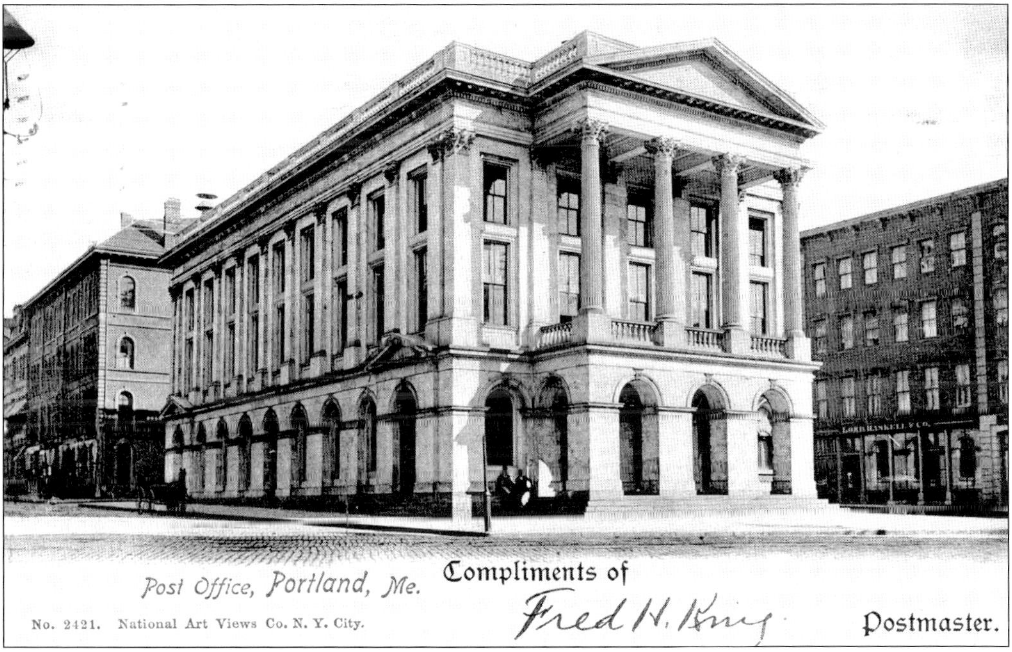


The marble post office at Middle and Exchange Streets was erected in 1868–1871. Designed by Department of the Treasury architect Alfred B. Mullett, the building served as Portland's main post office until the present one on Forest Avenue opened in 1934. After three more decades, the old building was demolished for a parking lot, which was recently transformed into Post Office Park.

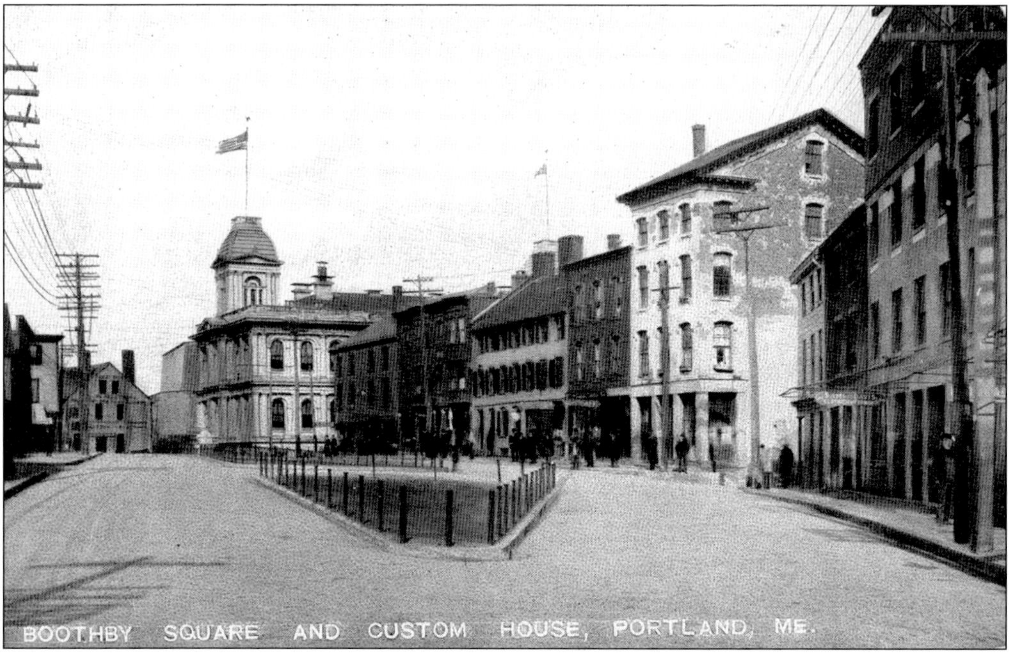


Boothby Square is a small park on Fore Street given to the city in 1902 by Col. Frederick E. Boothby. His gift included a granite water fountain, which was recently returned to the square. This view looking east on Fore Street from Market to Pearl Streets includes a row of commercial buildings dating from 1792 to 1902, ending with the granite U.S. Custom House of 1868–1871.

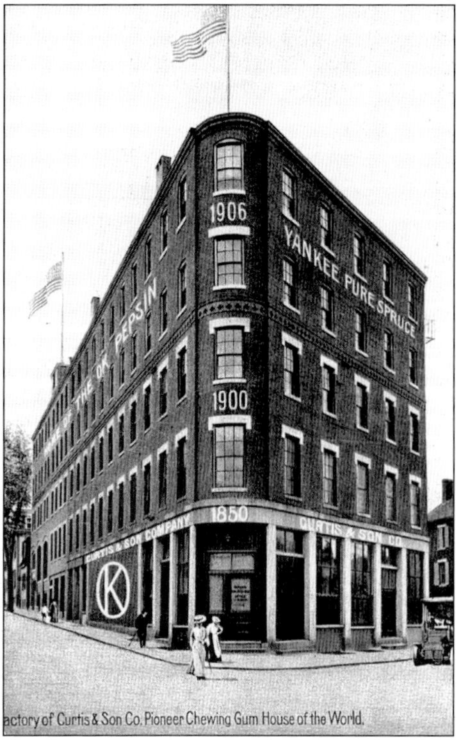


This five-story brick commercial block, still standing at Fore and Deer Streets, was the Curtis gum factory from 1866 until 1920. Founded in 1850, the Curtis factory at its height employed 200 people to make 1,800 boxes of spruce chewing gum a day. Derived from Maine spruce trees, the once-popular product was sold throughout the United States, Canada, and Mexico.

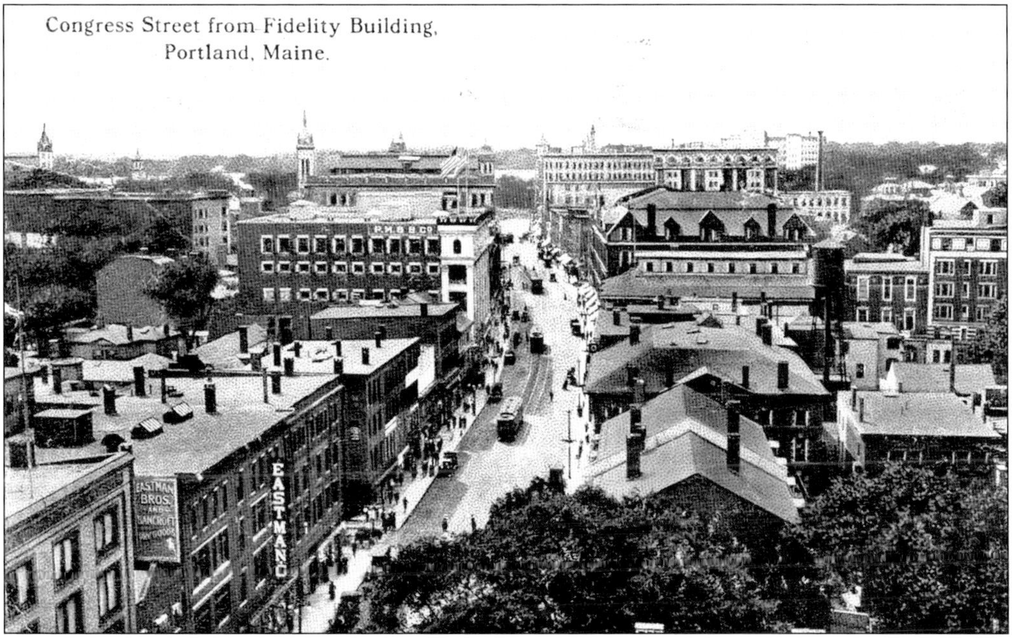


When this view was made, between 1910 and 1920, Congress Street from Monument Square to Congress Square was Portland's leading retail shopping district. This postcard includes four major department stores: Eastman Brothers and Bancroft; Porteous, Mitchell, and Braun; Rines Brothers; and J. R. Libby, none of which are in business today.

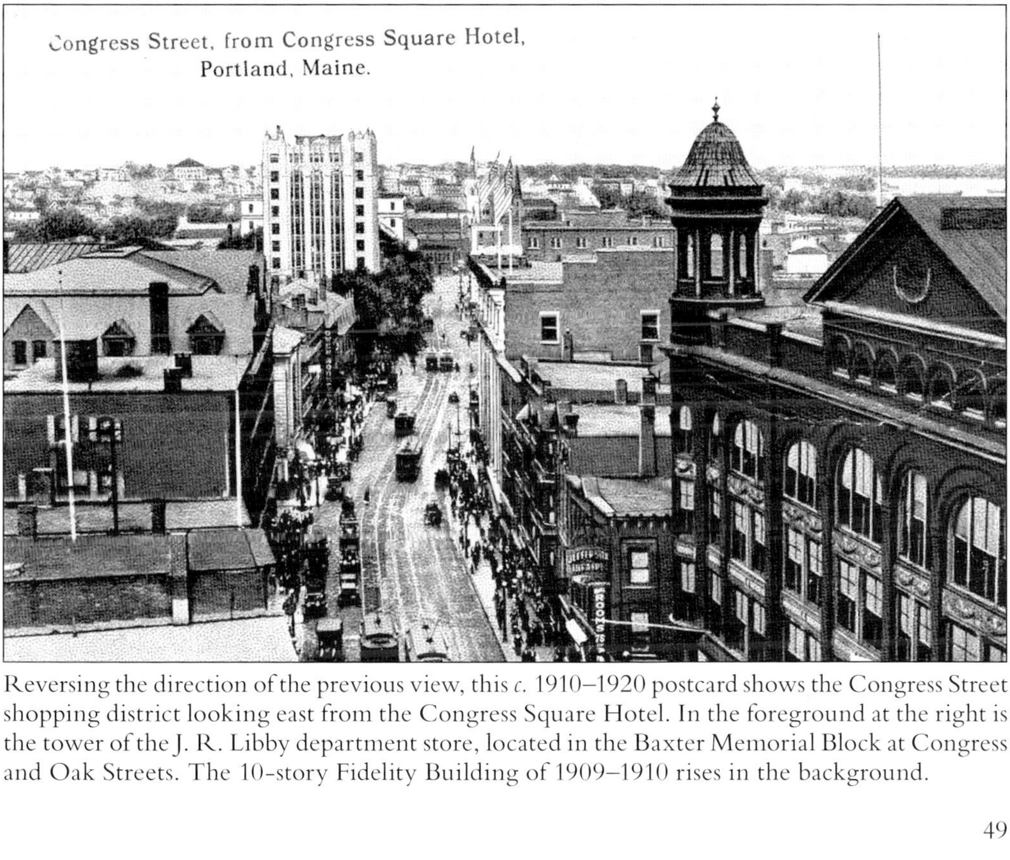


Reversing the direction of the previous view, this *c.* 1910–1920 postcard shows the Congress Street shopping district looking east from the Congress Square Hotel. In the foreground at the right is the tower of the J. R. Libby department store, located in the Baxter Memorial Block at Congress and Oak Streets. The 10-story Fidelity Building of 1909–1910 rises in the background.

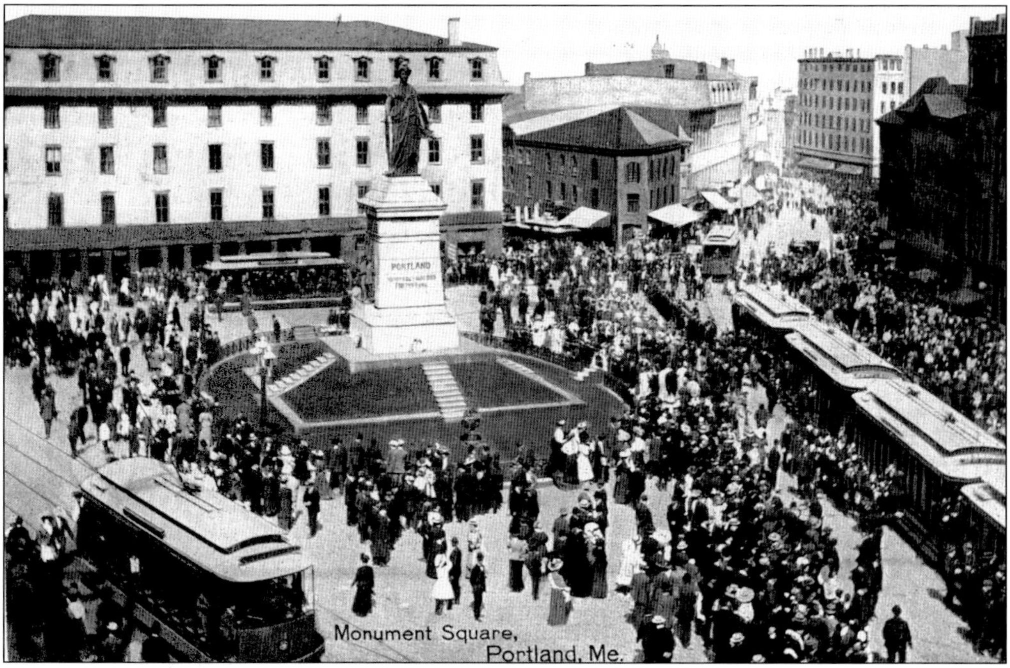


Every May 30 since 1892, Portlanders have gathered in Monument Square to observe Memorial Day. Here hundreds arrive by electric car and on foot to participate in the annual ceremony remembering those who served in the Civil War. Behind the monument is the Edwards and Walker hardware store, formerly the United States Hotel and since replaced by a Casco Bank building.

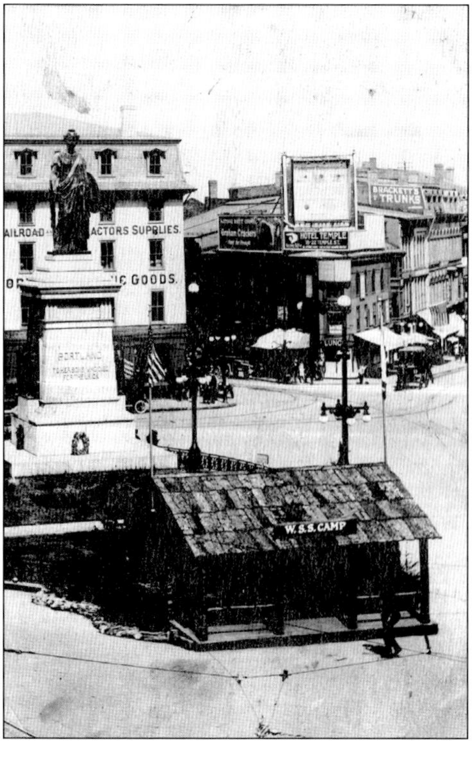


Shortly after America's entry into World War I in April 1917, the War Savings Stamp Camp was installed in front of the statue in Monument Square to serve as Portland's headquarters for the sale of stamps and bonds to help finance the war. This rustic log cabin was removed from the square when the armistice was achieved in November 1918.

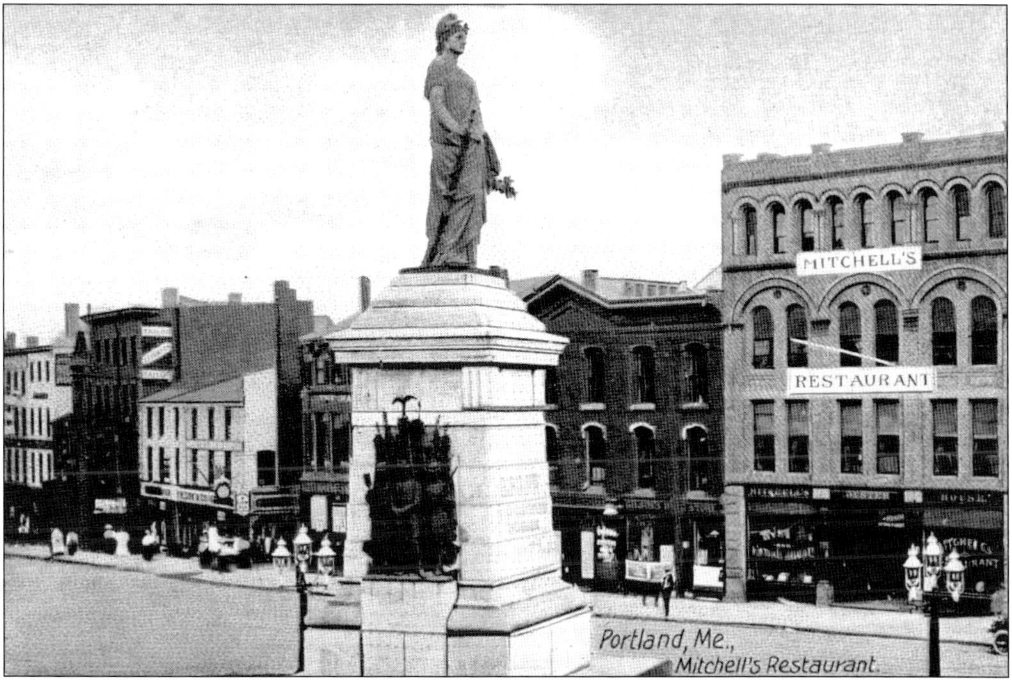


To honor the Portland men who died in the Civil War, the Soldiers and Sailors Monument was erected in Monument Square in 1889–1891. New York architect Richard Morris Hunt designed the granite pedestal. Bronze sculptures by Maine native Franklin Simmons—representations of army and navy men—are on the sides, with *Our Lady of Victories* crowning the composition.

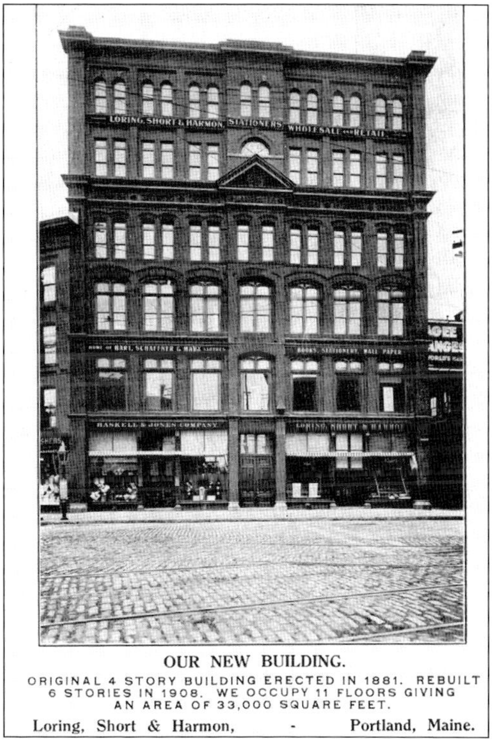


This postcard celebrates the 1908 addition of two new stories to the four-story Lancaster Block of 1881. Erected at Congress and Center Streets by J. B. Brown from designs by Francis H. Fassett and John Calvin Stevens, the brick Queen Anne–style building was named for Brown's New Hampshire birthplace and for years housed stationers Loring, Short, and Harmon.

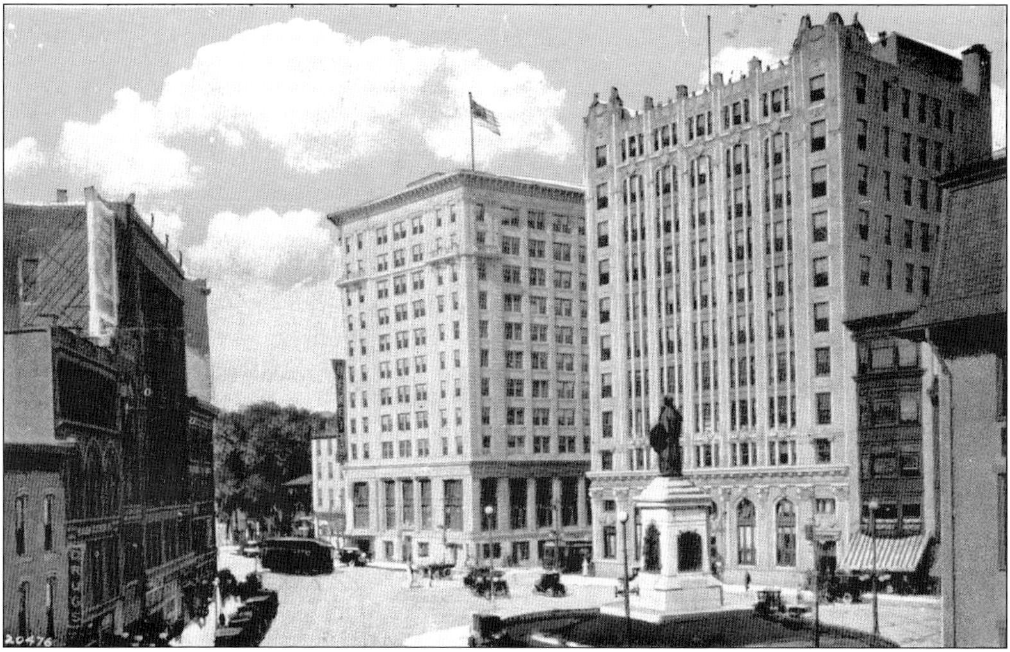


Maine's first two skyscrapers were built on Monument Square. G. Henri Desmond of Boston designed the Fidelity Building of 1909–1910 (right), while the Chapman Building of 1924 was the work of local architect Herbert W. Rhodes. Both were planned to have a bank at street level and offices above. The later building has received two more floors and a time and temperature sign.

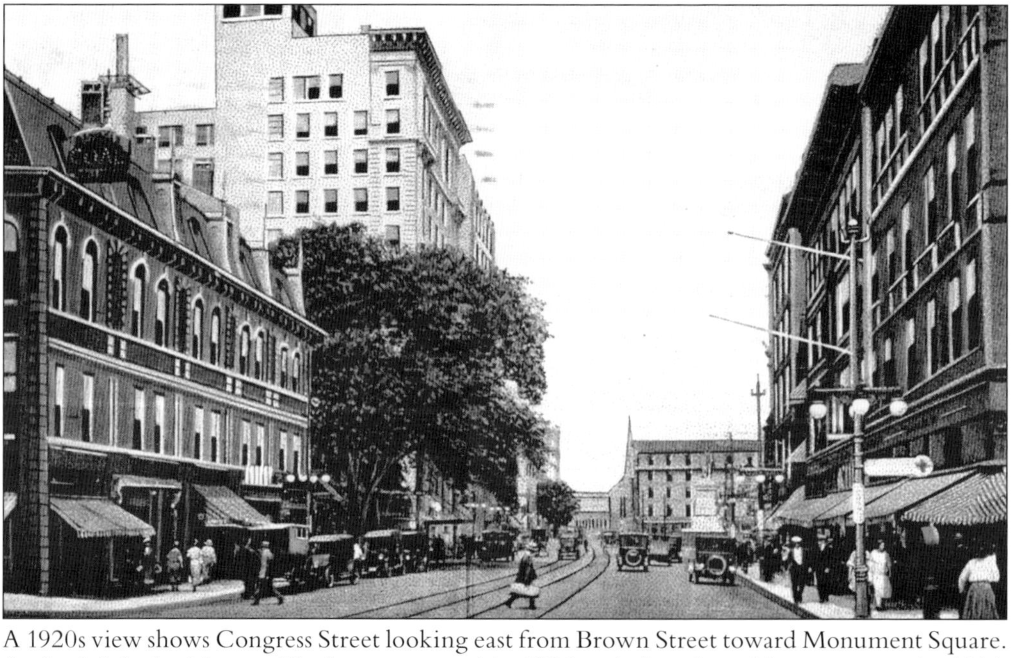

A 1920s view shows Congress Street looking east from Brown Street toward Monument Square. At the left is the Morton Block, constructed in 1826 and altered to this appearance in 1864. Two major remodelings later, it now houses the Maine Historical Society's museum and offices. The trees mark the Wadsworth-Longfellow House. On the right is the Eastman Brothers and Bancroft store.

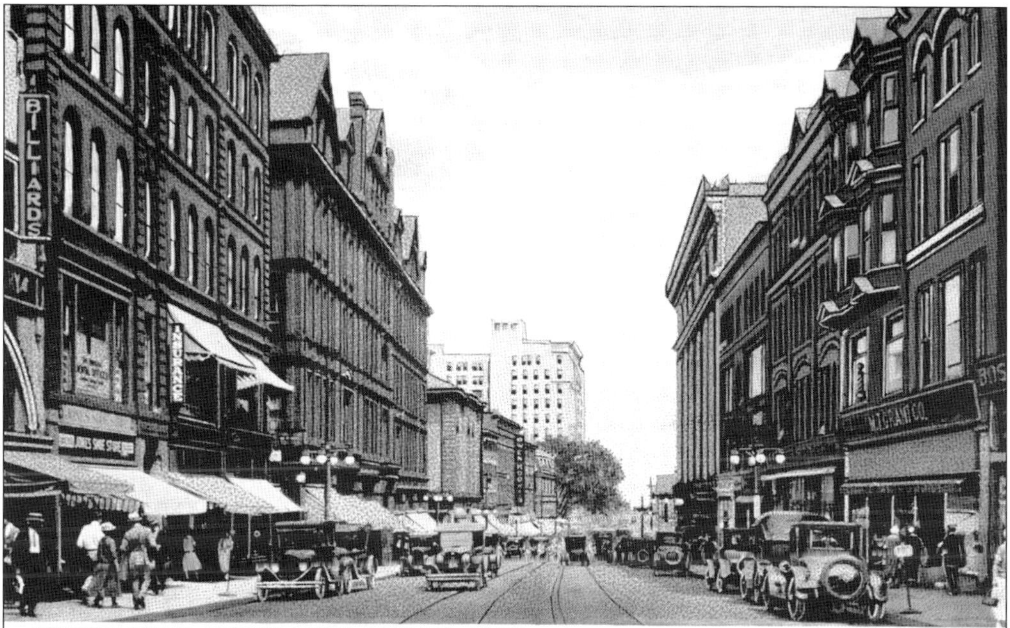


CONGRESS STREET, LOOKING NORTH, PORTLAND, MAINE.

More 1920s automobiles line both sides of Congress Street, viewed from slightly farther west. The second block from the left is the Brown Memorial Building, home to the Rines Brothers department store. Directly across from Rines is the Porteous, Mitchell, and Braun department store. The Chapman Building in the distance marks the location of Monument Square.

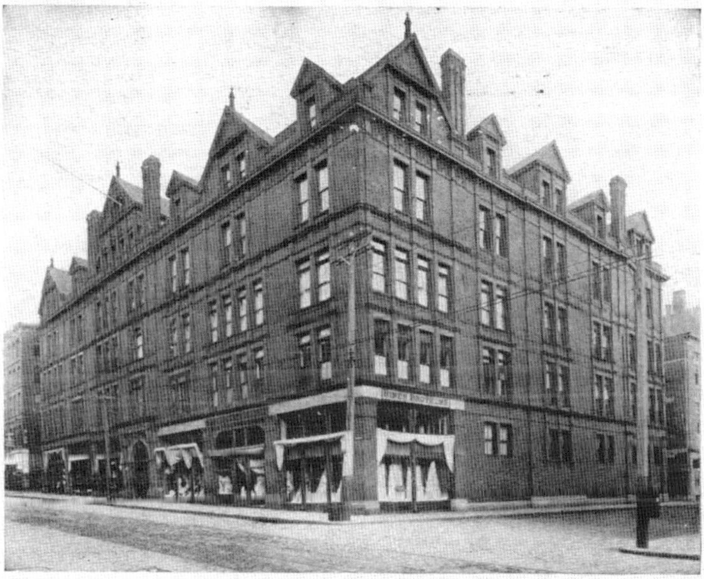

PORTLAND'S LEADING DEPARTMENT STORE, RINES BROS. COMPANY
529 to 535 Congress Street.

Make your headquarters here.

**Rest room on Second floor** for your convenience.

**Meet your Friends here**—Come in and rest.

**Free Telephone** for your use.

All electric cars stop at **RINES BROTHERS** or transfer to those which do.

After the death in 1881 of Portland's leading businessman, John Bundy Brown, his sons Philip Henry Brown and John Marshall Brown erected the Brown Memorial Building at Congress and Casco Streets in 1882–1883. Designed by John Calvin Stevens, this massive brick Queen Anne building was immediately (and for decades) occupied by the Rines Brothers department store.

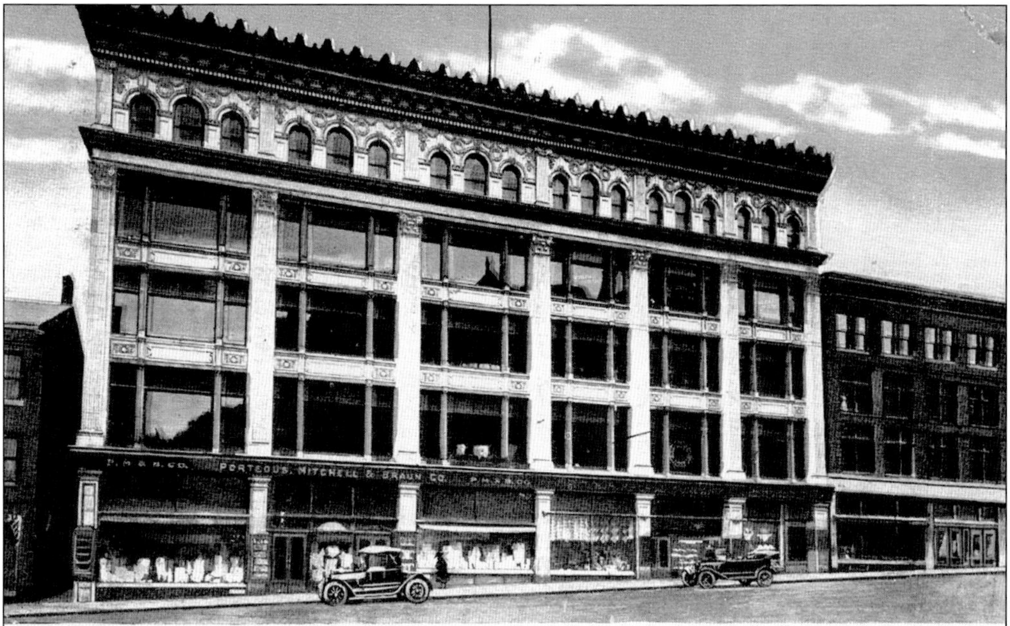

PORTEOUS. MITCHELL & BRAUN BUILDING. PORTLAND, ME.

The left half of this Congress Street department store was built in 1904 by William L. Miller, who operated the Boston Shoe Store there until 1906, when he sold to Porteous, Mitchell, and Braun, which added the right half in 1911. The Renaissance Revival terra-cotta facade was designed by Penn Varney of Lynn, Massachusetts, and carefully replicated in the expansion by George Burnham.

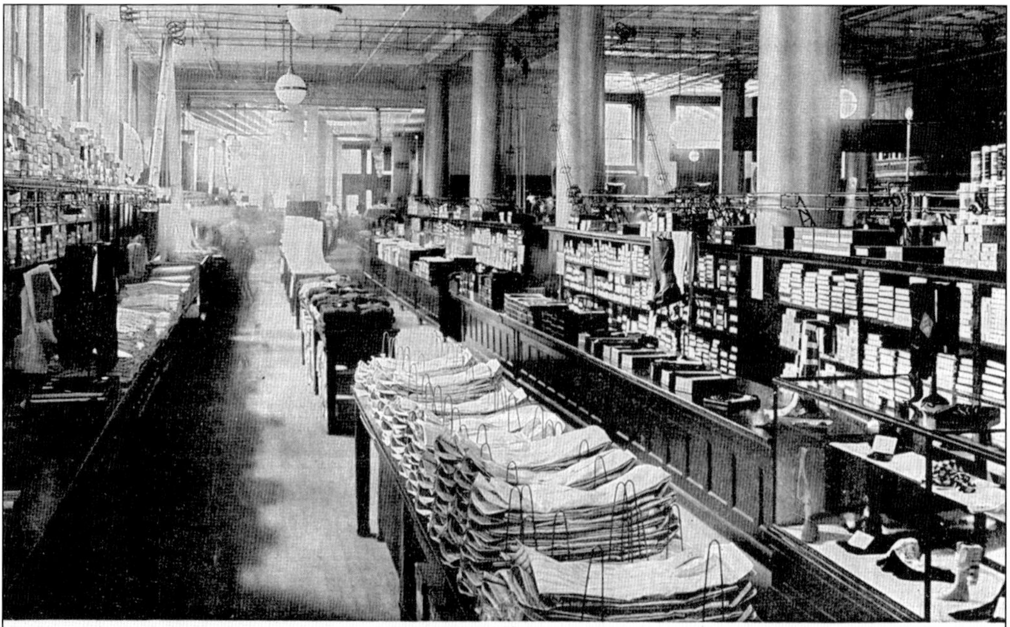

SHOWING OUR EAST AISLE. MAIN FLOOR. PORTEOUS. MITCHELL & BRAUN CO., PORTLAND. ME

The clothing department on the main floor was just one of Porteous, Mitchell, and Braun's many specialties. In 1909, the store employed 120 people and occupied more than 50,000 square feet of retail space. It closed its doors in 1991. The building was acquired three years later by the Maine College of Art, the state's largest art school.

The Baxter Memorial Block, on the right, was built in 1894–1896 by James P. Baxter in memory of his father, Dr. Elihu Baxter. The huge five-story brick building with a corner tower was designed by Francis H. and Edward F. Fassett. The prime tenant from 1896 to 1935 was the J. R. Libby department store, which occupied four floors and employed as many as 200 people.

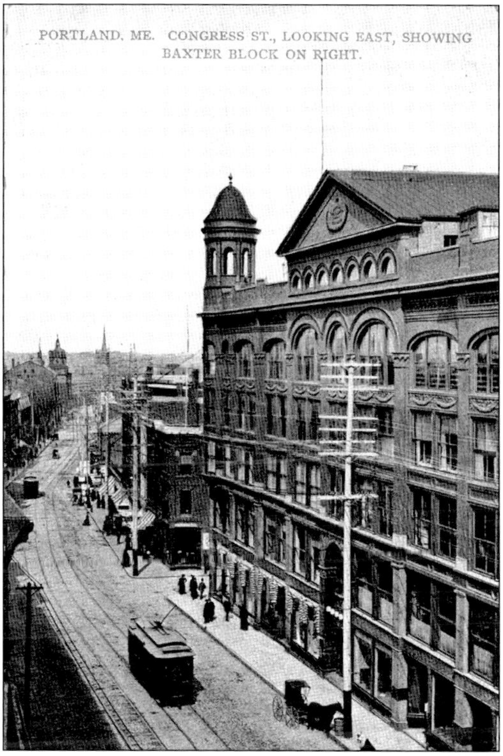


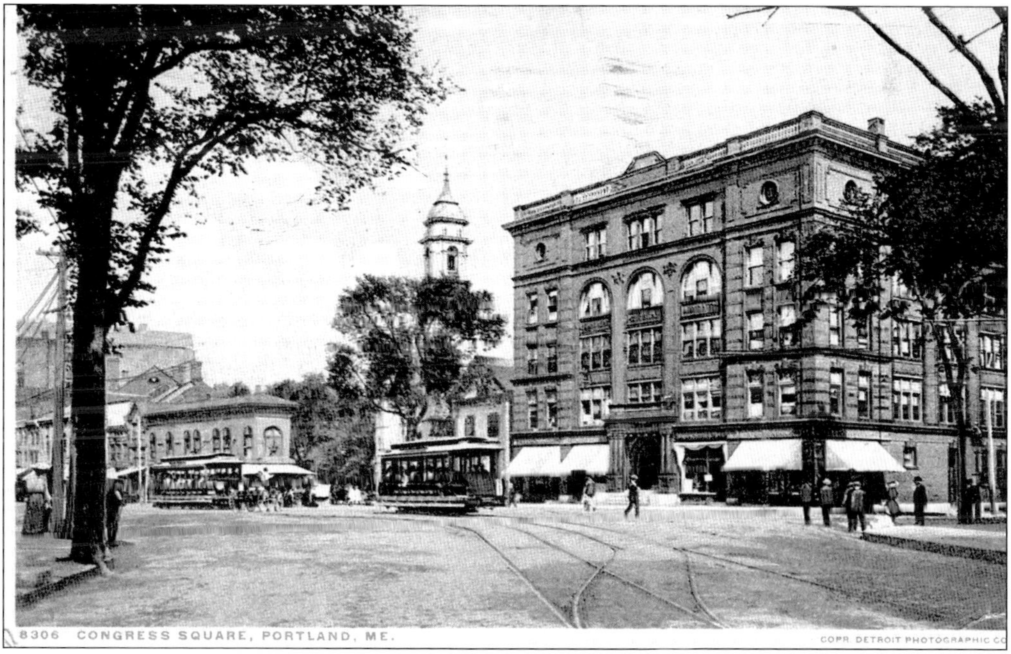


A view across Congress Square from farther west on Congress Street includes the H. H. Hay Building before it received a third floor, the Free Street Baptist Church, and the YMCA, erected in 1897 from designs by Frederick A. Tompson. Later the Libby Building, it was replaced in 1980 by the Payson Wing of the Portland Museum of Art.

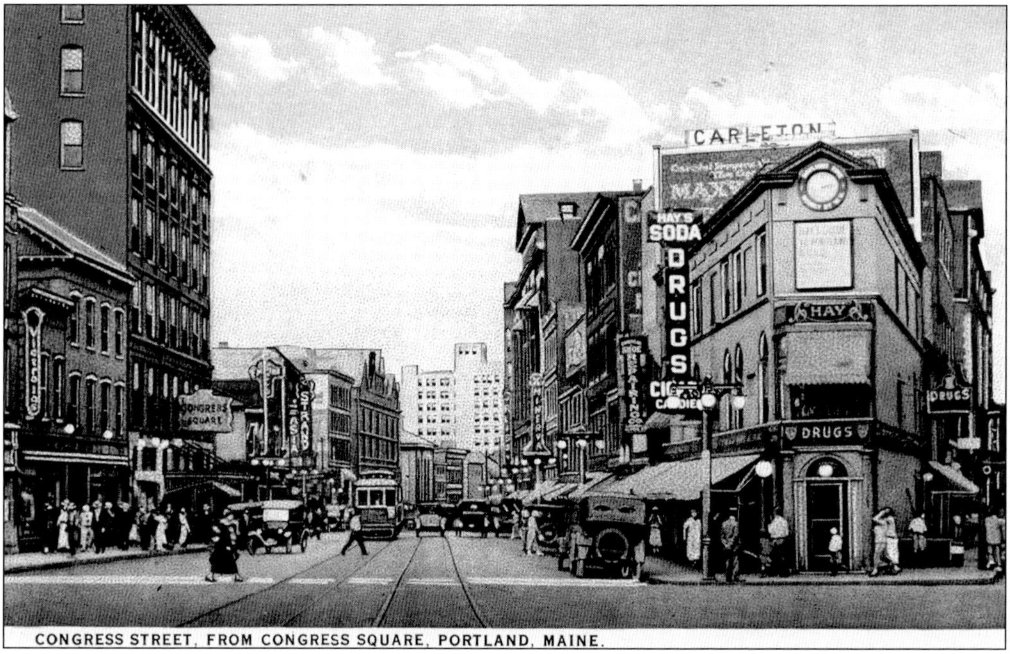


The upper H. H. Hay Building is on the right in this view of the east side of Congress Square in the 1920s. At the junction of Congress and Free Streets, Hay's was designed and constructed by Charles Q. Clapp in 1826, as the narrow two-story block of the previous picture. Hay opened this "uptown" drugstore in 1912 and added a third story in 1922, designed by the Stevens firm.

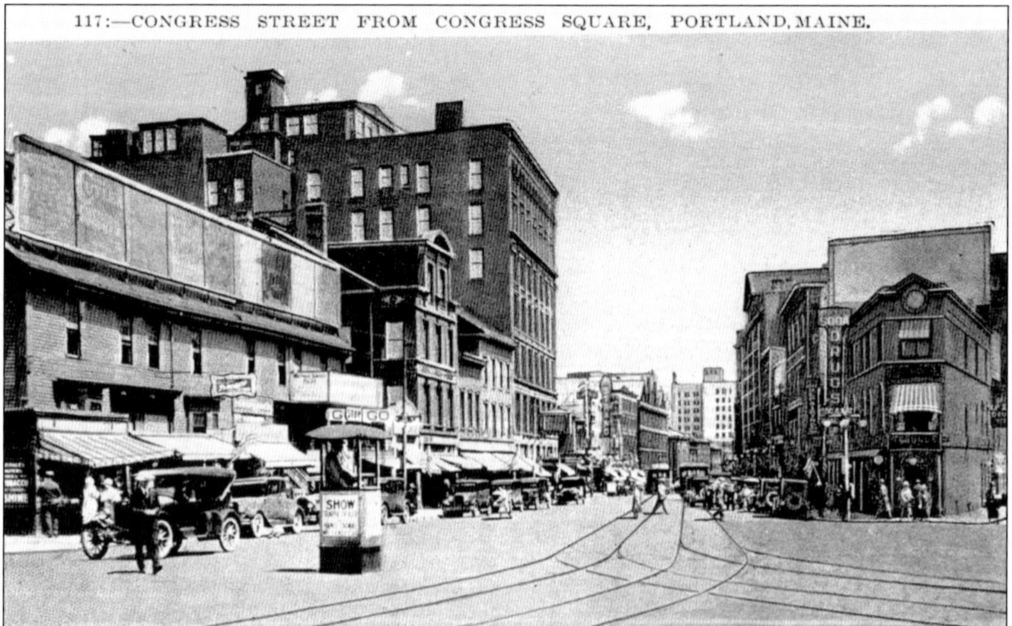


Trolley tracks run through Congress Square in the 1920s, and a policeman directs traffic from an open booth in the center. At the left stands a former row house, which became known as the League of Nations Building because of the varied nationalities of its shop owners. A small park now occupies the site. The tall building beyond is the Congress Square Hotel.

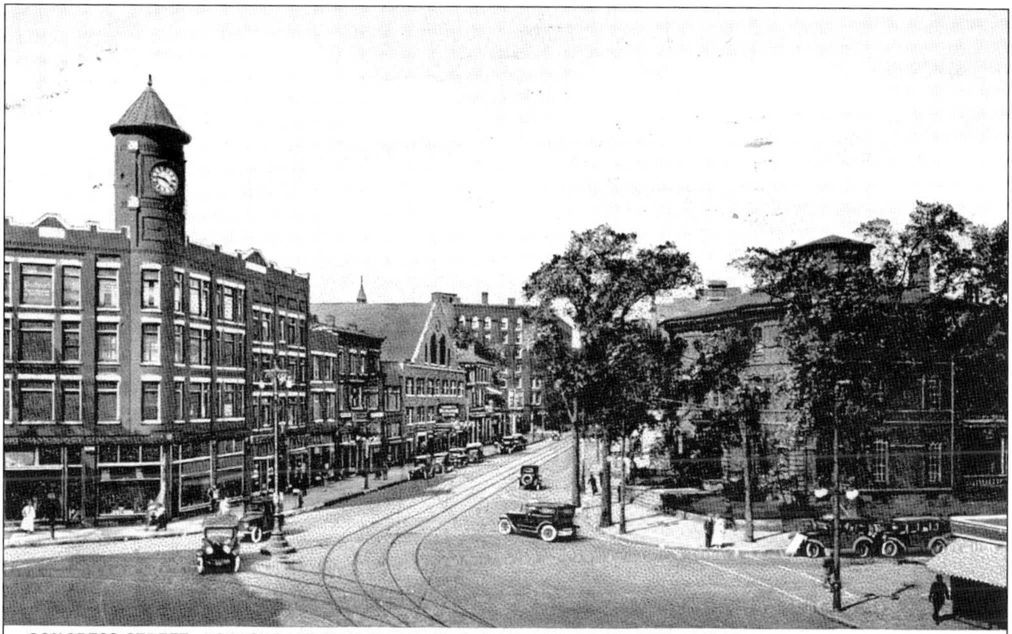


CONGRESS STREET, LOOKING WEST FROM CONGRESS SQUARE, PORTLAND, MAINE.

During the 1920s, Congress Square was in transition from residential to commercial use. In 1920, the four-story brick Schwartz Building at the left replaced an 1850 residence. On the opposite corner, H. J. Libby's Italianate double house of 1852–1853 (designed by Charles A. Alexander with elaborately painted wall decorations) would be demolished in 1929 for the State Building.

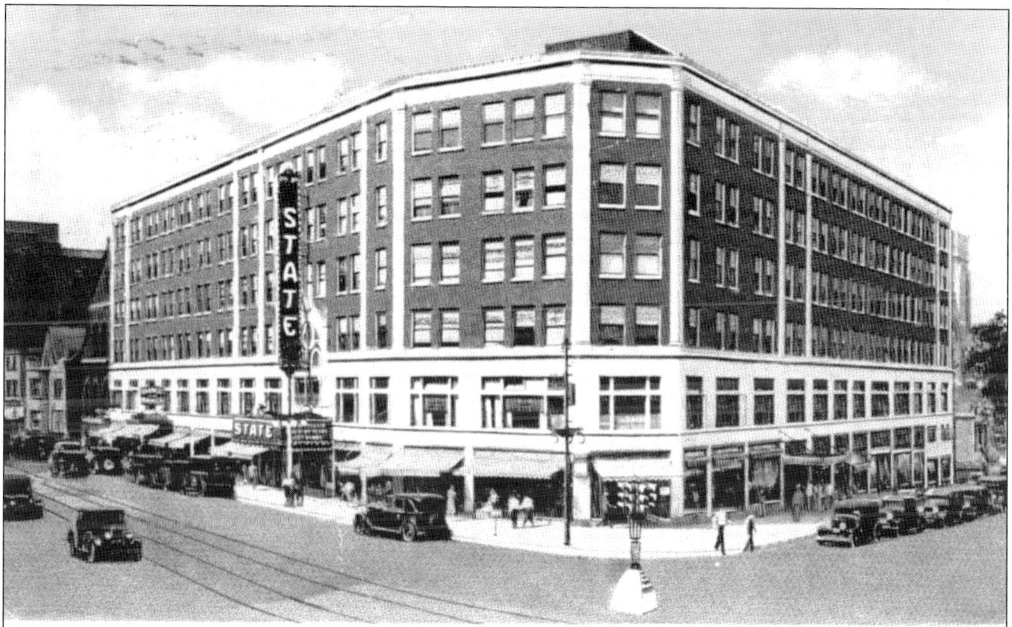


STATE BUILDING, PORTLAND, MAINE

OA4147

Dominating the northwest corner of Congress Square at Congress and High Streets is the Congress Building, also known as the State Building, which was constructed in 1929 from designs by Herbert W. Rhodes. The large brick block provides retail and office space and holds the State Theater, the last of the pre–World War II cinemas left in downtown Portland.

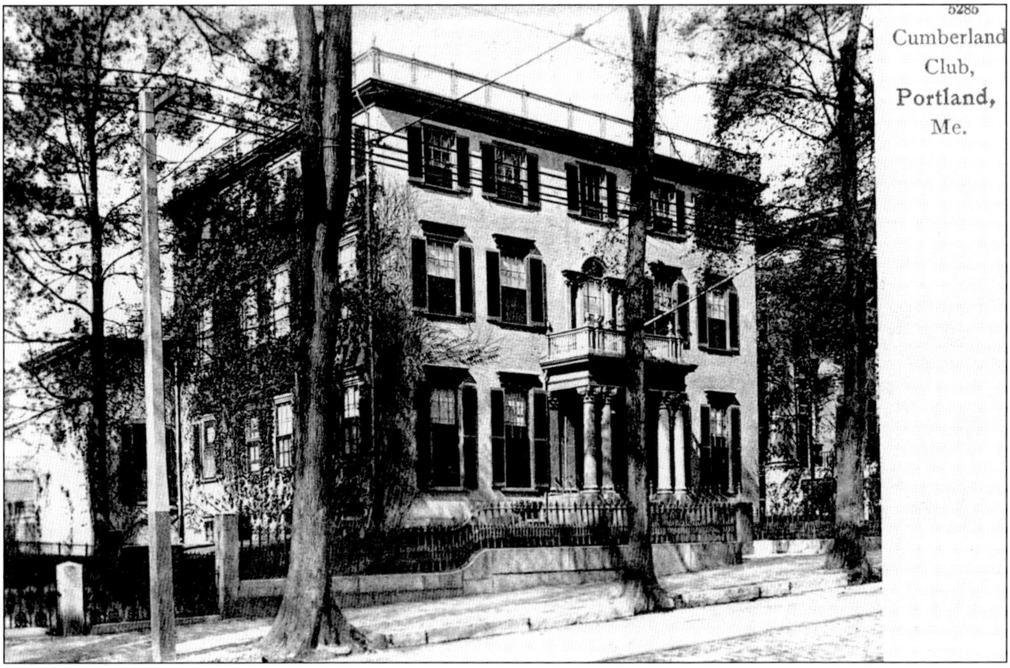


In 1800, the merchant brothers Hugh and Stephen McLellan built their three-story brick Federal mansions in the emerging Spring Street neighborhood. John Kimball Sr. was paid $20,000 apiece for the design and construction of each. Hugh's house (see page 14) became part of the art museum, while Stephen's (shown here) has been the Cumberland Club since 1895.

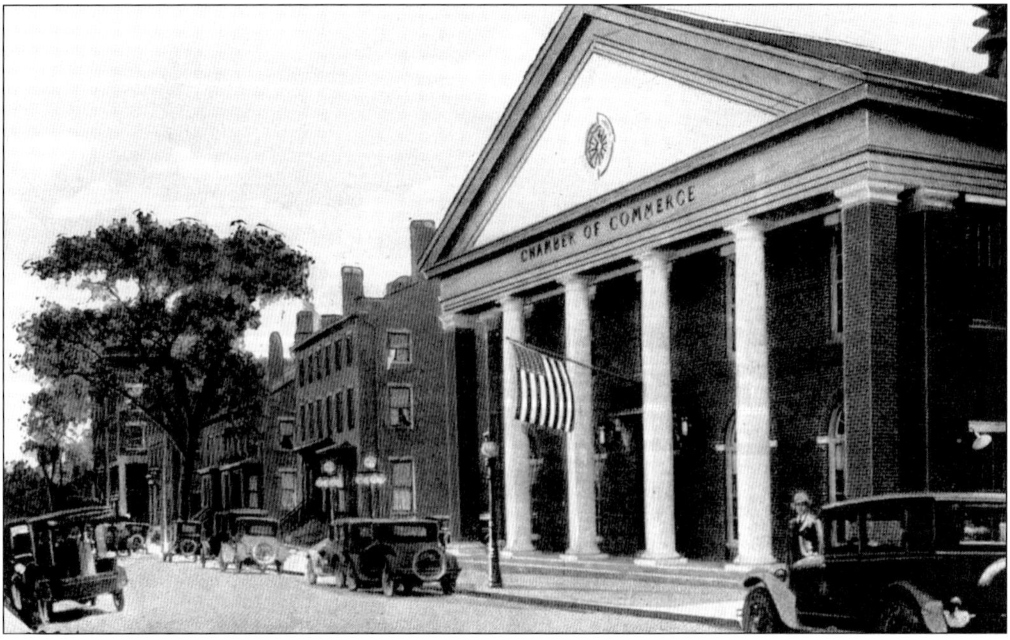


This columned building on Free Street has a long history of adaptive reuse. Built as the Portland Theater in 1830, it was the Free Street Baptist Church from 1836 to 1926. At that time, it was acquired by the Portland Chamber of Commerce, which hired the Stevens firm to remodel the structure to the appearance shown here. It now holds the Children's Museum of Maine.

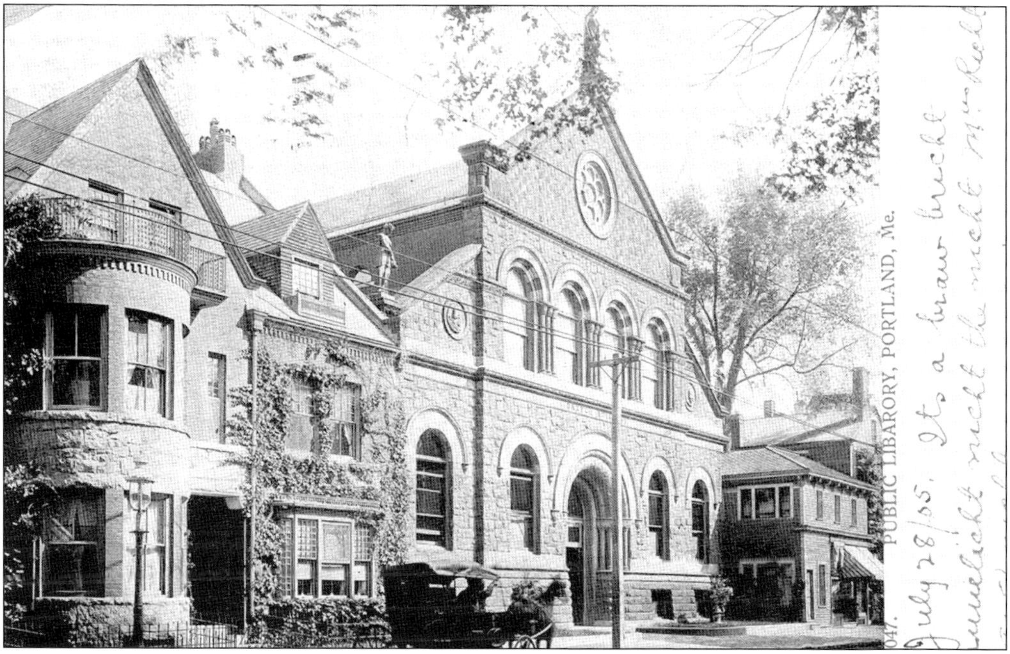


One of Francis H. Fassett's finest designs is his brownstone Romanesque facade for the Portland Public Library of 1887–1888 on Congress Street. A gift to the city by James P. Baxter, the building served readers for nearly a century before becoming part of the Maine College of Art. Designed by Stevens and Cobb, the Dr. James A. Spalding house of 1888 (left) was demolished in 1938.

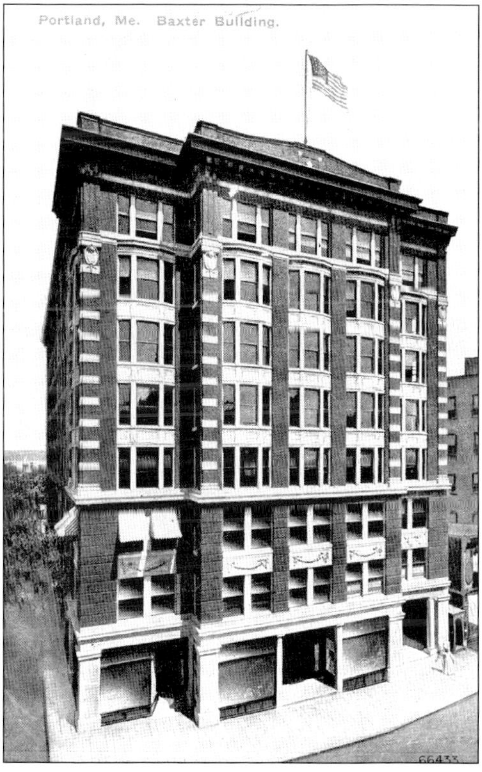


The eight-story Trelawny Building has overlooked Longfellow Square since 1909. Designed by Frederick A. Tompson, it was erected by James P. Baxter and named for Robert Trelawny, an English merchant who invested in the Portland area in the 1630s. Baxter's son, Gov. Percival P. Baxter, maintained his office on the top floor for many years.

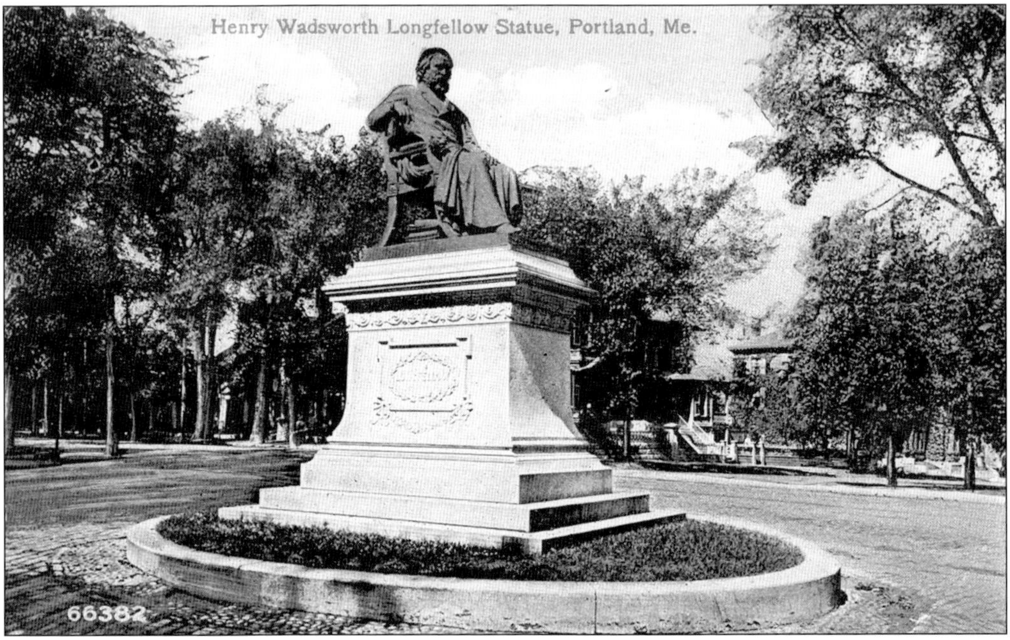


When Henry Wadsworth Longfellow died in 1882, Portland honored its most famous son by naming a square in his memory and placing a statue of him there. Since 1888, the bronze figure of the seated poet by Franklin Simmons has gazed down Congress Street from atop a granite pedestal designed by Francis H. Fassett. The money for the statue came from many small contributions.

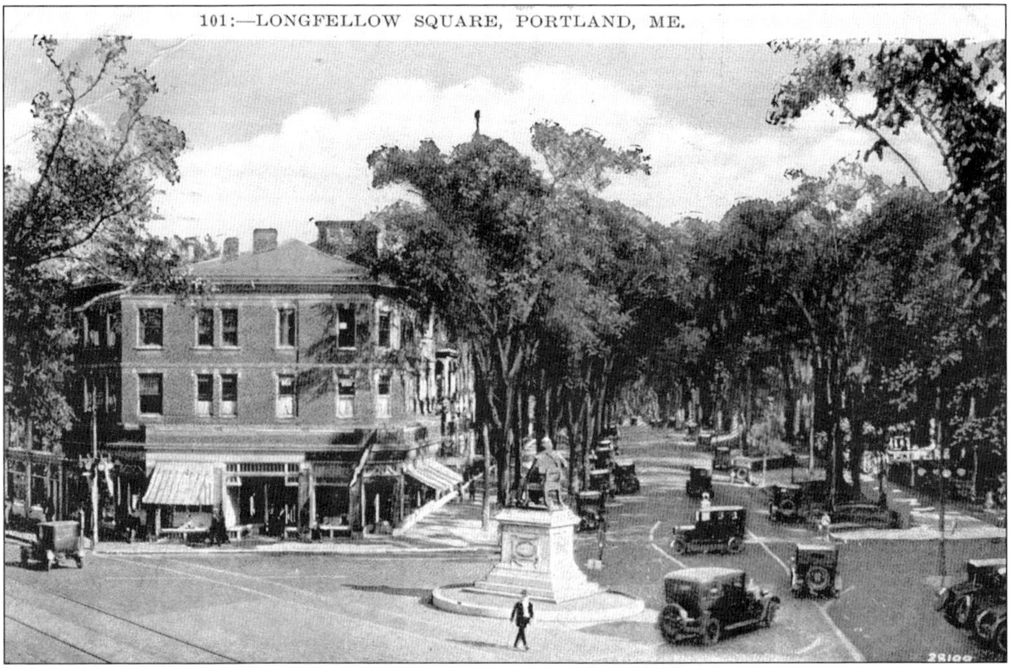


This 1920s view of Longfellow Square looks south down the original section of State Street from Congress Street toward York Street. The double rows of elms, planted in 1800, arch to meet above the center of the street. On the left, the Dr. Israel T. Dana house of 1878, by Francis H. Fassett, had been converted to commercial use by the time this postcard was made.

# Five

# Architecture

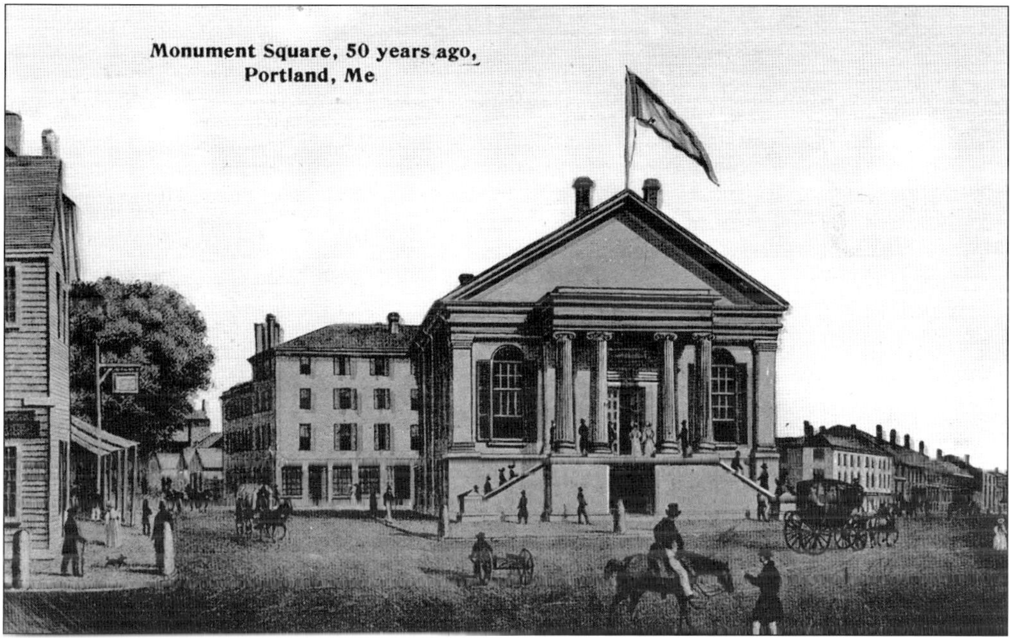


This historical view of Market (now Monument) Square was based on a picture that appeared on the 1838 award certificate for the Maine Charitable Mechanic Association fair. The columned building in the center was constructed as Portland's market house in 1825 to provide stalls for selling produce on the ground floor with a hall for militia training above. As designed by John Kimball Jr., the structure included a belfry on the roof, a feature that was removed in 1832 during its remodeling into the first city hall. This transformation from the Federal to the Greek Revival style was planned by Charles Q. Clapp. A real estate developer and architect, Clapp was also responsible for the 1835 expansion of the building behind the Portland City Hall from a tavern into the Cumberland House, a major hotel. To the left, Congress Street heads east, while to the right is the beginning of Middle Street.

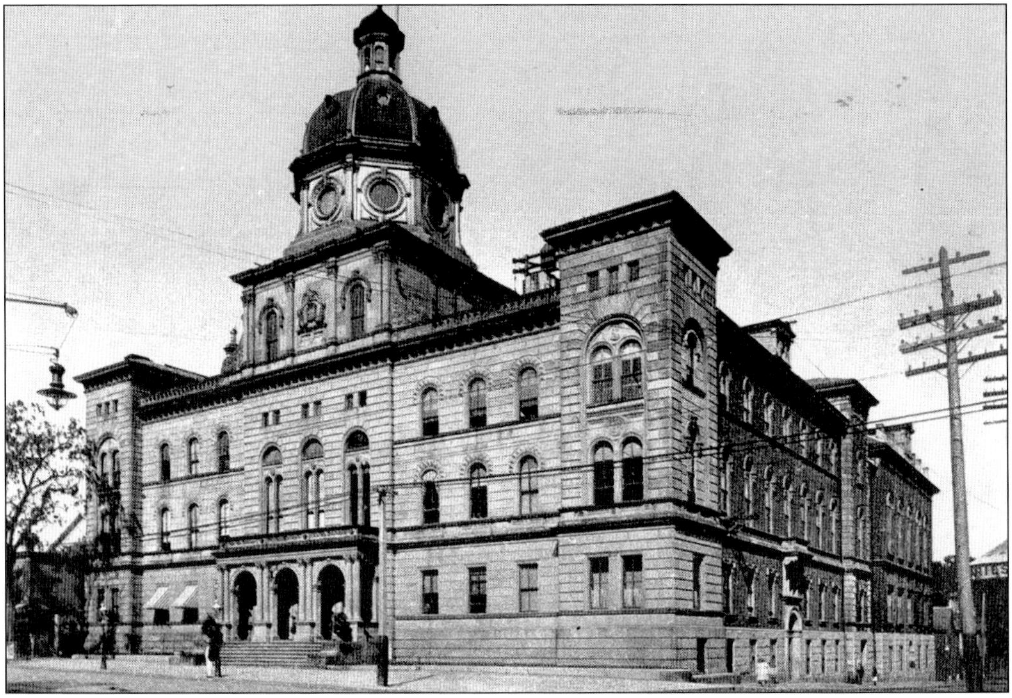

Between 1858 and 1860, Portland built a new city hall at Congress and Myrtle Streets. Designed by James H. Rand, it featured a 130-foot sandstone facade culminating in a large central dome. Six years later, Portland City Hall was gutted by the Great Fire of 1866. Reusing the burned-out walls, Francis H. Fassett supervised a reconstruction, employing a smaller dome on a square base.

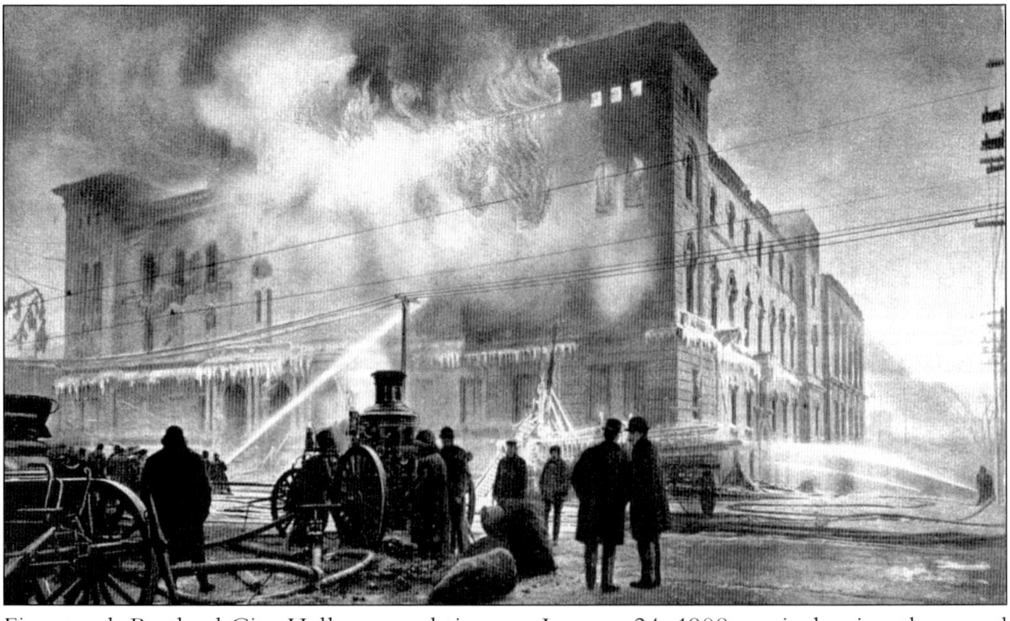

Fire struck Portland City Hall a second time on January 24, 1908, again leaving the proud structure an empty shell. As in 1866, fireproof vaults saved precious city and county records from destruction, the notable exception being the loss of Cumberland County's wills, dating back to 1760. After much public debate, the decision was made to build an entirely new city hall.

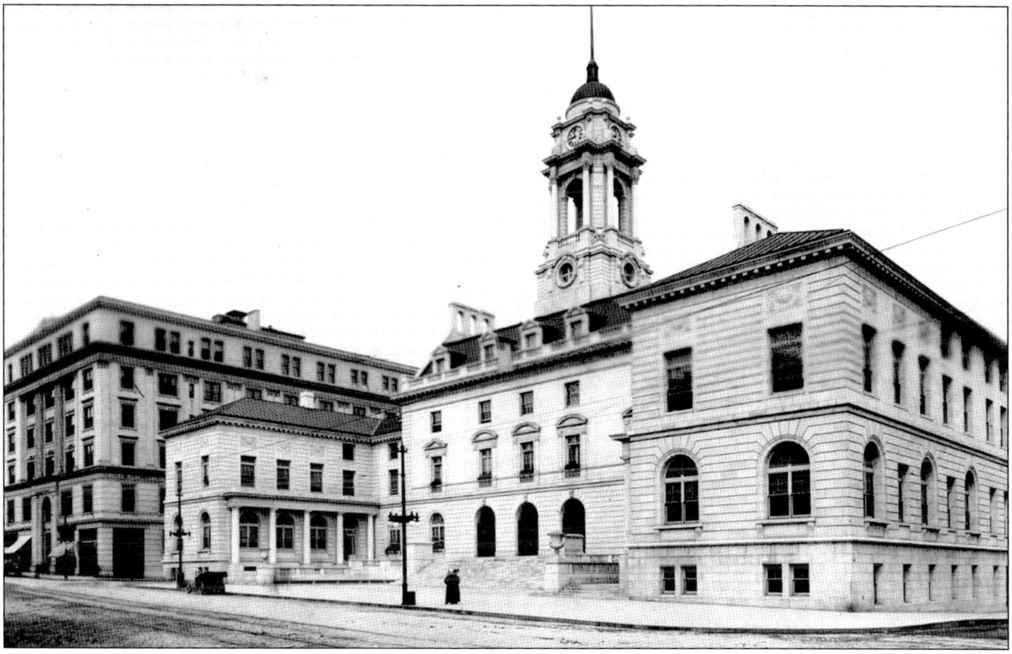

The new building was constructed on the site of the two previous ones. Planned by the New York firm of Carrere and Hastings in association with local architects John Calvin Stevens and John Howard Stevens, the city hall was built in 1909–1912 of granite from North Jay.

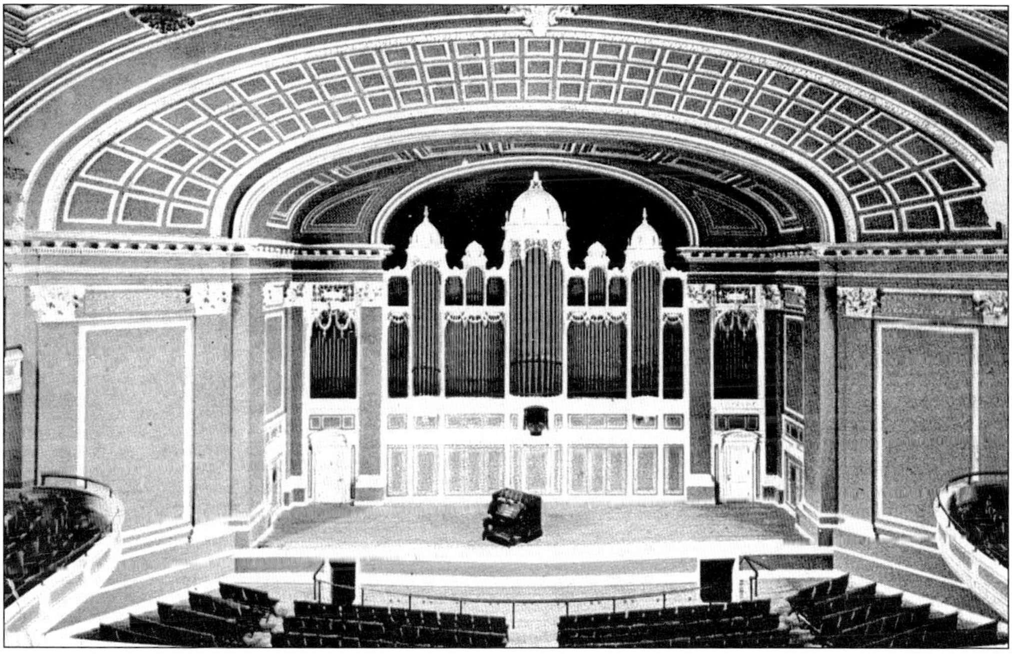

The rear of Portland City Hall is devoted to a great public auditorium, which has hosted countless events since its opening in 1912. The space focuses on a stage that contains one of the world's largest organs, given by Cyrus H. K. Curtis in memory of noted local musician Herman Kotzschmar. In the 1990s, the hall was renamed Merrill Auditorium in recognition of a bequest from Virginia and Paul Merrill, which inspired a major renovation of the facility.

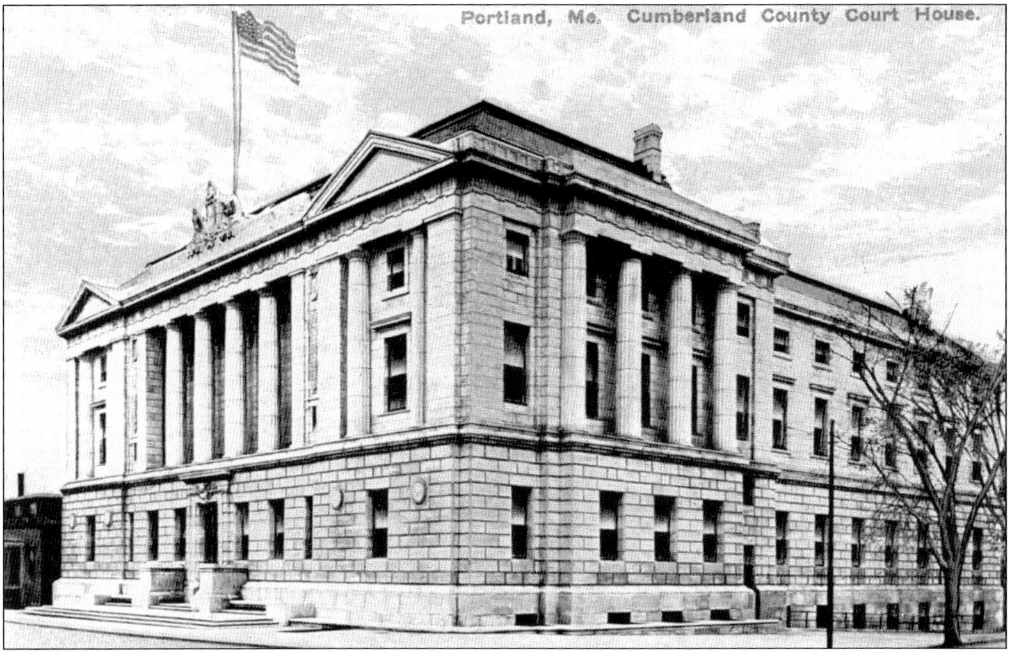


When Cumberland County was created in 1760, Portland (then Falmouth) became the county seat and has remained so to this day. In 1905, the county commissioners began this granite courthouse at Federal and Pearl Streets for the Maine Supreme Court, lower courts, and county offices. Completed in 1909, it was the work of George Burnham and Boston's Guy Lowell.

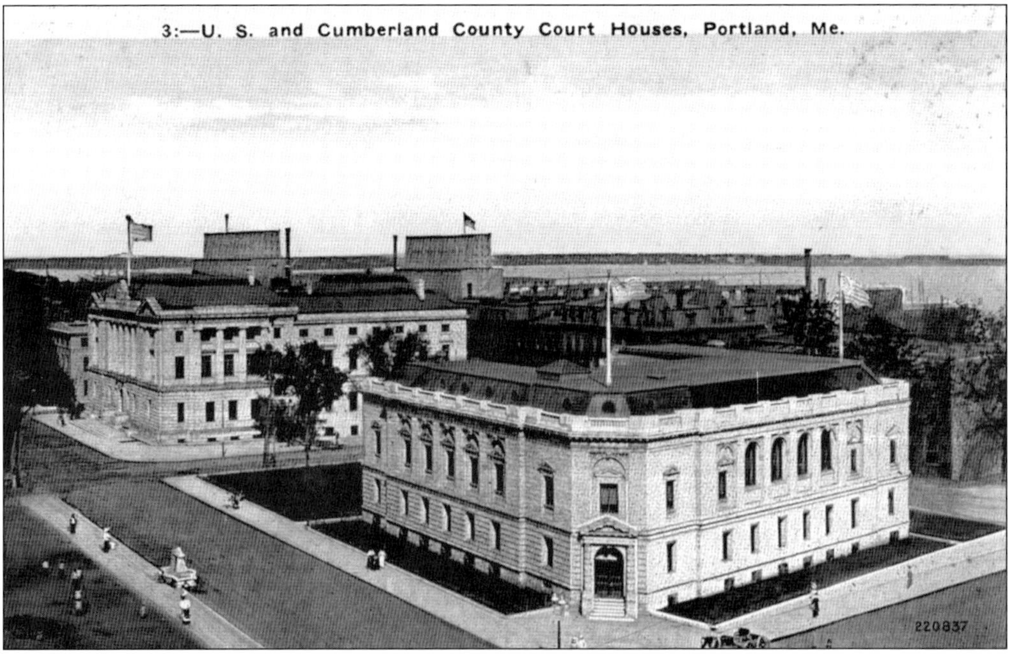


At about that time (1908–1911), the federal courthouse, seen in the foreground, was erected at Federal and Market Streets. In 1931–1932, government architect James Knox Taylor's distinctly French Beaux-Arts granite building was doubled in size by an addition that extended the courthouse to Pearl Street.

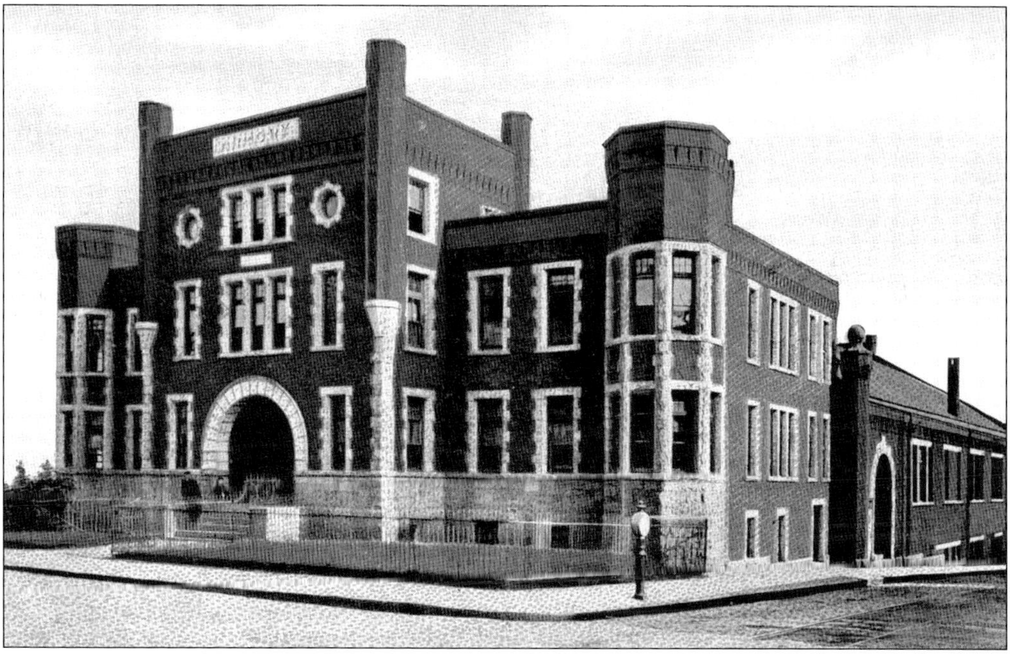

The 1895 State of Maine Armory, located on the block bordered by Milk, Silver, Fore, and Market Streets, was designed by Frederick A. Tompson to house the administrative and drill functions of several units of the Maine Militia, later part of the National Guard. Once its military functions ceased, the structure was a warehouse until converted into a hotel.

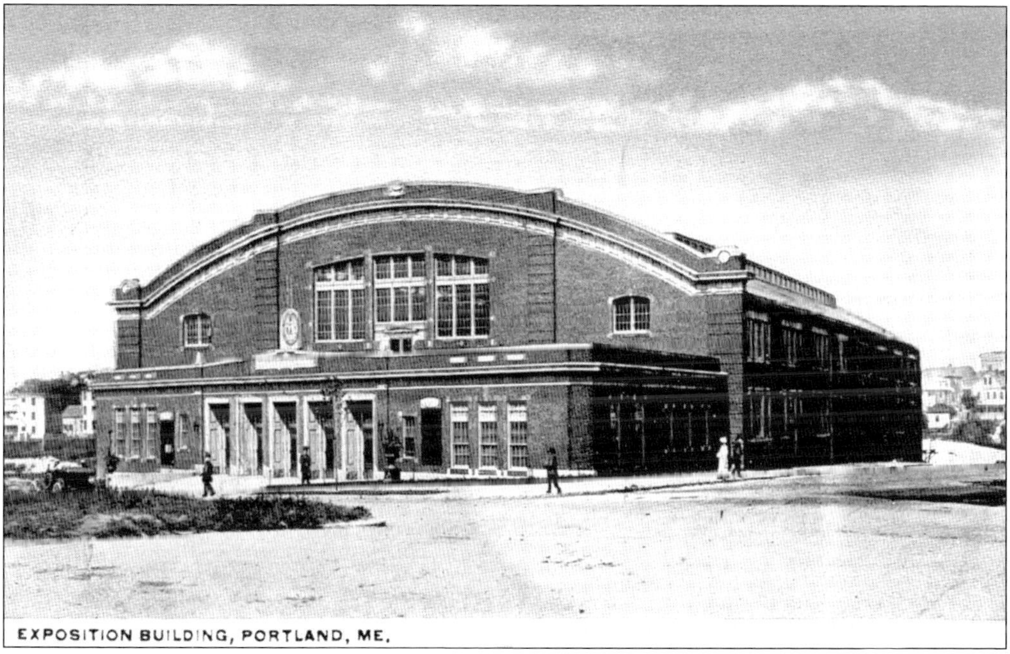


To address Portland's growing role as a convention center, the Exposition Building was constructed on Park Avenue in 1914. Also designed by Tompson, this massive brick structure, 132 feet wide by 206 feet long, can accommodate 5,000 people. Although superseded in size by the Cumberland County Civic Center in the 1970s, the "Portland Expo" still hosts many events.

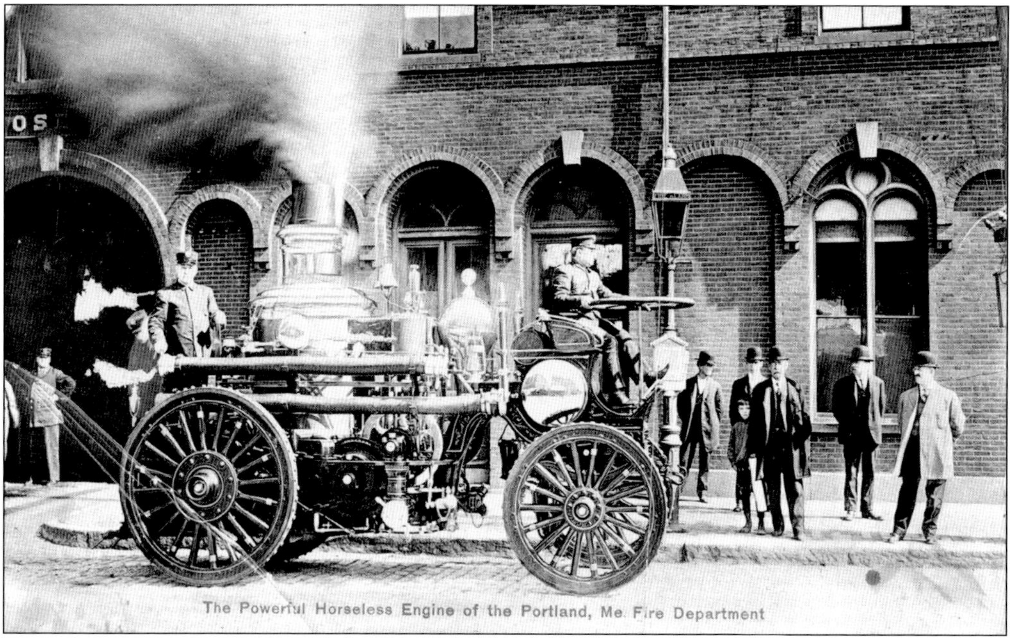


One of the measures that Portland took to prevent a recurrence of the Great Fire of 1866 was the establishment of a large central fire station at Congress and Market Streets. The first story of this arched brick Victorian building provides a backdrop for this scene of the city's "powerful horseless engine," a steam-driven pumper put into service in 1902.

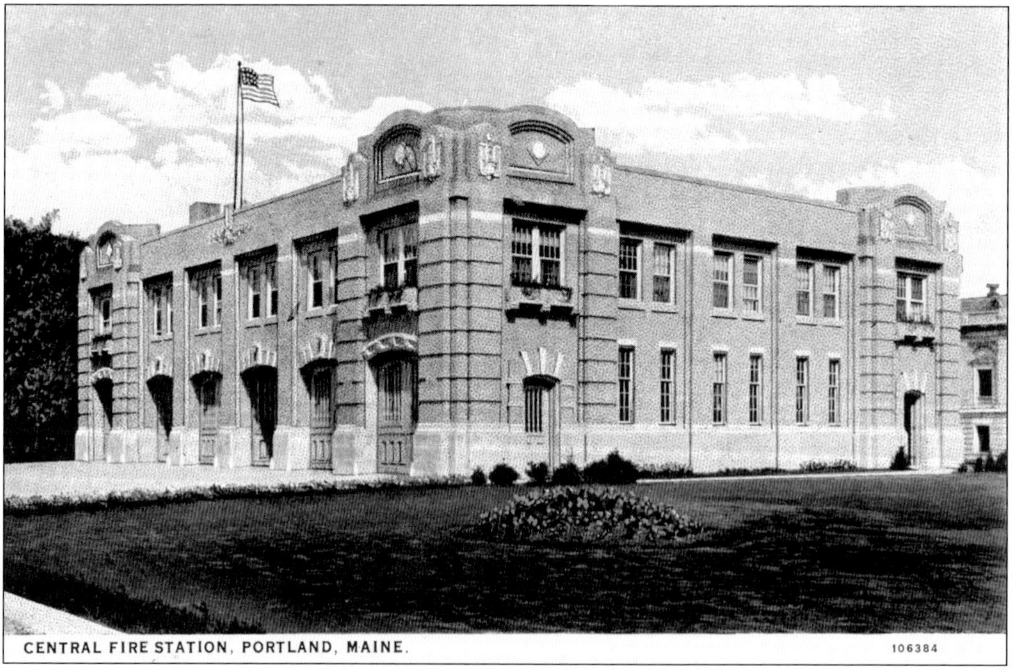


In 1923, the city replaced its old central fire station with a new one at Congress and Pearl Streets. Designed by William R. Miller and Raymond J. Mayo, the building was constructed to house the administrative offices of the Portland Fire Department and the firefighting apparatus for the downtown area. The Beaux-Arts style complements nearby government buildings.

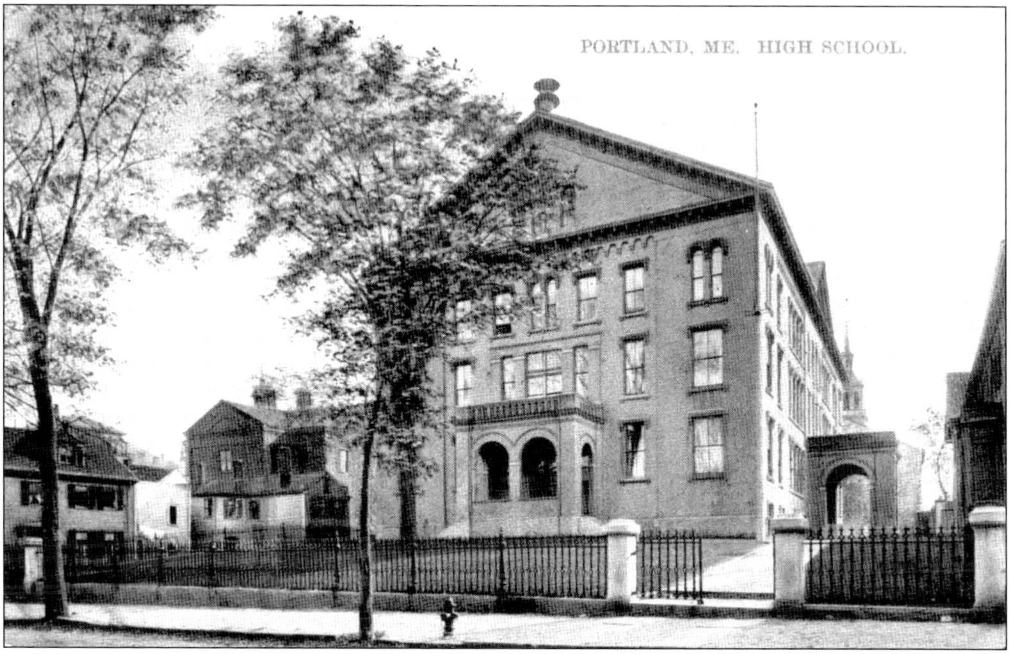


When Portland High School opened on Cumberland Avenue in September 1863, in its new brick Italianate-style quarters, the 135 boys and 161 girls were under the same roof for the first time, but a brick wall divided the building into a distinct half for each sex. Early students included future magazine publisher Cyrus H. K. Curtis and future Arctic explorer Robert E. Peary.

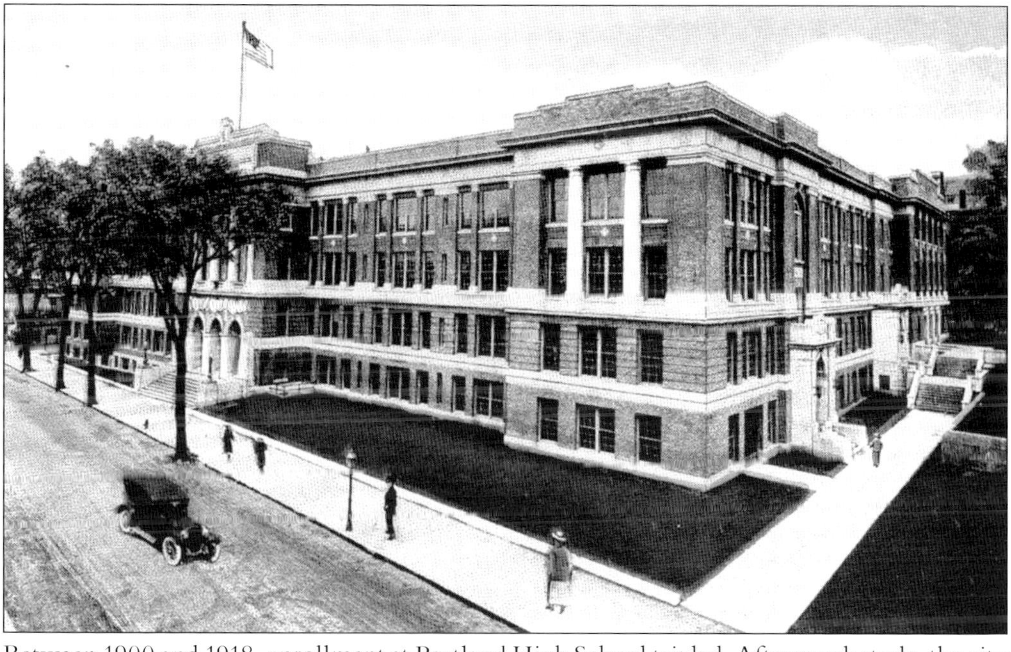

Between 1900 and 1918, enrollment at Portland High School tripled. After much study, the city decided to keep the 1862–1863 building by George M. Harding as the center of a much larger E-shaped structure. Designed by G. Henri Desmond of Boston and Miller and Mayo of Portland, the new Portland High School of 1918 contained 70 classrooms for 1,300 pupils.

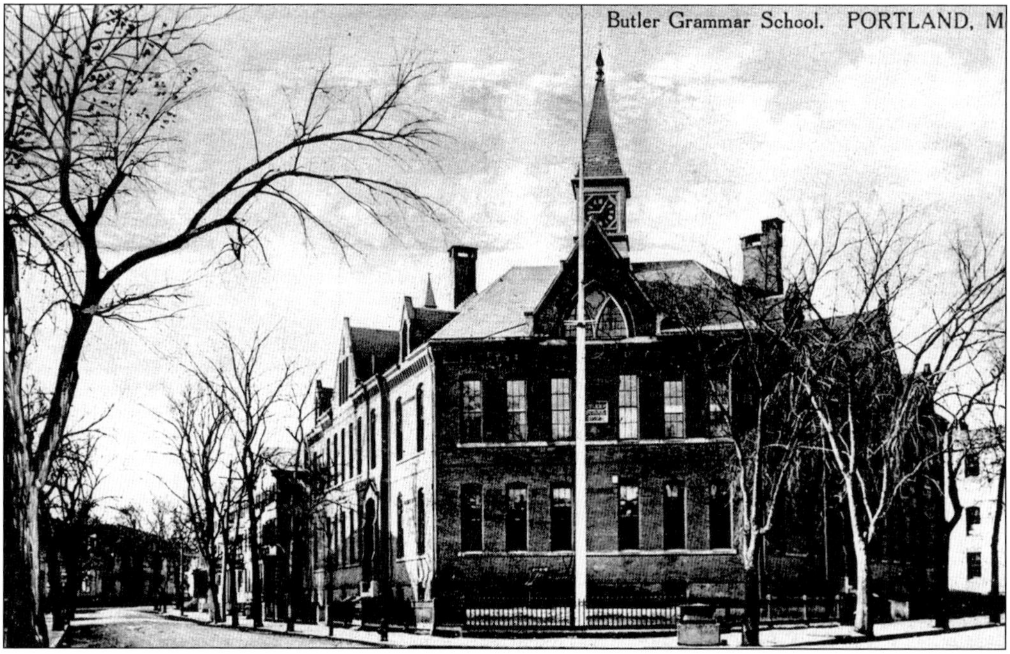


The Butler School occupies a commanding location at the intersection of Pine and West Streets. Constructed in 1878–1879 in the High Victorian Gothic style from designs by Francis H. Fassett, the large building addressed the educational needs of Portland's expanding West End. The school was named for Moses M. Butler, the mayor at the time. It now holds apartments.

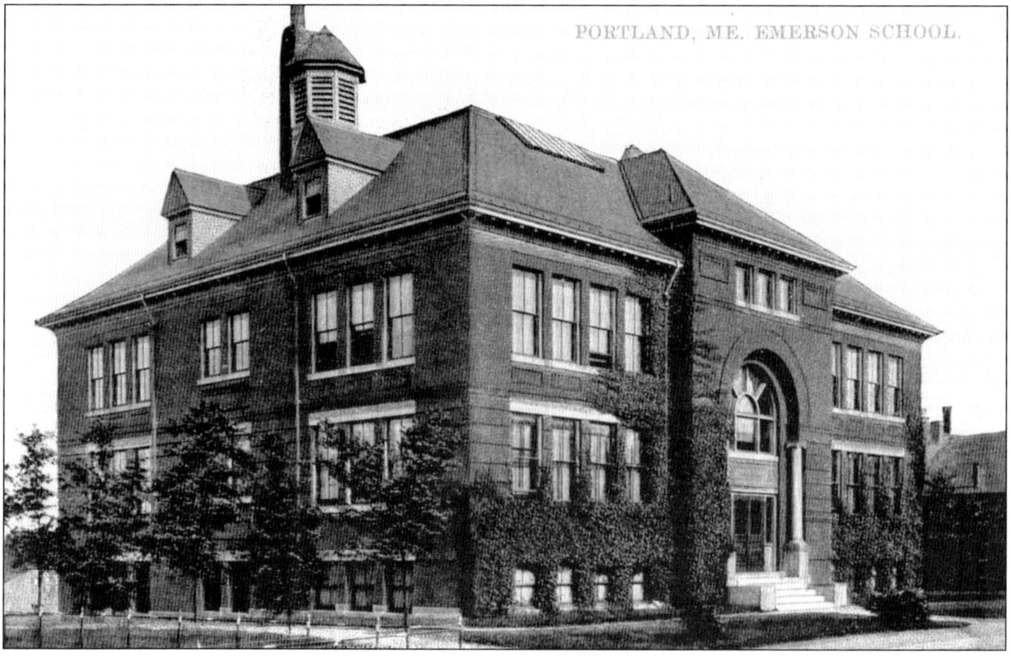


To Munjoy Hill's Monument Street, North, and Shailor grammar schools was added the Emerson School on Emerson Street in 1897—both named for Andrew L. Emerson, Portland's first mayor. Designed by Frederick A. Tompson, the brick and granite school contained eight classrooms and a third-floor assembly hall. It too was later converted into apartments.

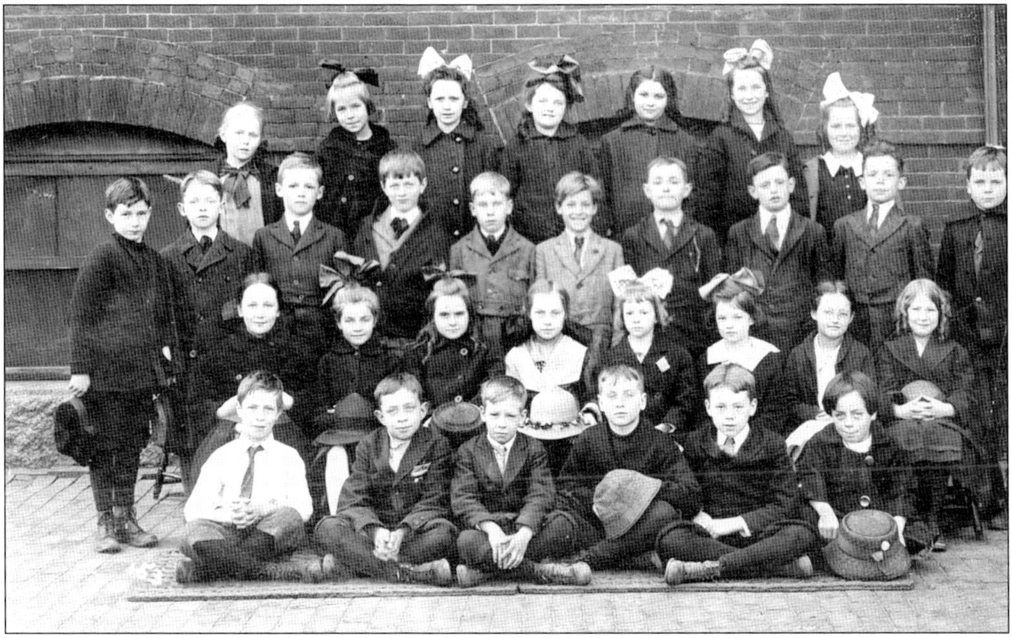

Less than a decade after the Butler School opened, another grammar school was needed in the West End. The McLellan School at Carroll and Neal Streets was built in 1886–1887 from designs by Fassett and Tompson. This 1918 postcard shows a class of well-dressed students, reflecting the affluent neighborhood. Named for Civil War mayor Jacob McLellan, the school is now residential.

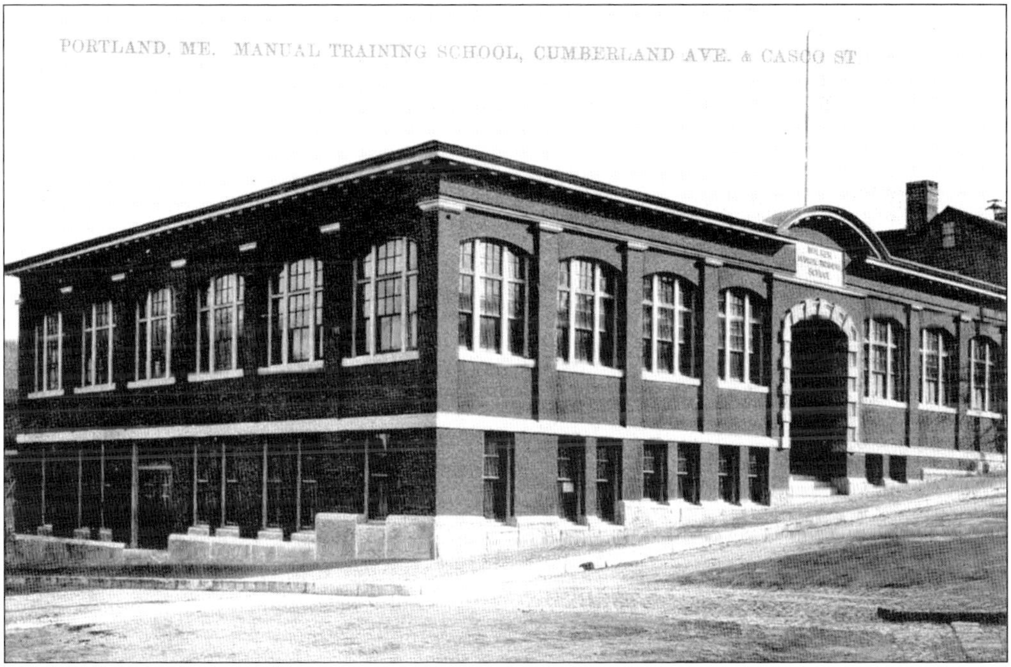


Nineteenth-century educators advocated public school training of young men for trades. After Westbrook businessman Joseph Walker died in 1891, his estate financed the construction of the Walker Manual Training School at Casco Street and Cumberland Avenue. Designed by Frederick A. Tompson, it opened in 1901 with four large workrooms and an evening school.

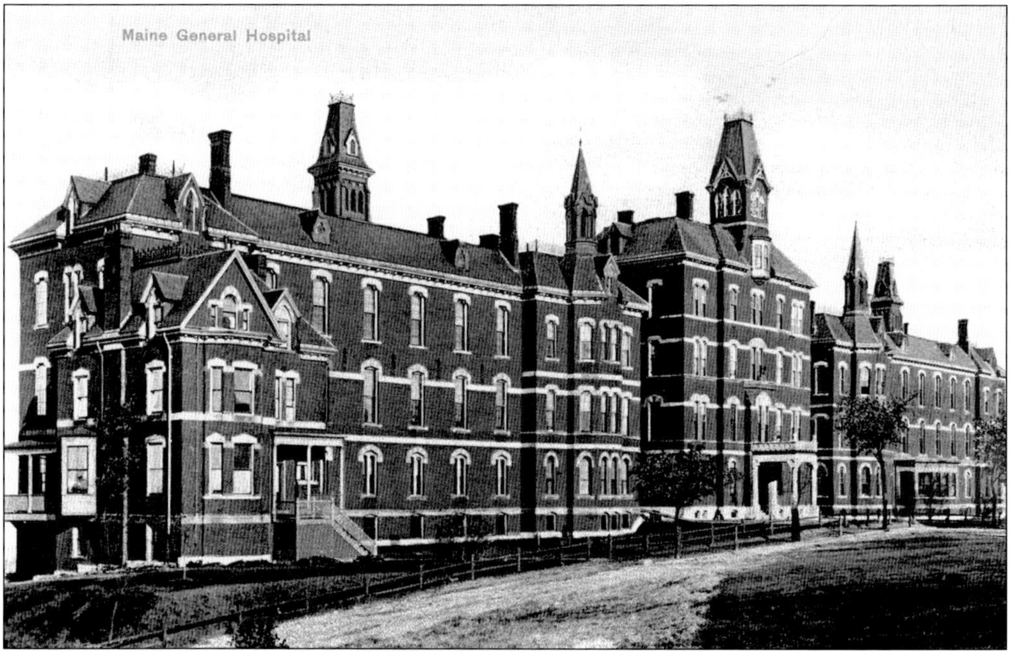


At the heart of today's Maine Medical Center complex is the Maine General Hospital, built on Arsenal Street between 1871 and 1892. Designed in the High Victorian Gothic style by Francis H. Fassett, the brick and stone building was based on state-of-the-art hospitals in Boston and New York. When the east pavilion opened in 1874, patients paid from $7 to $25 weekly.

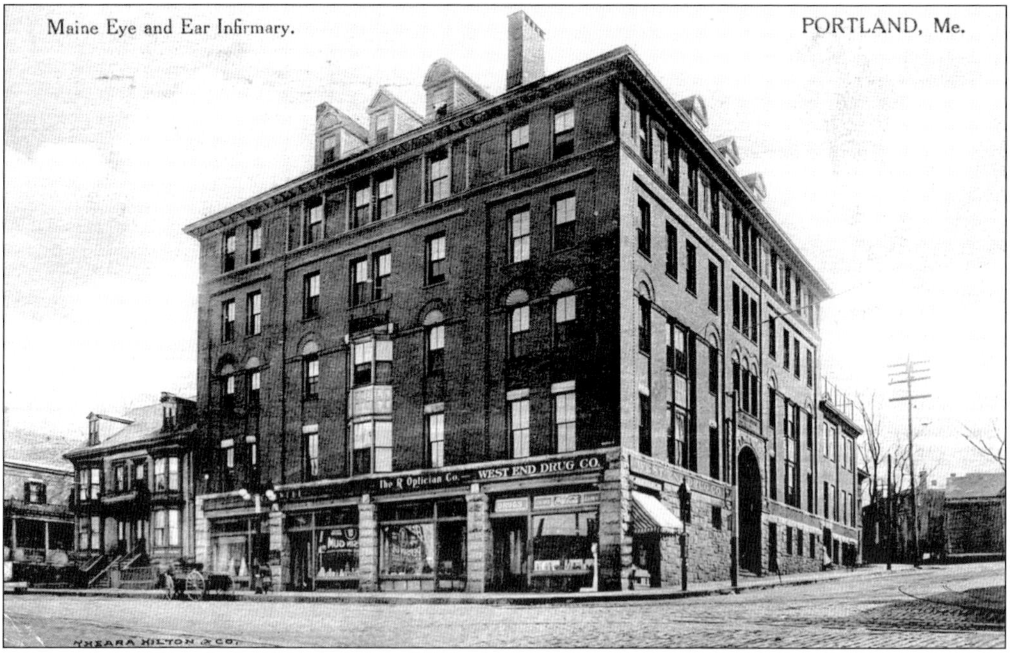


The five-story Maine Eye and Ear Infirmary of 1891–1892 at Congress and Vaughan Streets was erected as a medical facility for Dr. E. Eugene Holt, a noted authority on eye and ear diseases. It was designed by John Calvin Stevens in an eclectic blend of Romanesque and Colonial Revival styles. After many decades of medical service, Holt Hall was converted to apartments in 1998.

The First Parish Church on Congress Street is the oldest church on the Portland peninsula, having escaped the fire of 1866. Built in 1825–1826 by a Unitarian congregation, the church was constructed primarily of Freeport granite in the Federal style from designs by John Mussey. "Old Jerusalem," the Colonial meetinghouse previously on the site, hosted the Maine Constitutional Convention in 1819.

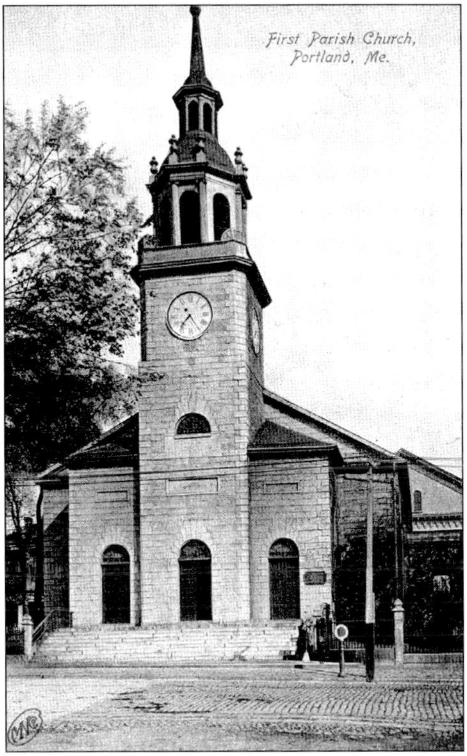


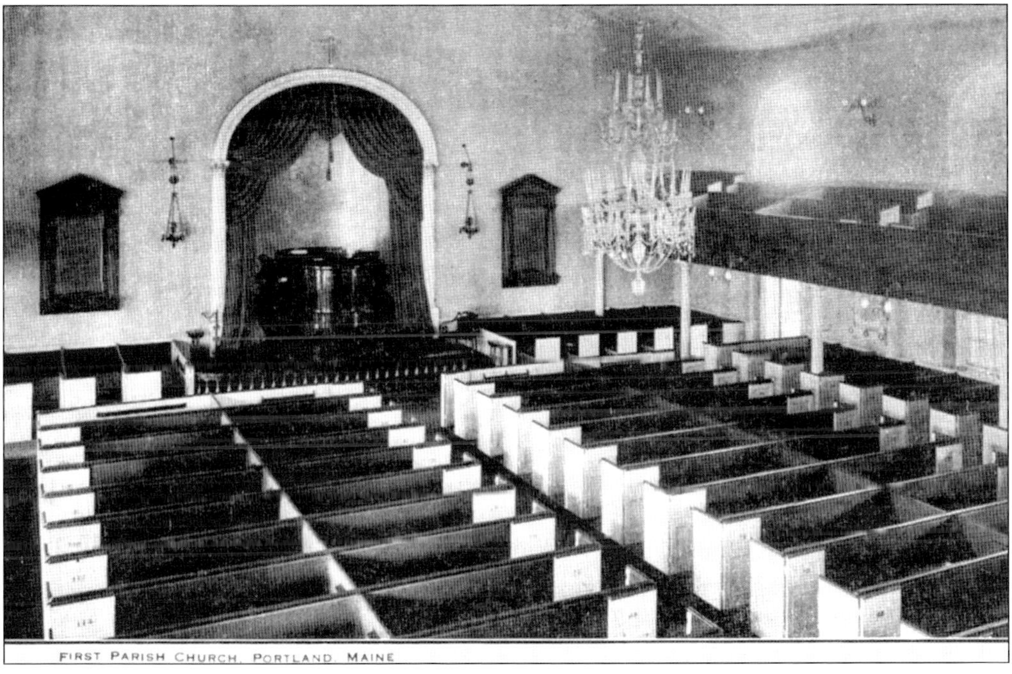

FIRST PARISH CHURCH, PORTLAND, MAINE

Although remodeled twice in the 19th century, the interior of the First Parish Church retains much of its original appearance. The 600-pound chandelier that hangs from the ceiling was installed shortly before the church was dedicated on February 8, 1826. Jefferson Davis (then secretary of war) used pew No. 75 when overseeing work on Fort Gorges in 1858.

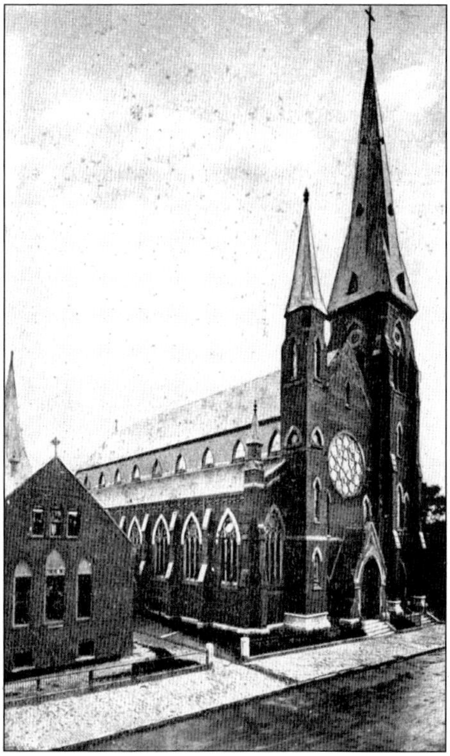

The soaring spires of the Cathedral of the Immaculate Conception at Cumberland Avenue and the Franklin Arterial have been part of the Portland skyline since 1869. The right tower rises to a height of 236 feet. Built of brick and stone in the Gothic Revival style, the cathedral was planned by Patrick C. Keeley of Brooklyn, New York, an Irish immigrant architect.

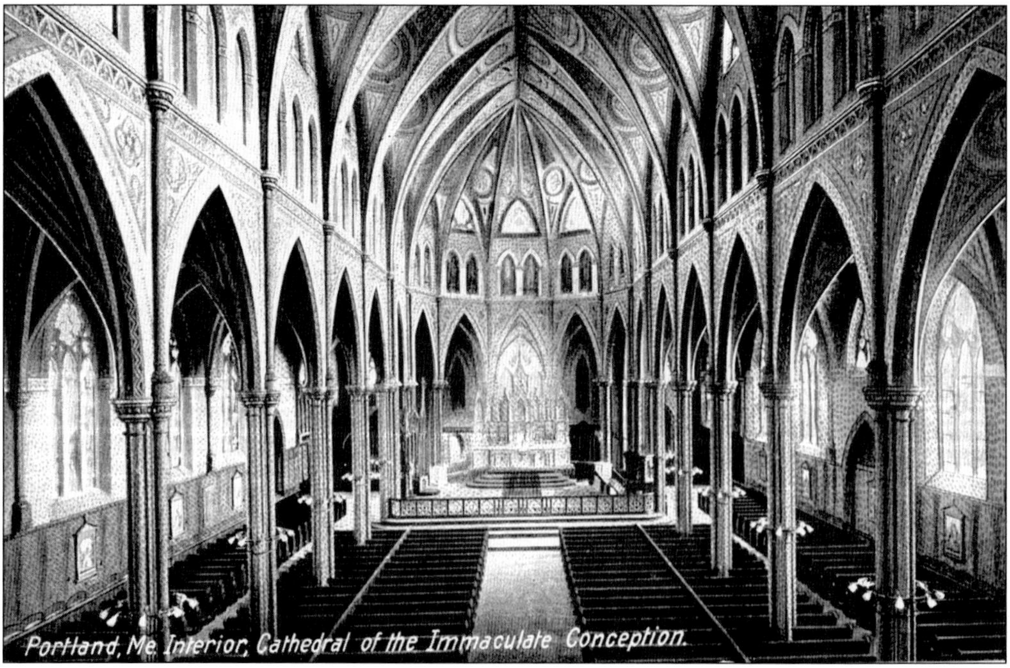


The cathedral was built for David W. Bacon, the first bishop of the Diocese of Portland, and has been the see of Maine's Catholic bishops since 1869. The church's interior is a masterpiece of Gothic Revival design—a broad nave flanked by clustered columns that support arched aisles. Lit by clerestory windows, the soaring space of the nave culminates in a vaulted ceiling.

The Chestnut Street Methodist Church is a graceful example of brick and brownstone Gothic Revival architecture. As originally built in 1856–1857 from designs by Charles A. Alexander, the church featured a pair of minaret-like spires, which were removed, leaving the two octagonal towers to frame the central entrance and the large arched window above it. The church is now closed, but an adaptive reuse will be found.

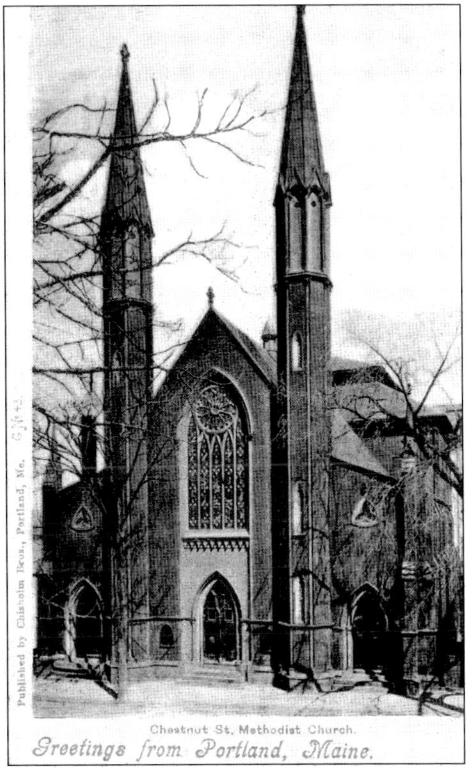


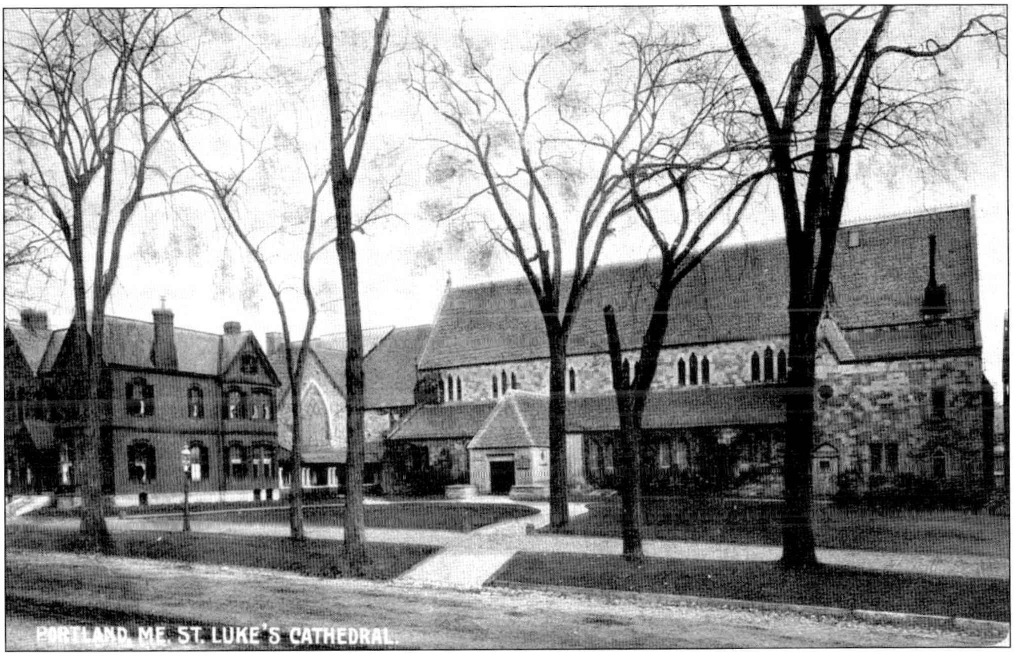


St. Luke's Cathedral was constructed on State Street in 1867–1868 for Rev. Henry Adams Neely, the second Episcopal bishop of Maine. This impressive stone Gothic Revival church was designed by Charles H. Haight of New York. The Emmanuel Chapel was added in 1905, through the generosity of Neely's successor, Bishop Richard Codman.

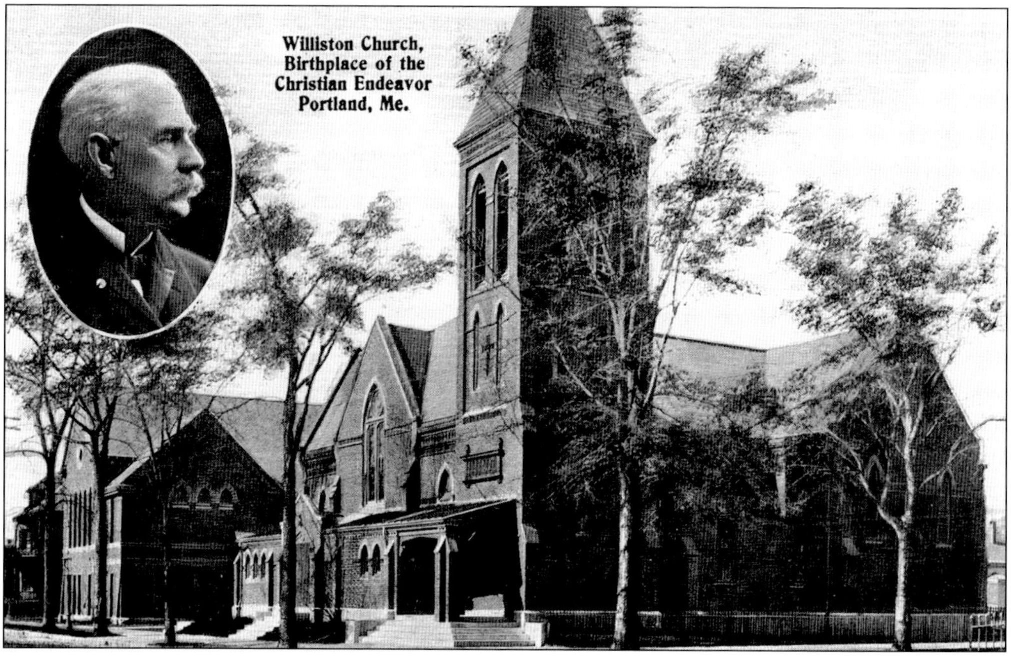


As the population of the West End increased, Congregationalists built the Williston Church at Thomas and Carroll Streets in 1877–1878, designed in High Victorian Gothic style by Francis H. Fassett. In 1881, Rev. Francis E. Clark (inset) founded the Young People's Society of Christian Endeavor there. The 1905 brick parish house at left was designed by Stevens and Stevens.

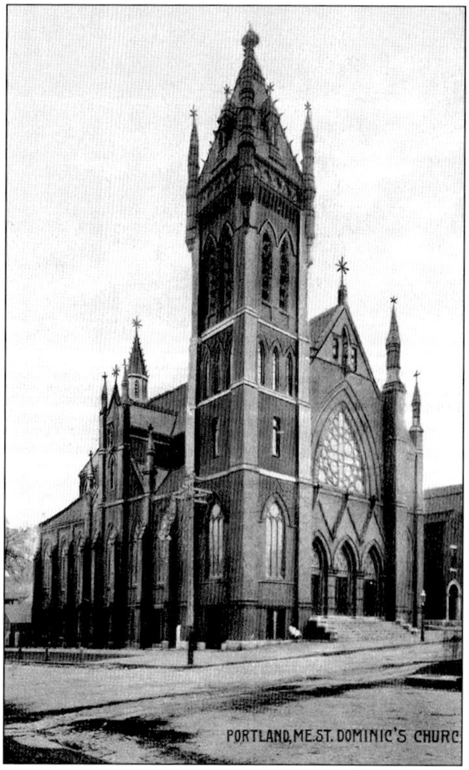


To minister to the needs of Portland's burgeoning Irish Catholic population, St. Dominic's Church was built at State and Gray Streets in 1830. That modest building was replaced in 1888–1893 by the present St. Dominic's, an elaborate brick and stone Gothic Revival edifice constructed from designs by P. W. Ford of Boston. It has recently become the Irish Heritage Center.

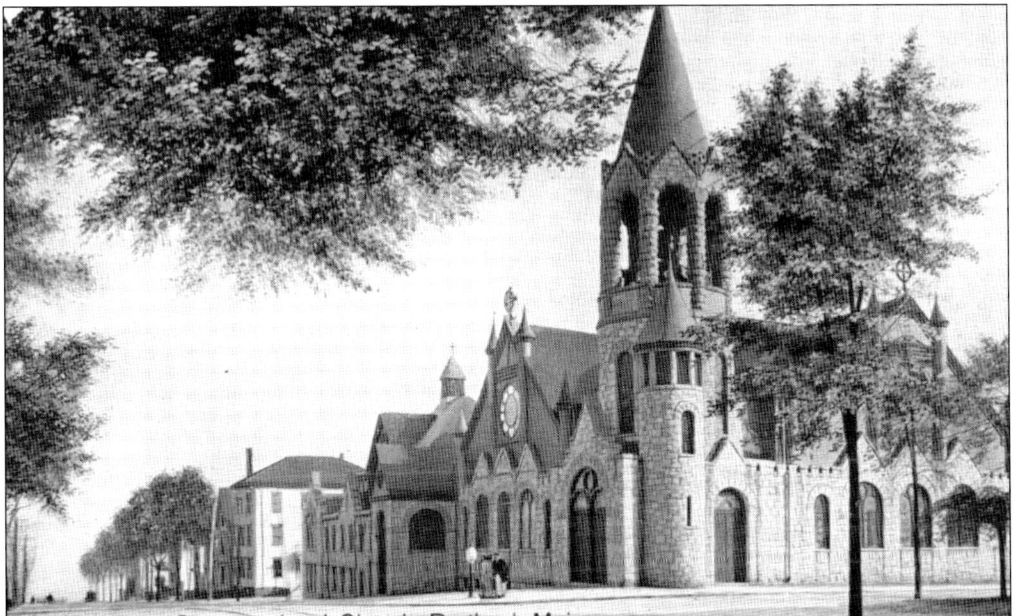

St. Lawrence Congregational Church, Portland, Maine.

The St. Lawrence Church at Congress and Munjoy Streets is one of the city's most distinctive. Erected by Congregationalists in 1897 from designs by Arthur Bates Jennings of New York, the stone Romanesque Revival building is defined by its picturesque roofline and circular tower. The parish house became a performing arts center after the church closed in 1985.

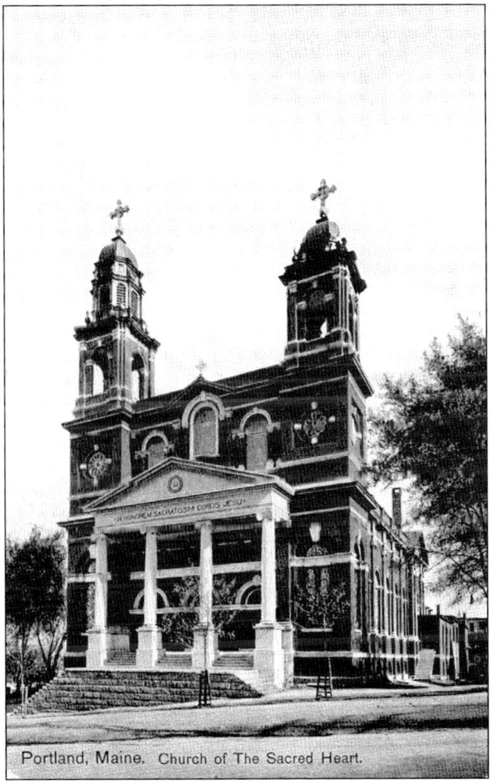

Portland, Maine. Church of The Sacred Heart.

The Church of the Sacred Heart at Mellen and Grant Streets is one of the last major buildings by Francis H. Fassett, who practiced architecture in Portland from 1863 until his death in 1908. Constructed between 1896 and 1915, the elaborate brick and stone Catholic church combines Fassett's baroque-style exterior design with a classical interior by Boston's Charles D. McGinnis.

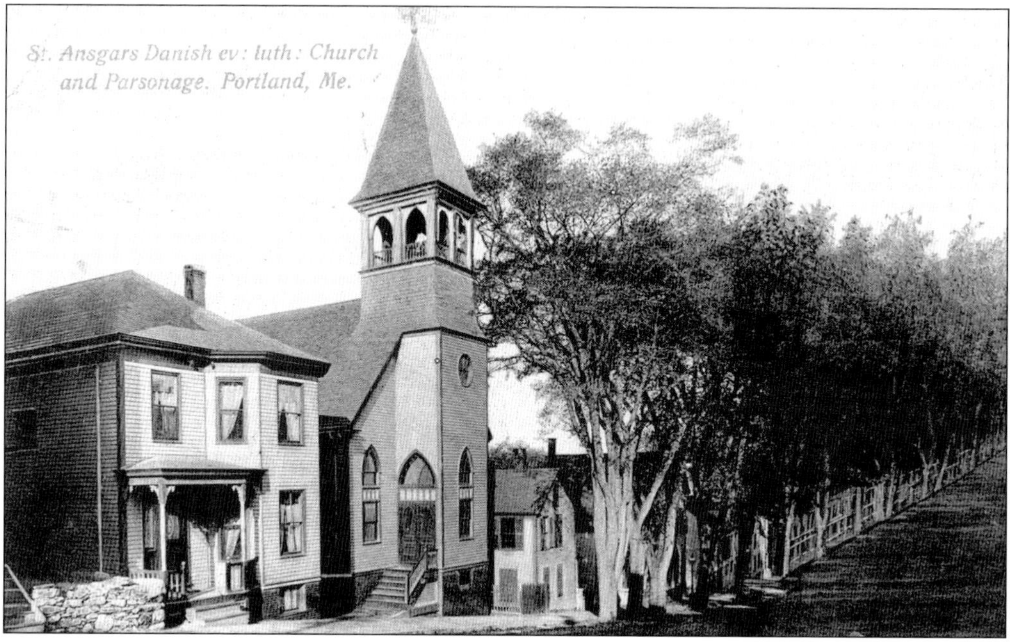


St. Ansgars Danish Lutheran Church was one of three Danish churches serving an immigrant community of 1,500. Located on Mayo Street near Cumberland Avenue, this frame Gothic Revival church of 1897–1898 drew its members from the Bayside and Munjoy Hill neighborhoods. Its first pastor lived in the parsonage at left. Today the church is a performing arts center.

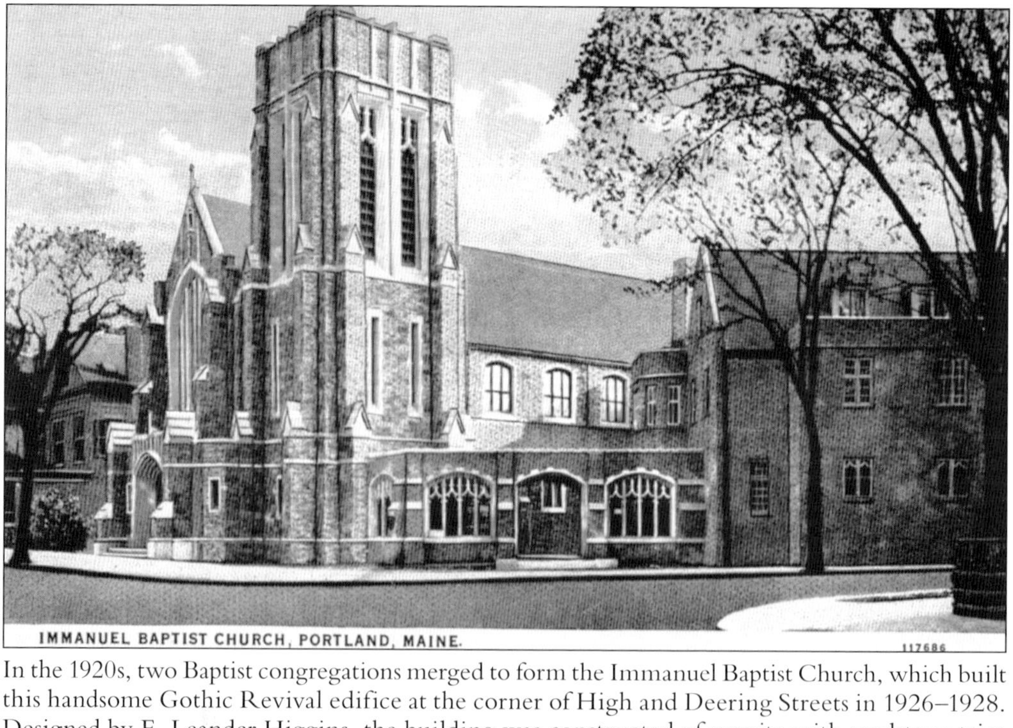


In the 1920s, two Baptist congregations merged to form the Immanuel Baptist Church, which built this handsome Gothic Revival edifice at the corner of High and Deering Streets in 1926–1928. Designed by E. Leander Higgins, the building was constructed of granite with sandstone trim and consists of a church, parish house, cloister, and courtyard.

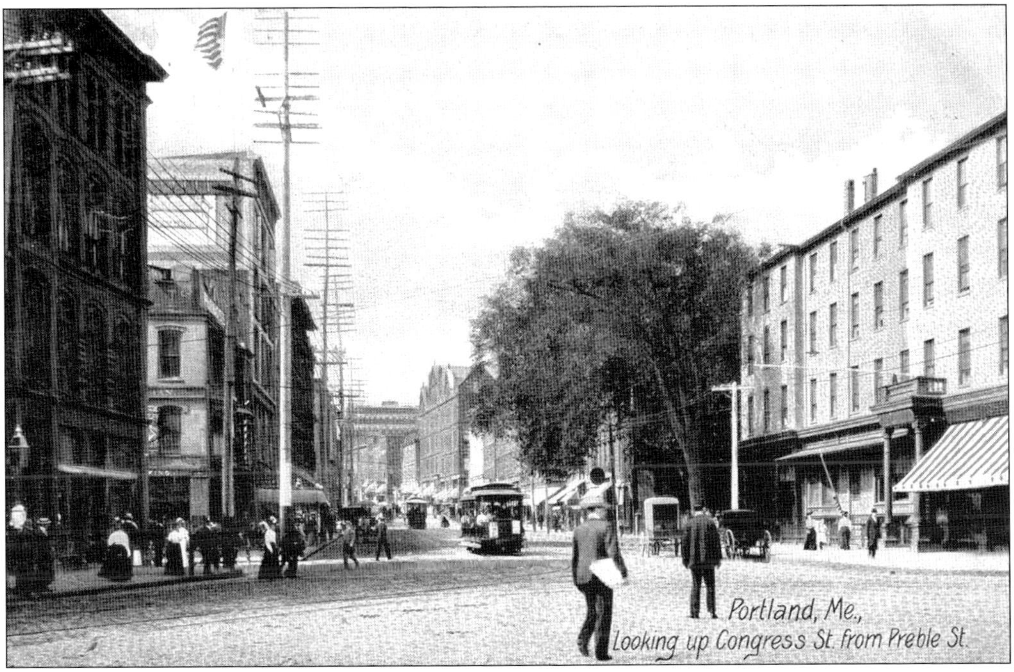


The Preble House stands in the foreground at the right in this view looking up Congress Street from Preble Street. Erected in 1806–1808 as a residence for Commodore Edward Preble, the Federal mansion was given an addition on either side and made into a hotel in 1860. Most of it was demolished in 1924 to make way for the Chapman ("Time and Temperature") Building. Below, the same view is transformed into a night scene through the retoucher's art. Its caption holds a double meaning: lights shining through windows and two staggering figures added at the left are all "lit up."

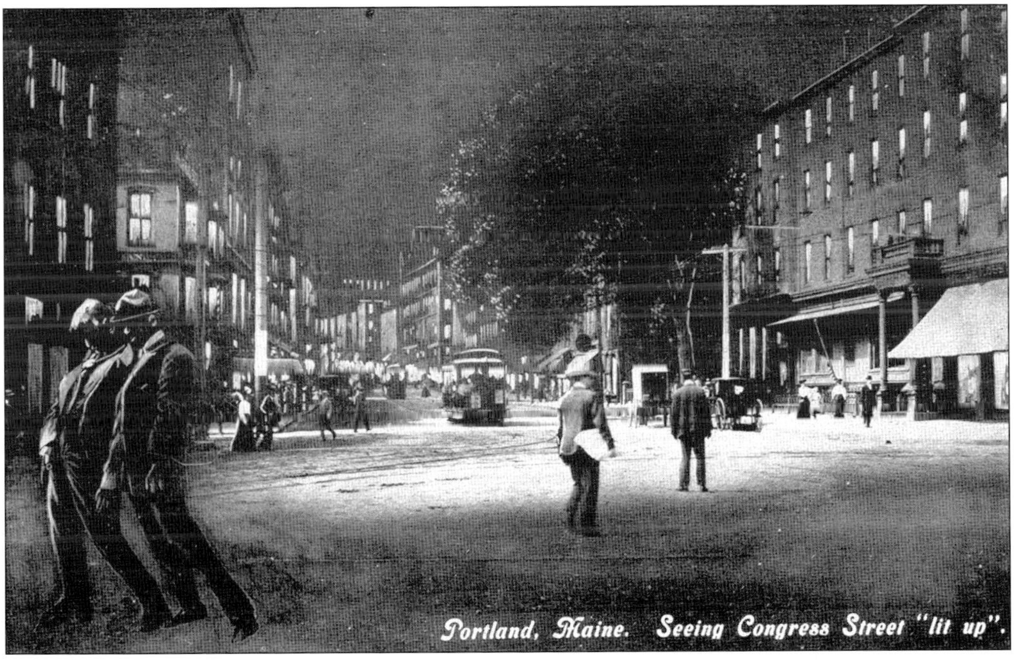

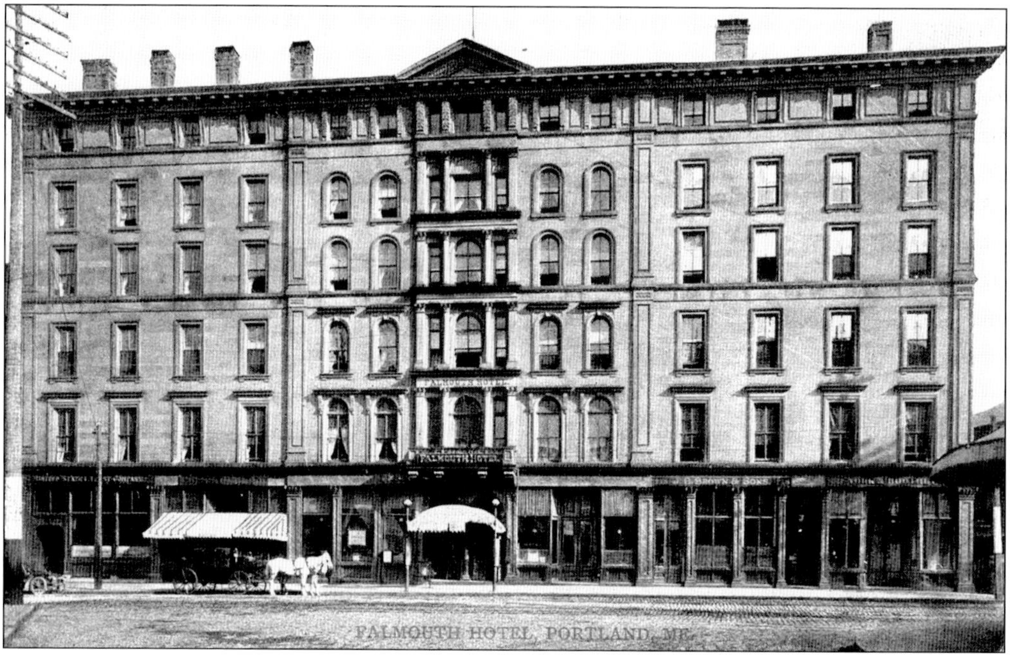


No building better symbolized the rebirth of Portland's commercial district after the 1866 fire than the Falmouth Hotel at Middle and Union Streets. Erected in 1867–1868 by J. B. Brown, the six-story Falmouth featured a grand sandstone facade and contained 240 guest rooms, a dining room, a billiard room, and 10 stores. It was razed in 1963–1964 after almost a century of service.

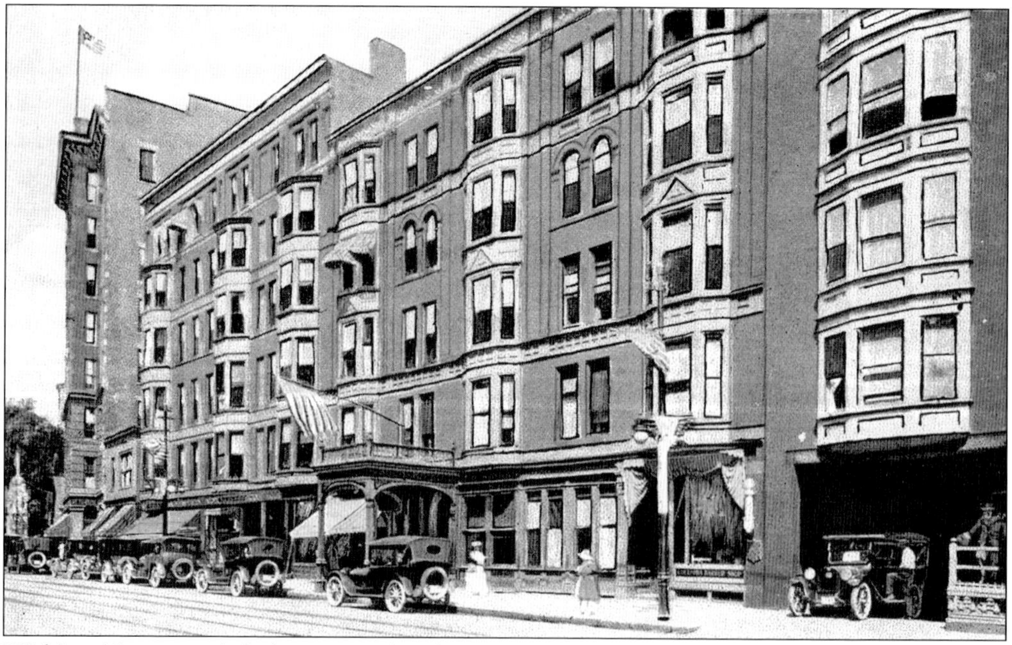

Within a 10-year period, three major hotels were built on Congress Street between Congress and Longfellow Squares. The first was the Columbia, which was constructed by the Rines brothers in two parts, the first section of five stories in 1893–1894, with a six-story west wing added in 1899–1900. The architects were Fassett and Fassett. Its rooms now serve as a college dormitory.

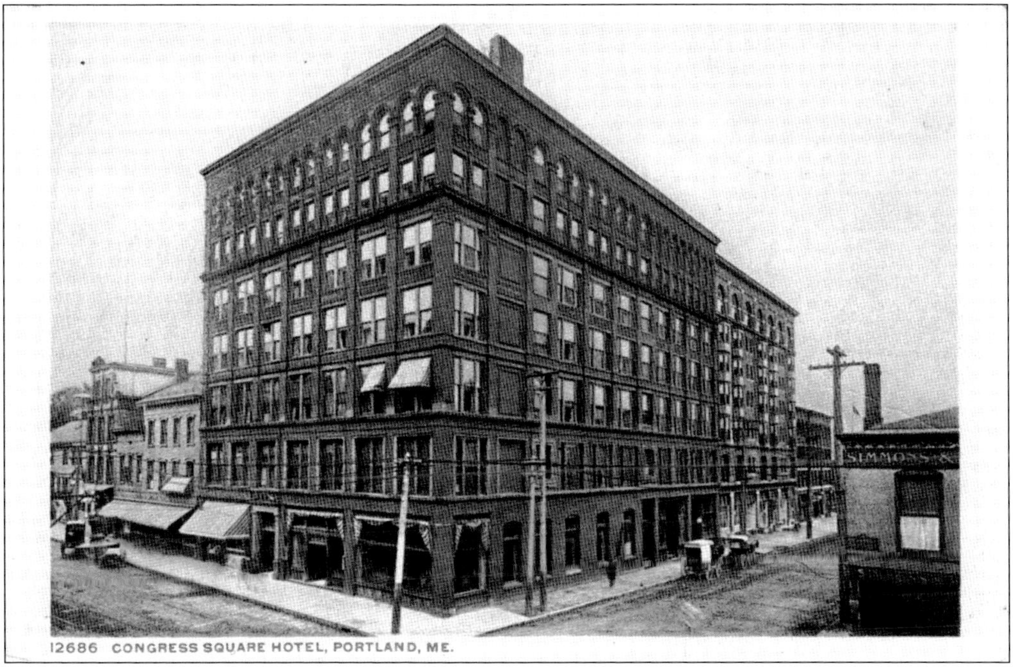


The year the Columbia Hotel opened, the Rines brothers set out to replace the City Hotel at Congress Street and Forest Avenue with a seven-story brick hotel also designed by the Fassetts. Built between 1894 and 1896, the Congress Square Hotel was Maine's tallest building, with more than 100 guest rooms. A large Forest Avenue addition was made in 1907–1909.

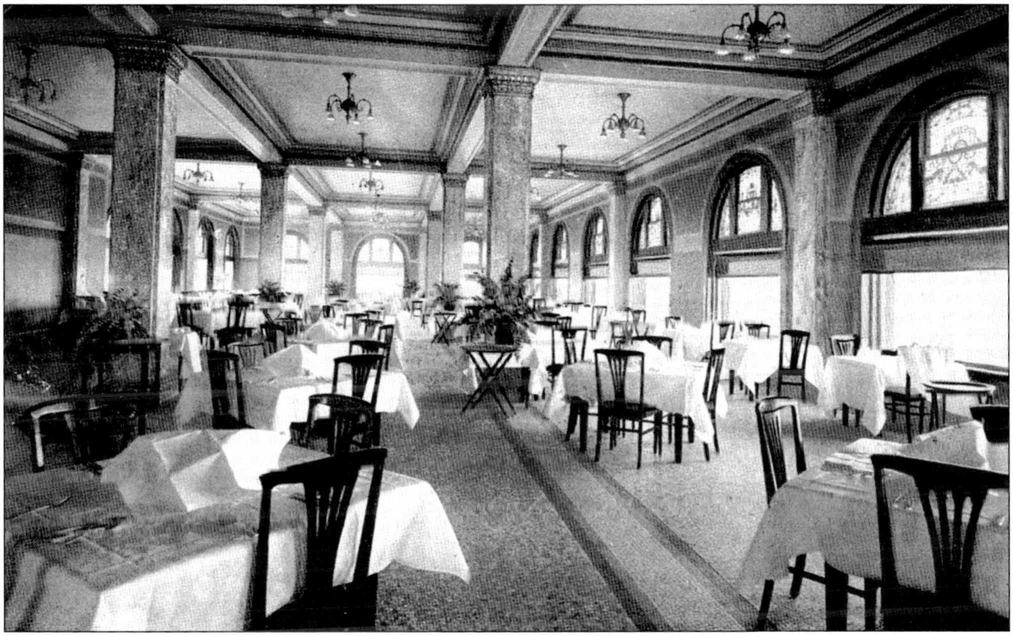

This view captures the elegance of the 250-seat, seventh-floor dining room of the Congress Square Hotel, which opened in 1909 atop the new addition. Guests dined amid tile floors, marble columns, stained glass, and picture windows that afforded spectacular views of the city and the harbor.

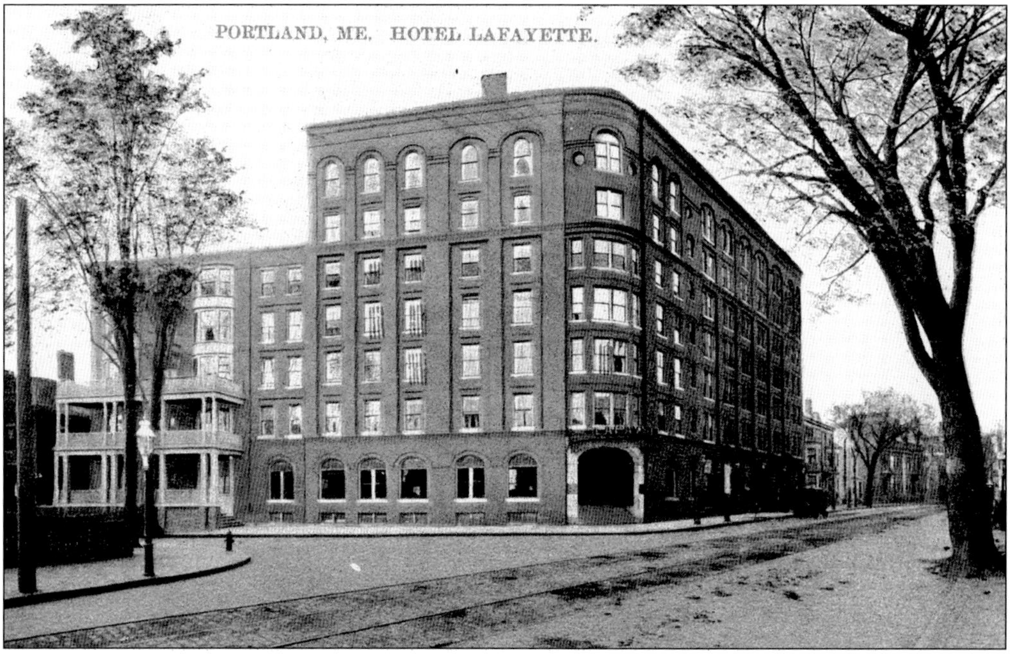


In 1902–1903, James Cunningham built the Lafayette Hotel at Congress and Park Streets on the site of an inn where the Marquis de Lafayette stayed in 1825. Designed by Francis H. Fassett and Edward F. Fassett, this seven-story brick structure offered 95 rooms and a seventh-floor dining room from which the guests could view the city and Portland Harbor.

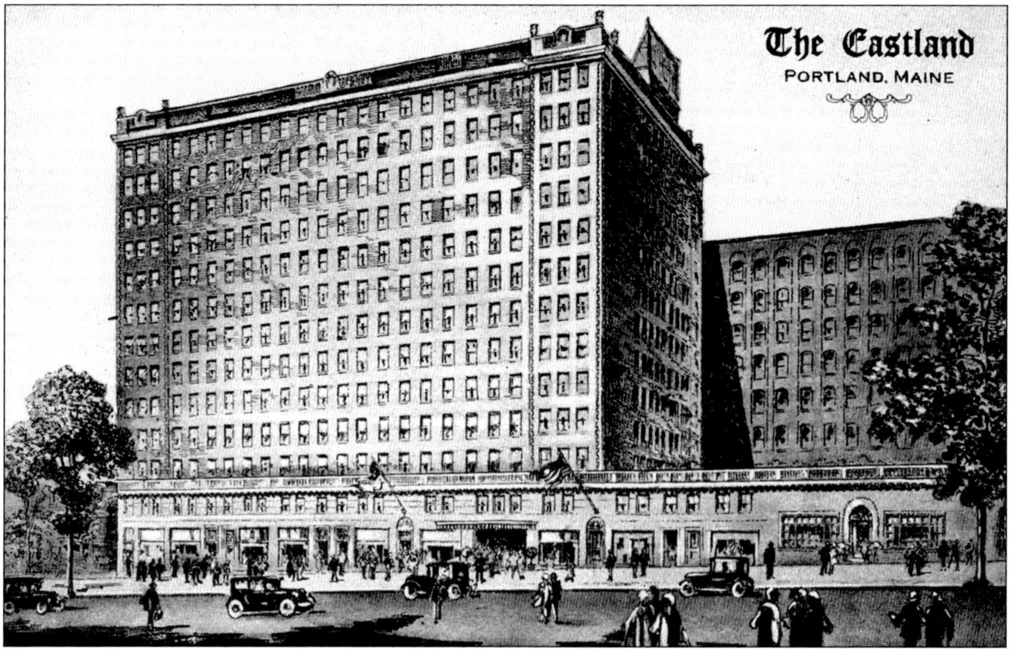


The Eastland, on High Street between Congress Square and Cumberland Avenue, opened in 1927. Designed by Herbert W. Rhodes, the 12-story brick building was constructed by the Rines family. It contained 369 guest rooms, a Spanish lobby, the State of Maine Function Room, the Egyptian Dining Room, the Danish Tea Room, and the rooftop Sun Room.

Portland once supported several theaters presenting plays and vaudeville acts. From 1897 to 1933, the Jefferson Theater at Free and Oak Streets offered the finest dramatic performances in the city, featuring big-name stars. Financed by local businessmen, the elegant 1,500-seat "Old Jeff" was designed by Chicago theater architects James M. Wood and Sidney Lovell.

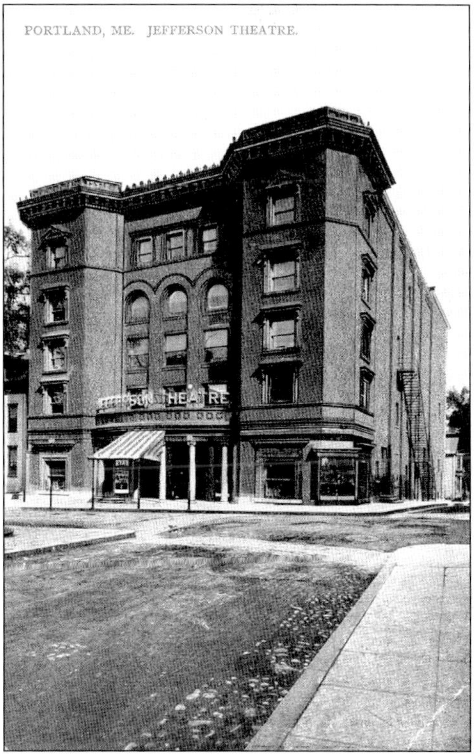


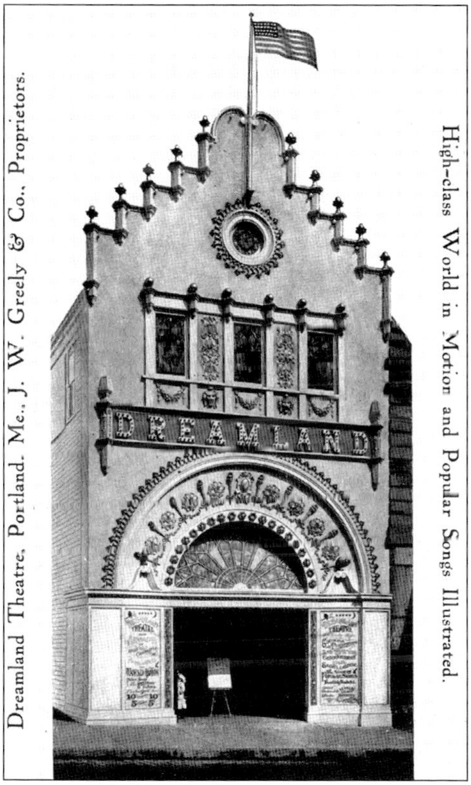


The welcoming arched entrance and fanciful architectural features of the Dreamland captured the spirit of amazement and delight experienced by early moviegoers. In 1908, with the help of architect John Calvin Stevens, James W. Greeley transformed a wooden building at Congress and Oak Streets into Portland's first moving picture theater.

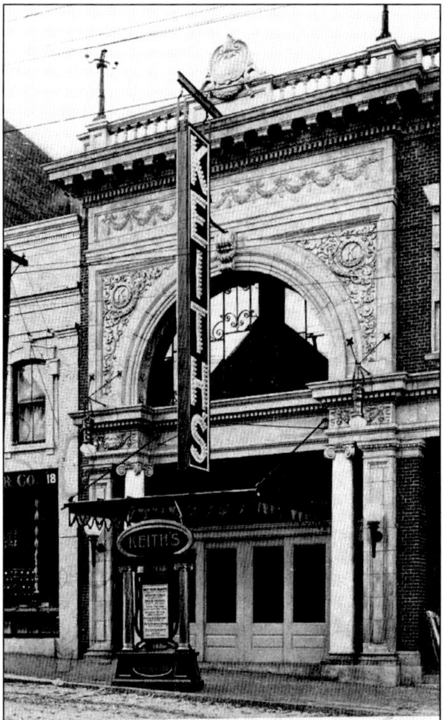


MAIN ENTRANCE, KEITH'S NEW THEATRE, PORTLAND, MAINE.
Published by James F. Edrehi. Photo Copyright, 1908, The Hugh C. Leighton C

Between 1906 and 1908, B. F. Keith of Boston constructed an elegant vaudeville theater on Preble Street from designs by Francis H. Fassett and Edward F. Fassett. This elaborate Beaux-Arts facade of brick, stone, and terra-cotta and the long corridor behind it, which connected the Preble Street entrance to the theater, are all that remain of this once-popular place of entertainment.

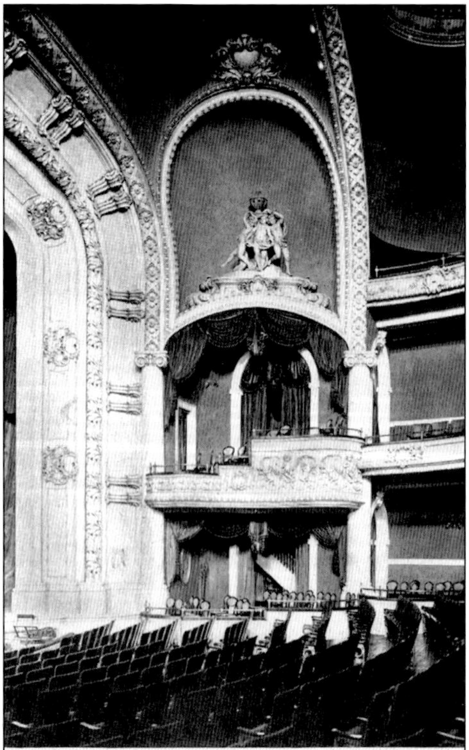

INTERIOR VIEW, KEITH'S NEW THEATRE, PORTLAND, MAINE.
The Ornamental Plaster Work by C. & W. B. Jackson.

Here is the interior of Keith's Theatre, showing some of its elaborate plasterwork. Billed as "the Amusement Center of Portland" in the 1920s when vaudeville was declining, it was also showing moving pictures. Later known as the Civic Theater, it was eventually torn down for a parking garage.

A longtime real estate agent, Ingram B. Wheelock was first listed in this location at 104 North Street in 1882 in what appears to have been a two-family dwelling. In 1911, Wheelock decided to maximize the financial return on his narrow Munjoy Hill lot by constructing a four-story apartment house, with corner tower, where he lived along with tenants until his death in 1923.

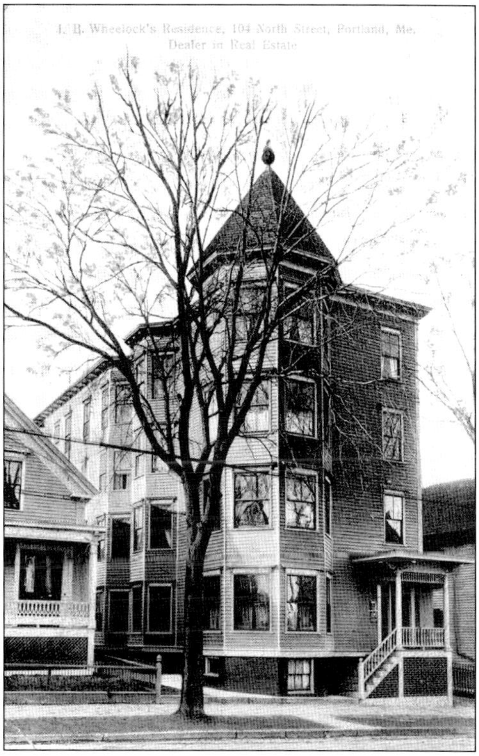


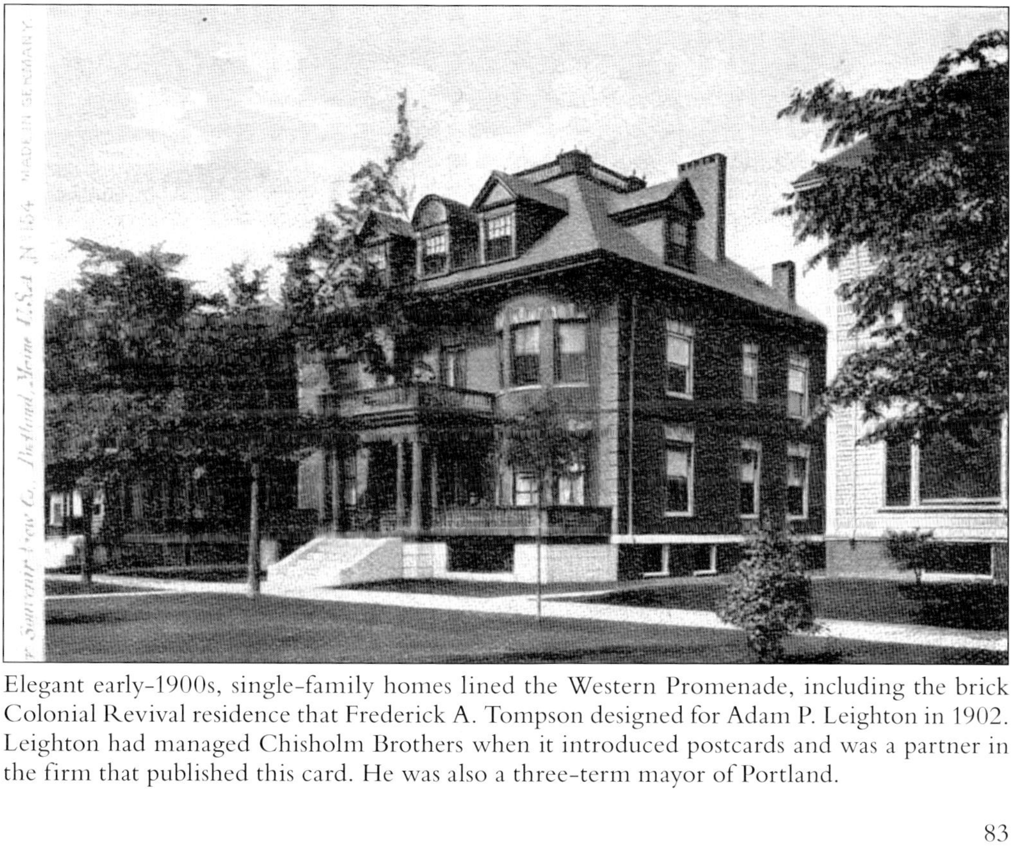

Elegant early-1900s, single-family homes lined the Western Promenade, including the brick Colonial Revival residence that Frederick A. Tompson designed for Adam P. Leighton in 1902. Leighton had managed Chisholm Brothers when it introduced postcards and was a partner in the firm that published this card. He was also a three-term mayor of Portland.

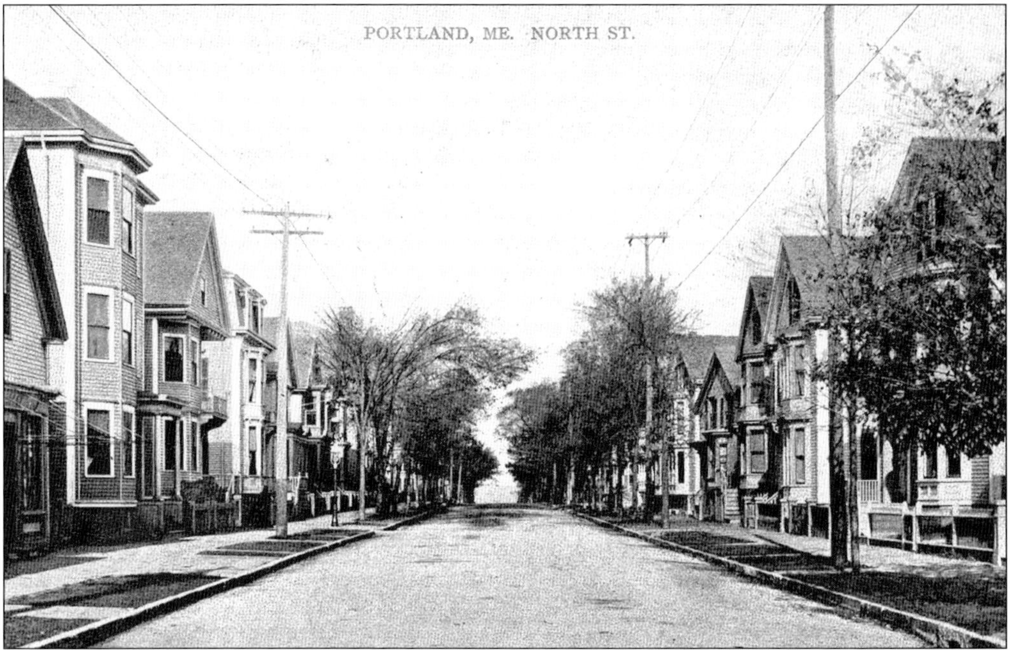


Running from Congress Street to the Eastern Promenade, North Street was laid out in 1795 as one of the first streets on Munjoy Hill. However, it held few homes until after 1866. This view looking north from Congress Street shows two- to three-story frame houses tightly sited on narrow lots, similar to most other residences in the east end of the city.

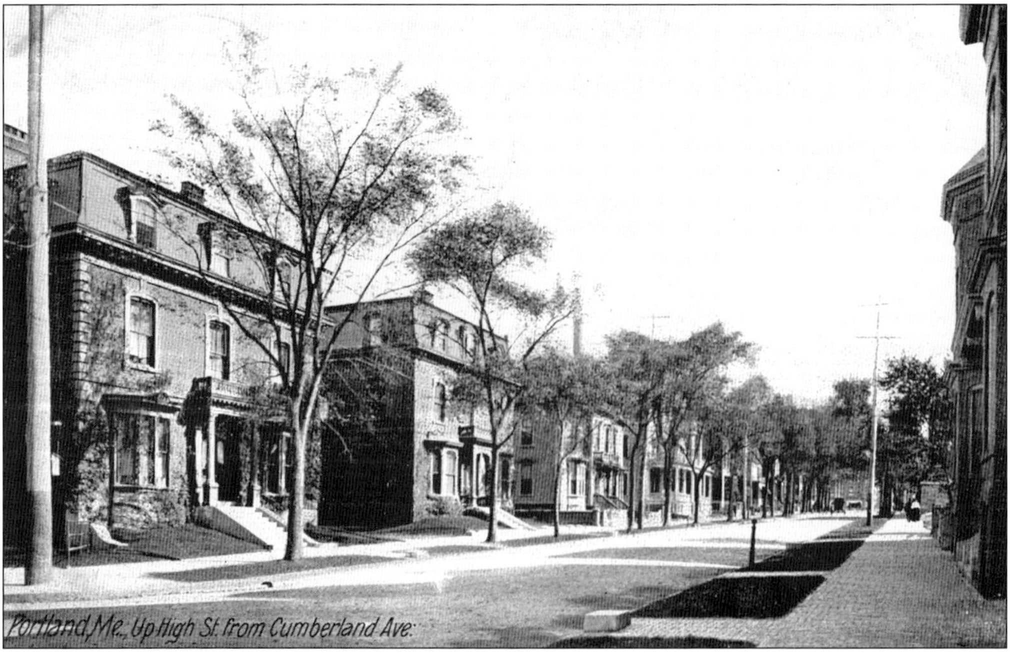


The area bordered by Deering, Mellen, and High Streets and Park Avenue was known as Deering Pasture until residential construction spread westward after the great fire. The neighborhood was developed with substantial homes like those shown on the east side of High Street, looking from Cumberland Avenue to Congress Square—now a parking garage and the Eastland Hotel.

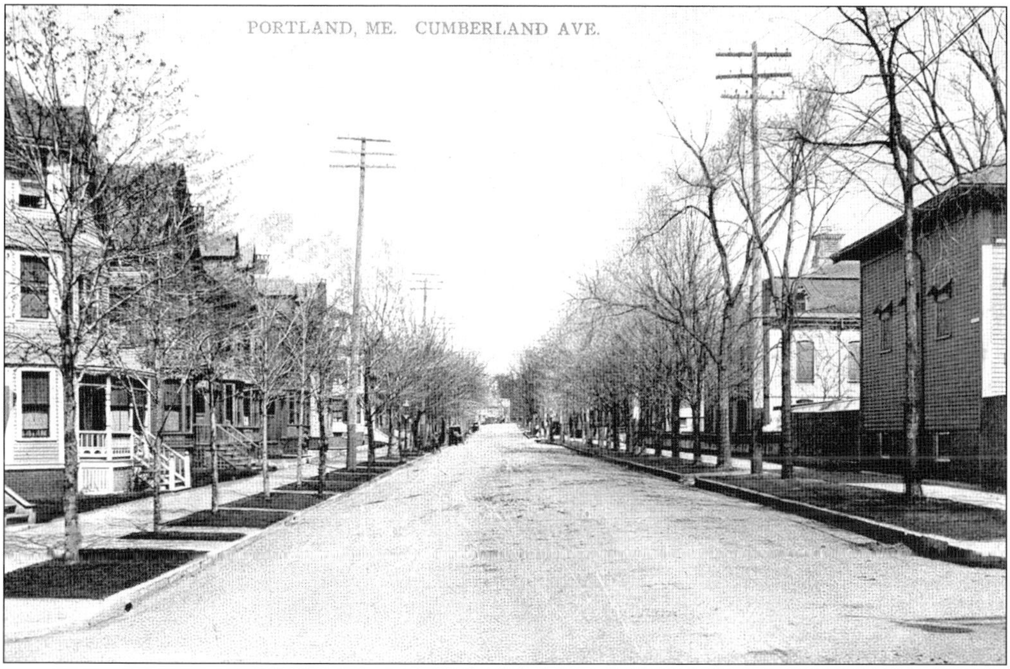


This view of Cumberland Avenue, looking east from Mellen Street toward High Street, depicts another section of the neighborhood that emerged from Deering Pasture in the late 19th century. Most of the wood and brick houses lining this section of Cumberland Avenue were built between 1880 and 1900.

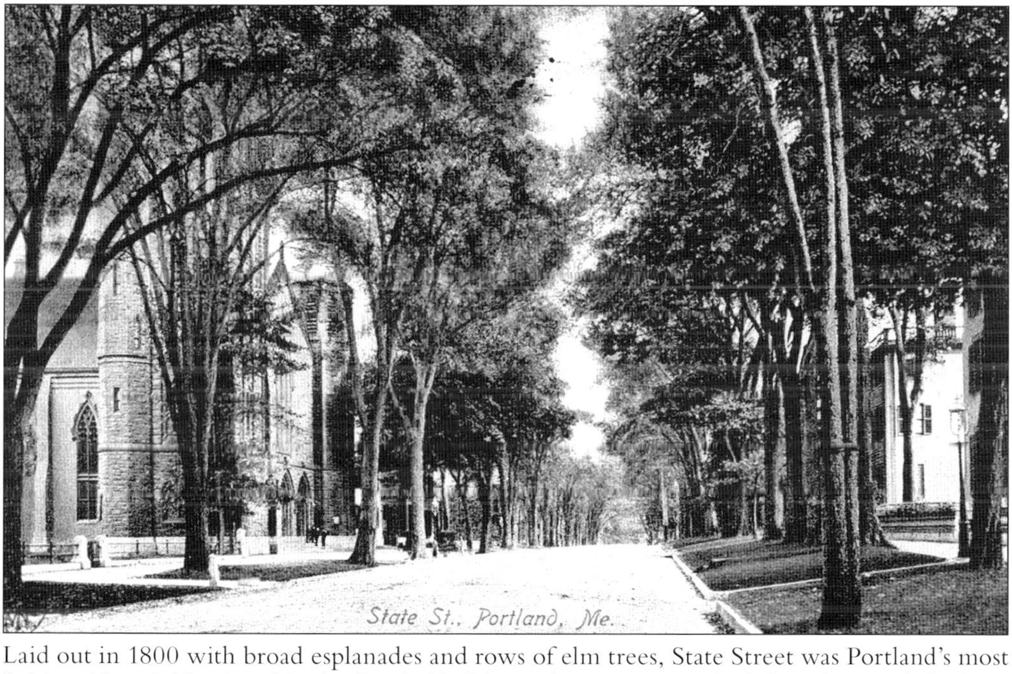


Laid out in 1800 with broad esplanades and rows of elm trees, State Street was Portland's most fashionable neighborhood in the first half of the 19th century. On the left in this south-looking view is the State Street Church of 1851, designed by William Washburn of Boston and in 1892–1893 given a brownstone facade by John Calvin Stevens.

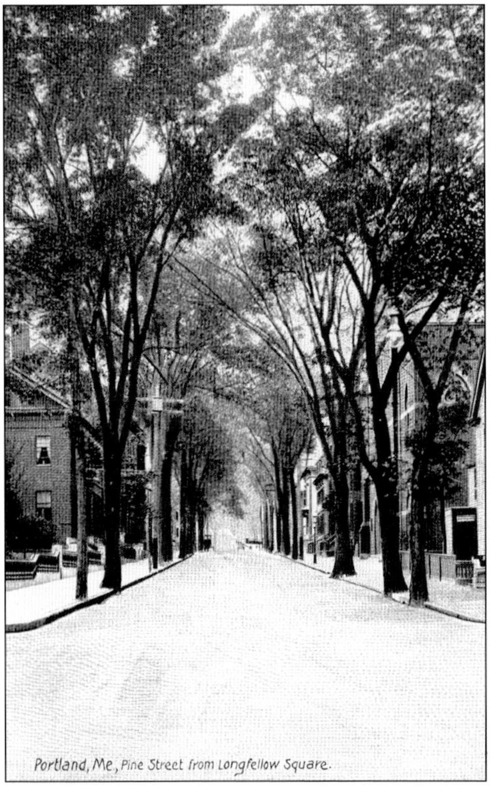


Tree-lined streets throughout Portland gave the community its 19th-century title of "Forest City." Graceful elms dominated this view of Pine Street looking west from Longfellow Square to the intersection of Brackett Street. At the right is the Pine Street Methodist Church of 1875, a High Victorian Gothic brick building designed by the Kenway Brothers, now a parking lot.

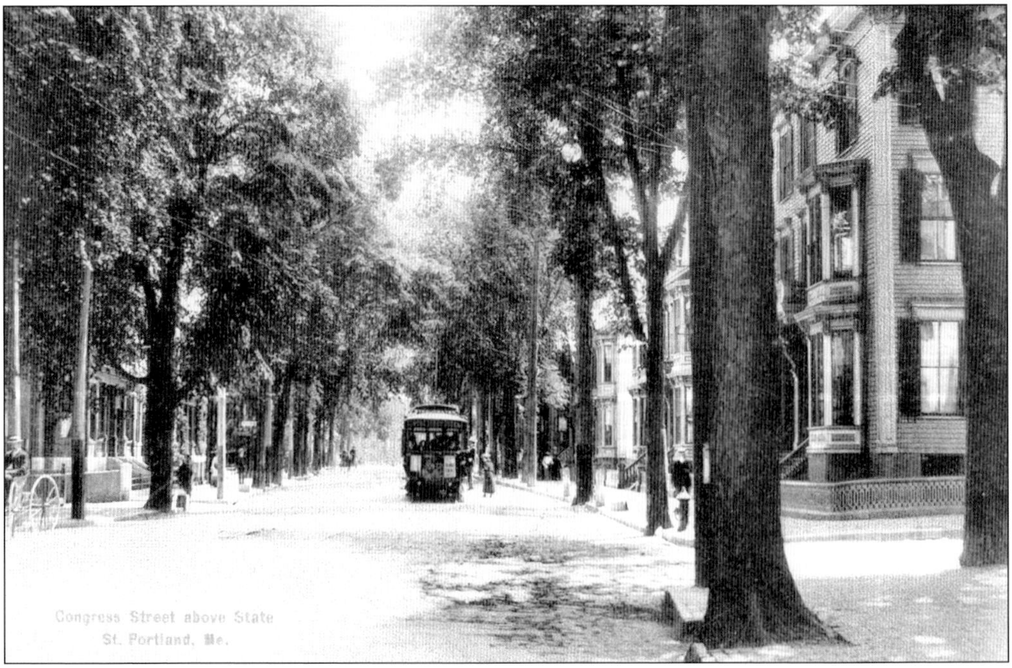


An electric trolley car makes its way along a tree-lined Congress Street in this view looking east from Dow Street to Longfellow Square. In the early 1900s, the section of Congress Street from Longfellow Square to Bramhall Square was predominantly residential.

# *Six*

# The Park System

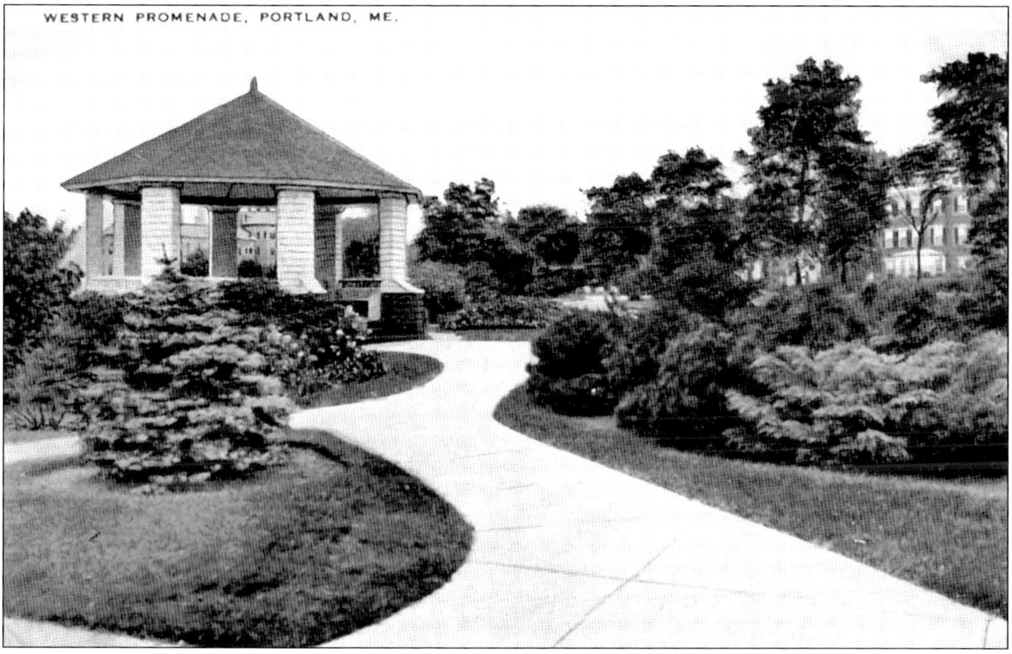


Lush plantings and an attractive shingled bandstand characterize the park along the Western Promenade in this 1925 postcard. Such beautiful park space in Portland was typical of the municipal park system created in the 19th and early 20th centuries to include the Eastern and Western Promenades, Lincoln Park, Deering Oaks, Fort Allen Park, and Baxter Boulevard. Designed by John Calvin Stevens and Albert Winslow Cobb in 1890, the now lost bandstand shown here was the counterpart to the one the architects planned for the Eastern Promenade that same year.

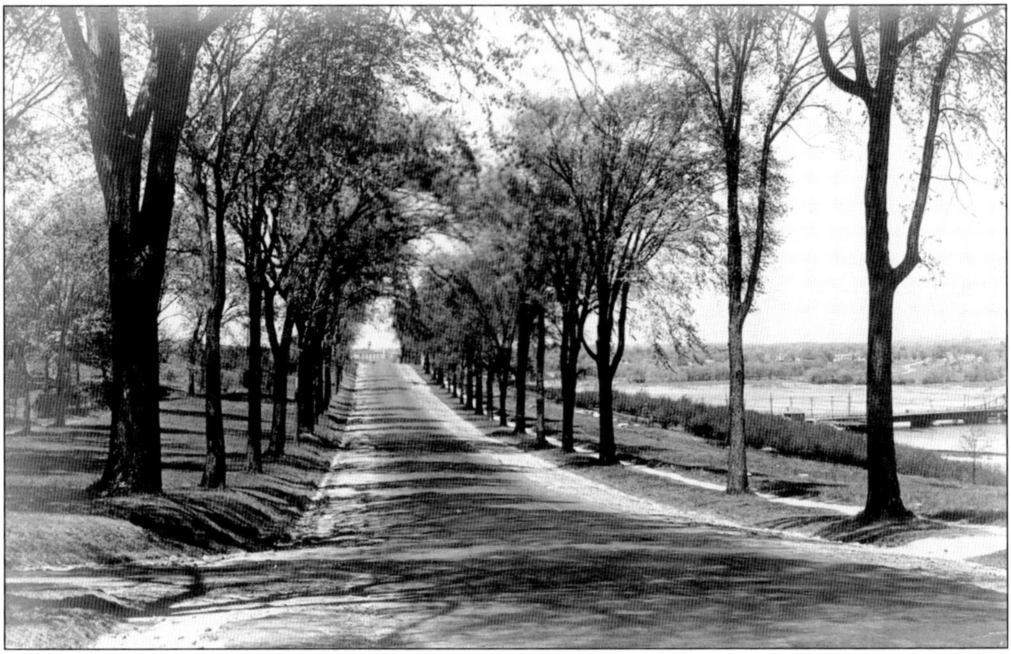

Portland's first public land was acquired on Munjoy Hill in 1828 and contributed in 1837 to the formation of the Eastern Promenade, a tree-lined drive extending from Fore Street to Washington Avenue. To this day the Eastern Promenade offers spectacular views of Portland Harbor and the Casco Bay islands.

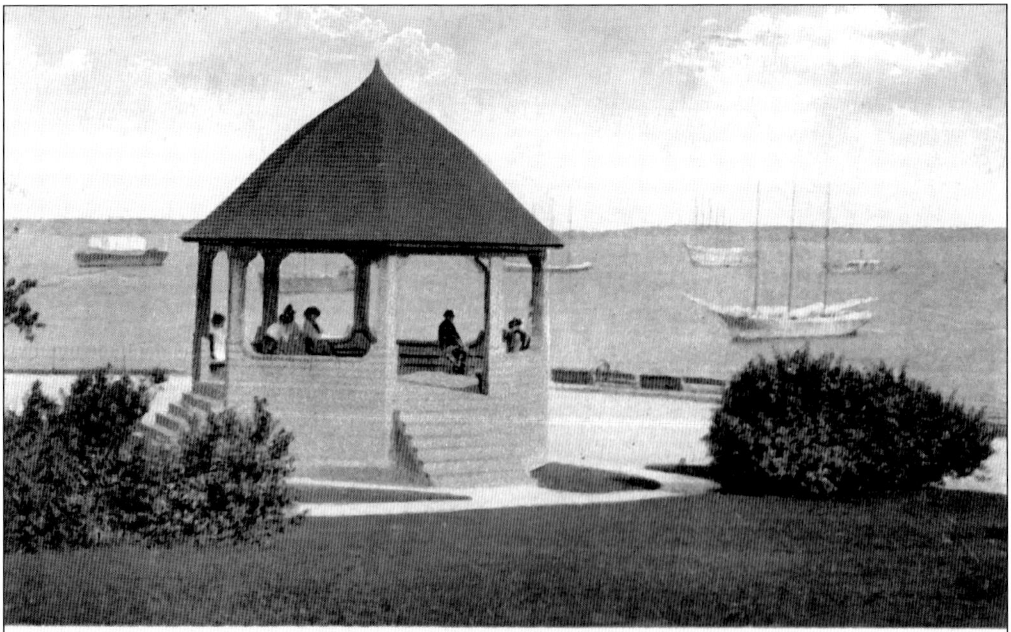

HARBOR FROM FORT ALLEN PARK, PORTLAND, MAINE.

To enhance the Eastern Promenade, Portland created Fort Allen Park in 1890, the four-and-a-half-acre site of artillery batteries erected in the Revolutionary War and the War of 1812 to protect the town from British invasion. Recently restored, the picturesque bandstand was designed for the park in 1890 by architects John Calvin Stevens and Albert Winslow Cobb.

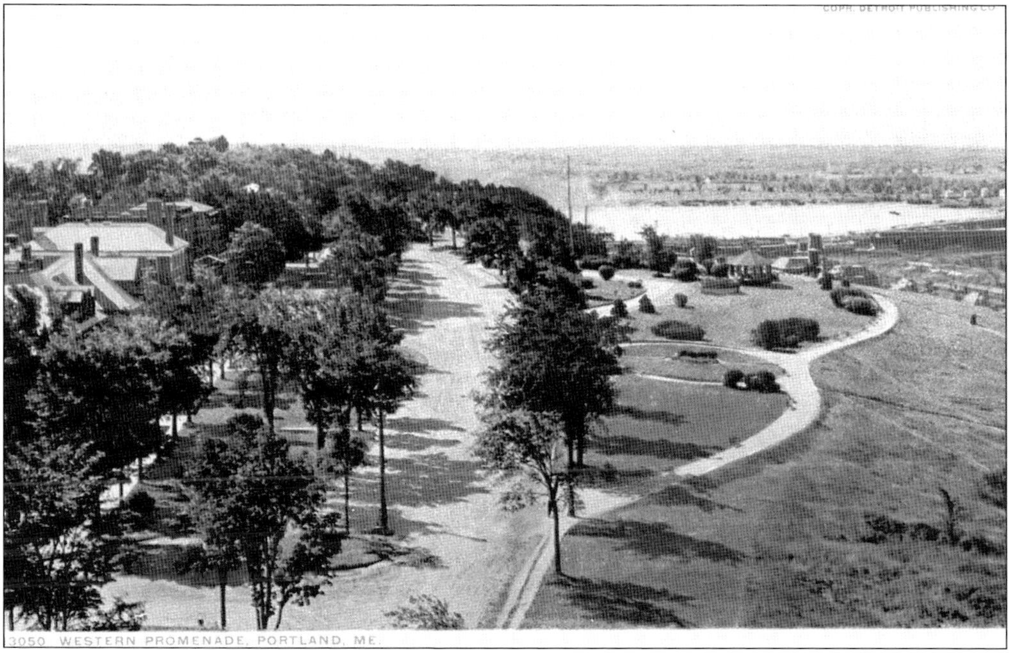


The Western Promenade in summer is viewed from the tower of the Maine General Hospital (now Maine Medical Center). Now extending from Bramhall Street to Danforth Street, the promenade was laid out by the city in 1837 as the west end counterpart to the Eastern Promenade. The new promenade afforded views of the Maine countryside to the White Mountains.

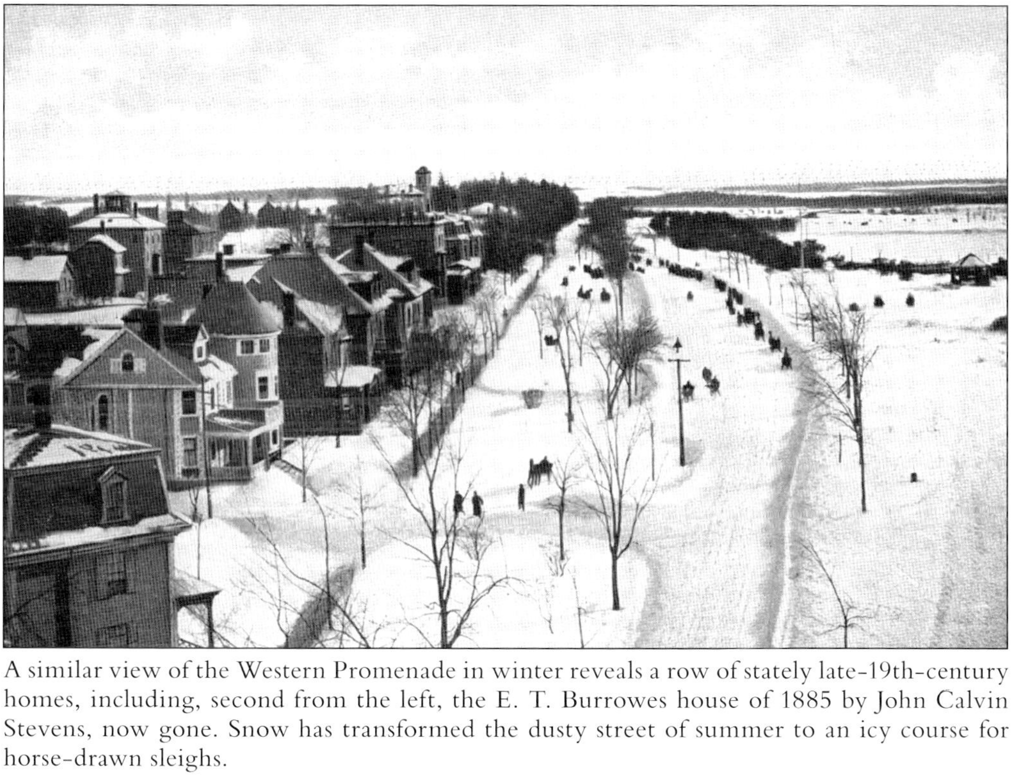

A similar view of the Western Promenade in winter reveals a row of stately late-19th-century homes, including, second from the left, the E. T. Burrowes house of 1885 by John Calvin Stevens, now gone. Snow has transformed the dusty street of summer to an icy course for horse-drawn sleighs.

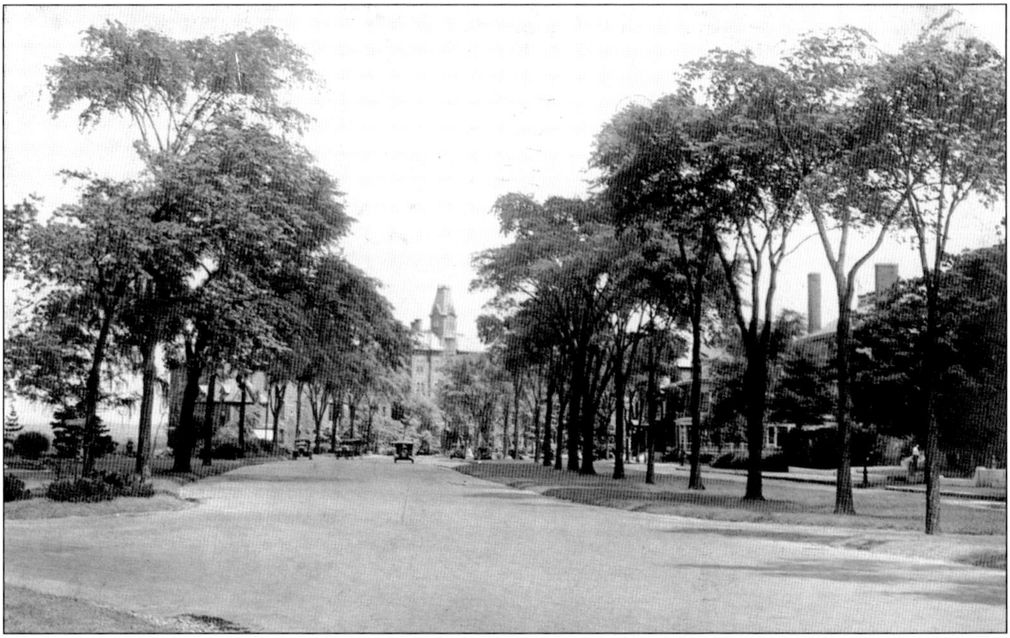

Well after its 1837 construction, the Western Promenade received landscaping improvements from city civil engineer William A. Goodwin and the Olmsted Brothers of Massachusetts. By the time this real-photo postcard was made in the 1920s, the view toward the Maine General Hospital was framed by rows of graceful elms—which were lost to disease in the 1960s.

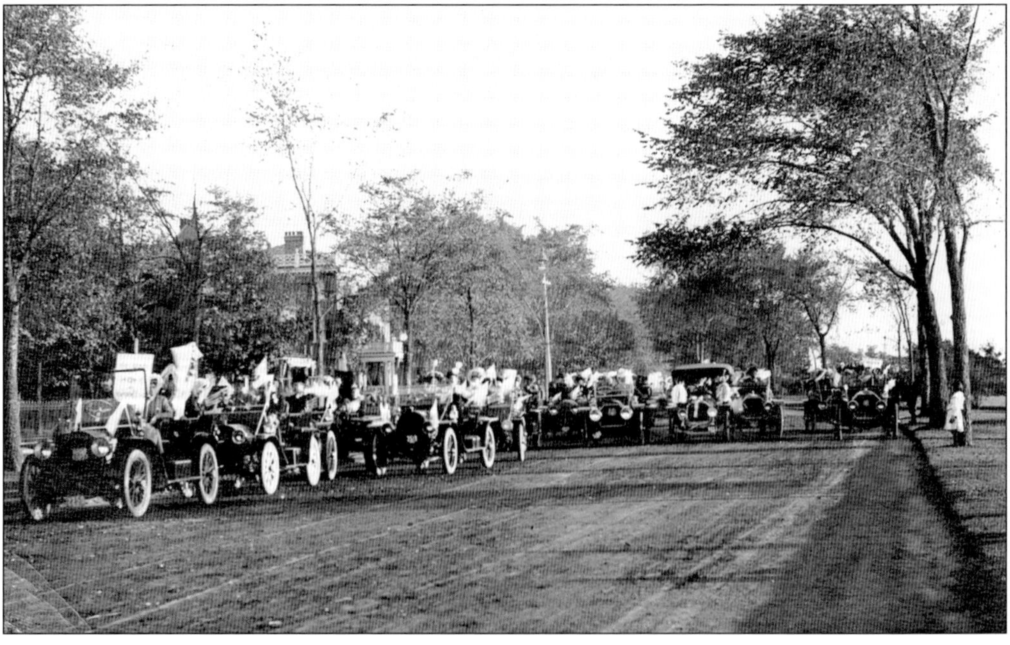

By 1910, the 20th-century automobile had invaded the 19th-century serenity of the Western Promenade. This parade of early cars, staged by the Women's Christian Temperance Union in support of a ban on the sale of alcoholic beverages, reflected the historic roles of Portland residents in promoting the national Prohibition movement.

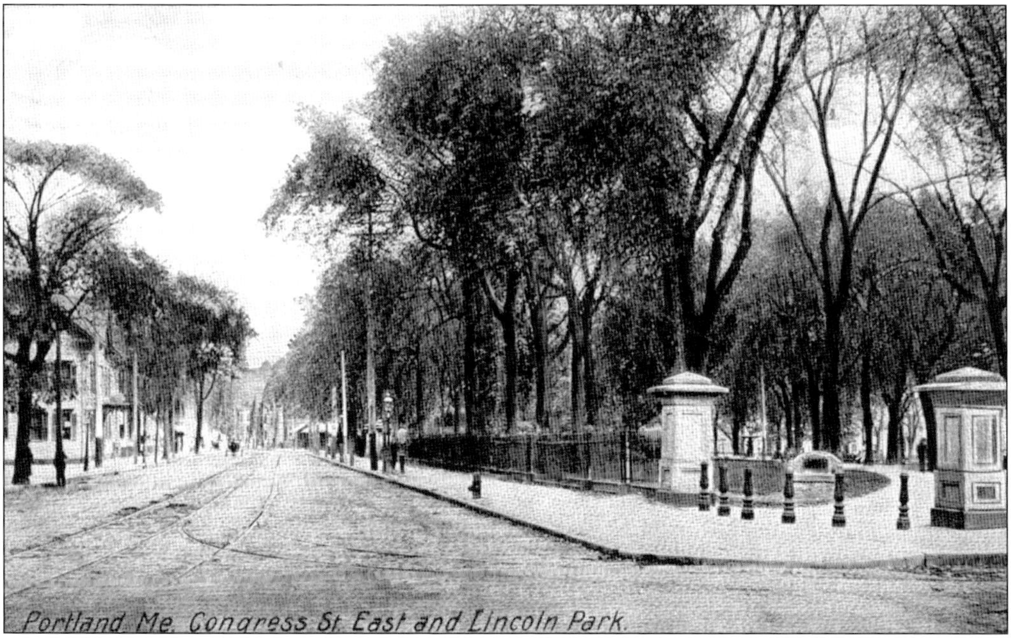


After the Great Fire of 1866, the city acquired the land bounded by Congress, Franklin, Federal, and Pearl Streets to make a firebreak in case of another conflagration as well as to provide public open space in the center of the city. First called Phoenix Square, the area was renamed Lincoln Park in 1867 to honor Pres. Abraham Lincoln. The view looks toward Munjoy Hill.

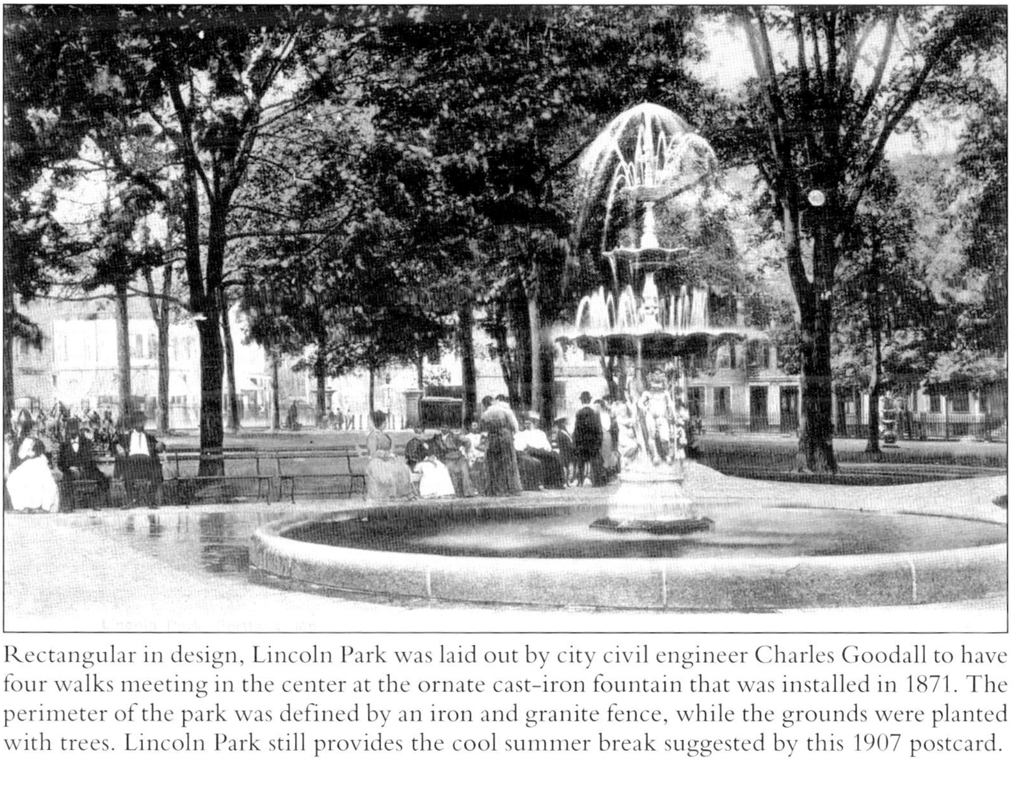

Rectangular in design, Lincoln Park was laid out by city civil engineer Charles Goodall to have four walks meeting in the center at the ornate cast-iron fountain that was installed in 1871. The perimeter of the park was defined by an iron and granite fence, while the grounds were planted with trees. Lincoln Park still provides the cool summer break suggested by this 1907 postcard.

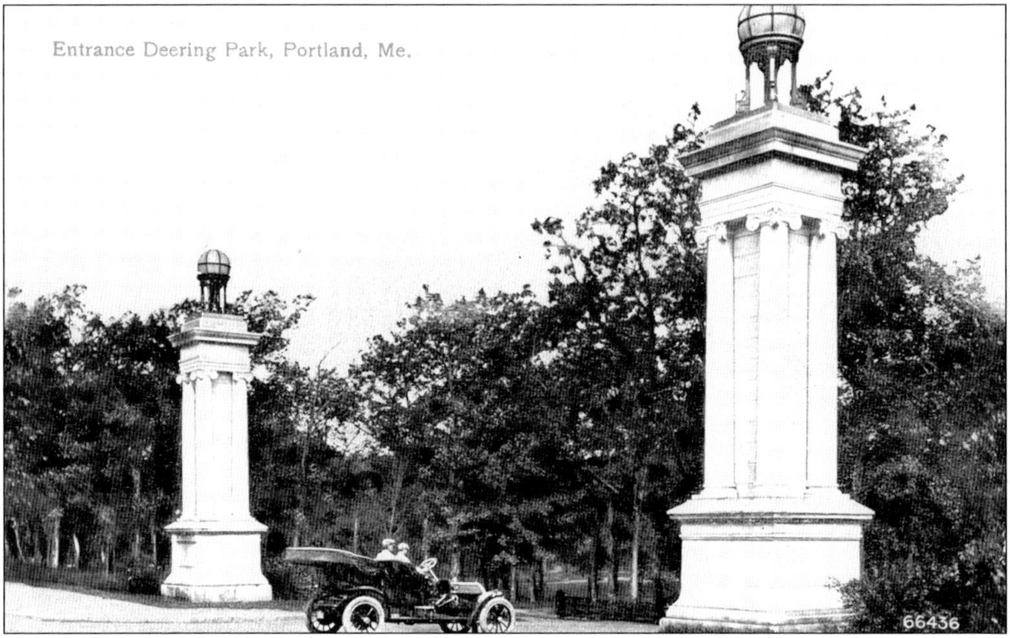


Stately granite pillars of 1902–1904, designed by Frederick A. Tompson, mark the Park Avenue entrance to Deering Oaks, the 46-acre park that Portland acquired from the Deering heirs in 1879 in exchange for a tax abatement agreement with the family. This remarkable bargain gave the city a public breathing space in the spirit of New York City's Central Park.

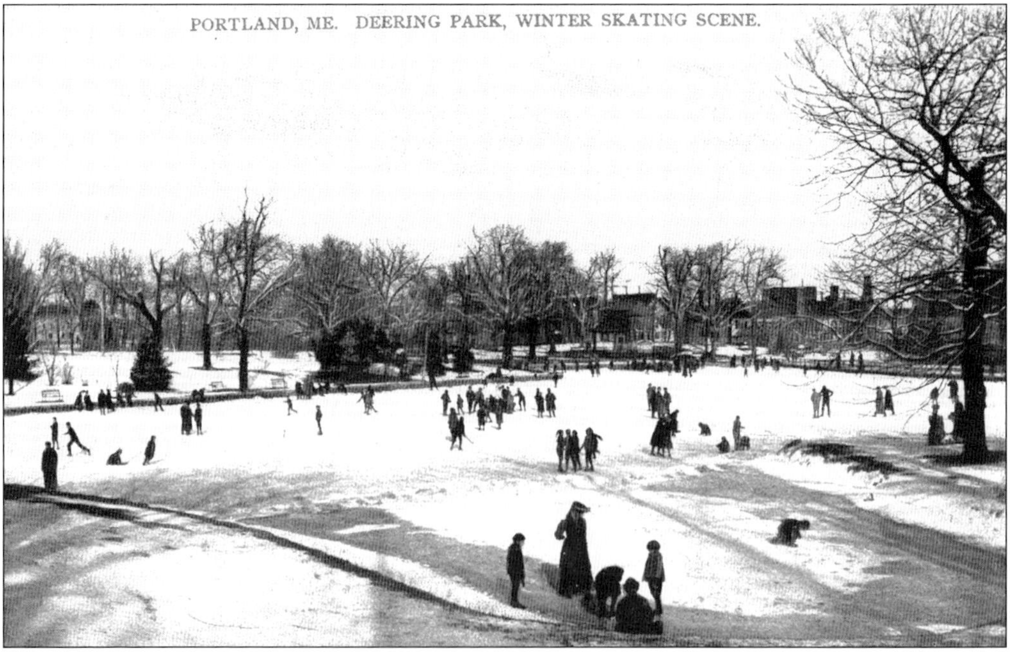


City civil engineer William A. Goodwin transformed Deering Oaks into a multifaceted pleasure ground for Portland's growing populace. By closing the tidal gates at Deering Bridge, Goodwin created one of the park's most favorite features, a four-acre pond that was cleared in winter to provide a safe haven for ice-skating by both children and adults.

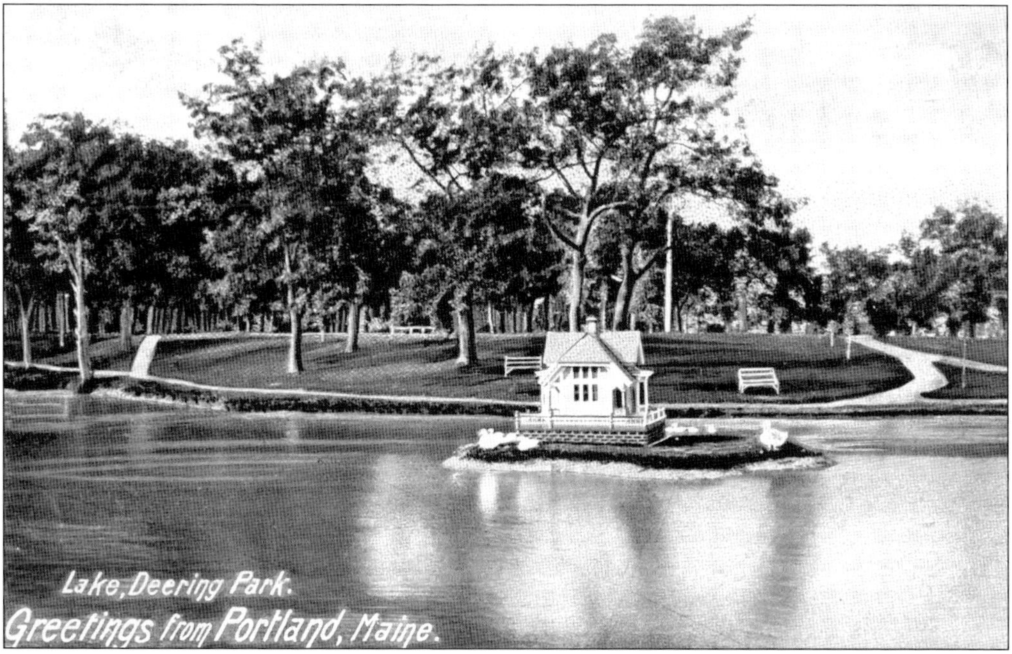


An enduring landmark of Deering Oaks is the Duck House. In 1887, Goodwin constructed a riprap island to accommodate a wooden model of a stylish Queen Anne residence, built by the Legrow Brothers Lumber Company as part of its float in the 1886 Portland Centennial Parade. A modified version of that structure still shelters the park's waterfowl during summer months.

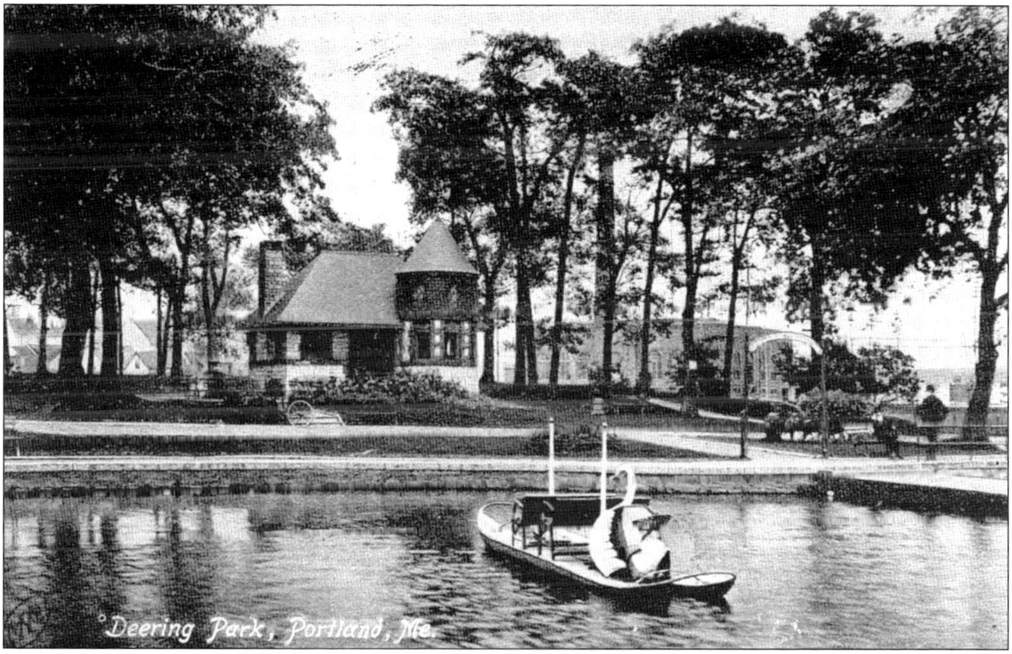


A shelter for humans was built on the shore of Deering Oaks' pond in 1894. The picturesque, towered, Queen Anne–style brick and granite building contained an ornamental fireplace at which skaters could warm themselves on winter afternoons. Designed by Frederick A. Tompson, Portland's Castle in the Park has recently been restored to its original appearance.

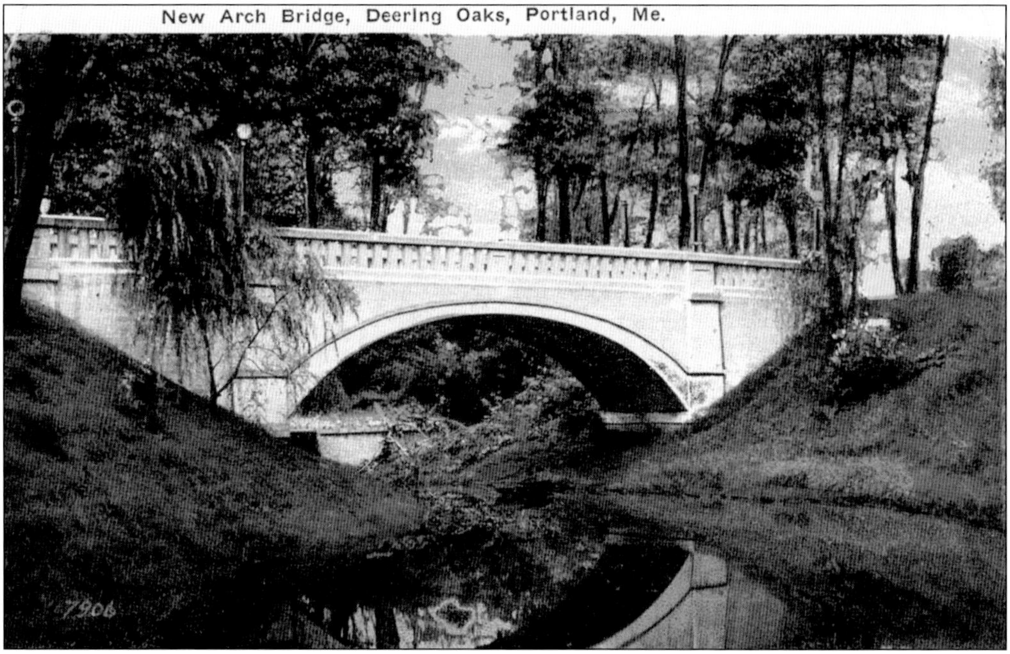


One of William A. Goodwin's first improvements to Deering Oaks was the construction of two wooden bridges over the gully at the west end of the pond. These were replaced in 1891 by an arched wooden bridge that, in turn, gave way to the present concrete bridge in 1911. Eight feet wide, it has an 80-foot span.

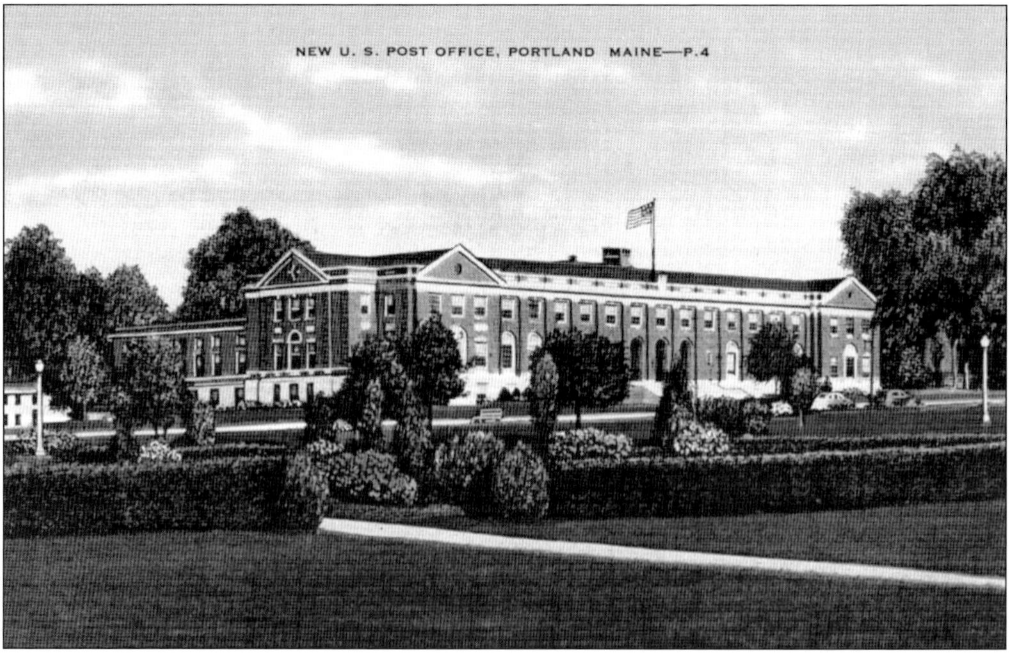


Between 1893 and 1923, Portland expanded Deering Oaks by eight acres to include the section between State Street and Forest Avenue. This 1930s view shows the 1931 rose circle in the new portion of the park as the foreground for the recently constructed Portland Post Office of 1933–1934 on Forest Avenue. The building was designed by Stevens and Stevens.

From 1889 to the 1950s, this wooden column in Deering Oaks served as a reminder of Portland's old city hall (see page 61). The slate tablet at the base explained, "Above is a model of the Market Hall built in 1825 from which this column was taken when it was removed from the spot now occupied by the Soldiers and Sailors Monument."

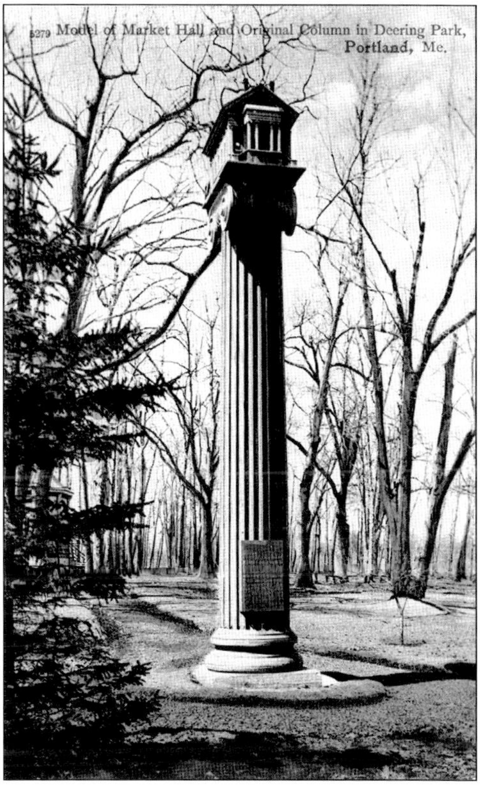

5279 Model of Market Hall and Original Column in Deering Park, Portland, Me.

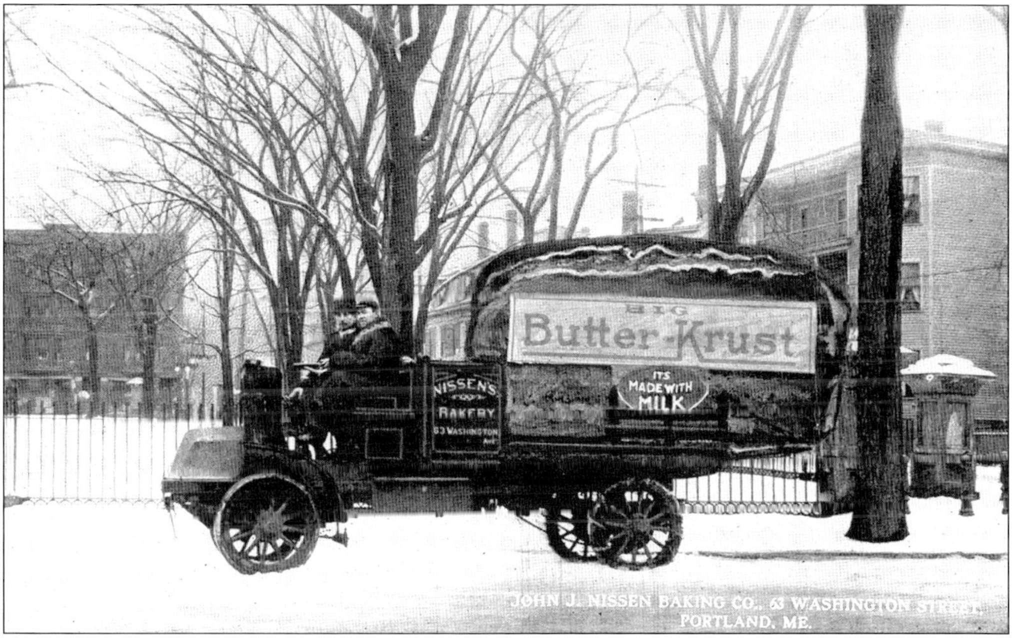


JOHN J. NISSEN BAKING CO., 63 WASHINGTON STREET, PORTLAND, ME.

From their inception, postcards were used for advertising, and this view of an early truck fitted out to promote Nissen's Big Butter-Krust bread is a classic example. Bundled in heavy coats to ward off the winter cold in an open cab, these two men have parked their vehicle at Lincoln Park. The address given for the bakery dates the picture to between 1910 and 1919.

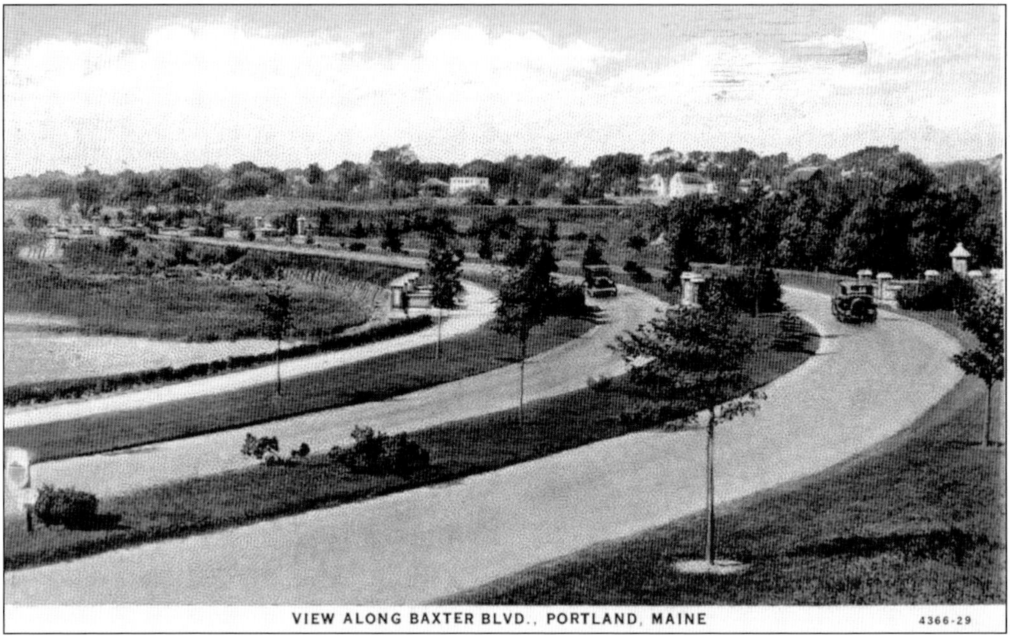


Envisioned by Mayor James P. Baxter in the 1890s, a boulevard was constructed around the shore of Back Cove in 1916–1917. Linking Forest Avenue to Washington Avenue, the two-and-one-quarter-mile roadway helped to open the Deering suburbs to residential development and provided a beautiful drive from which to view the city.

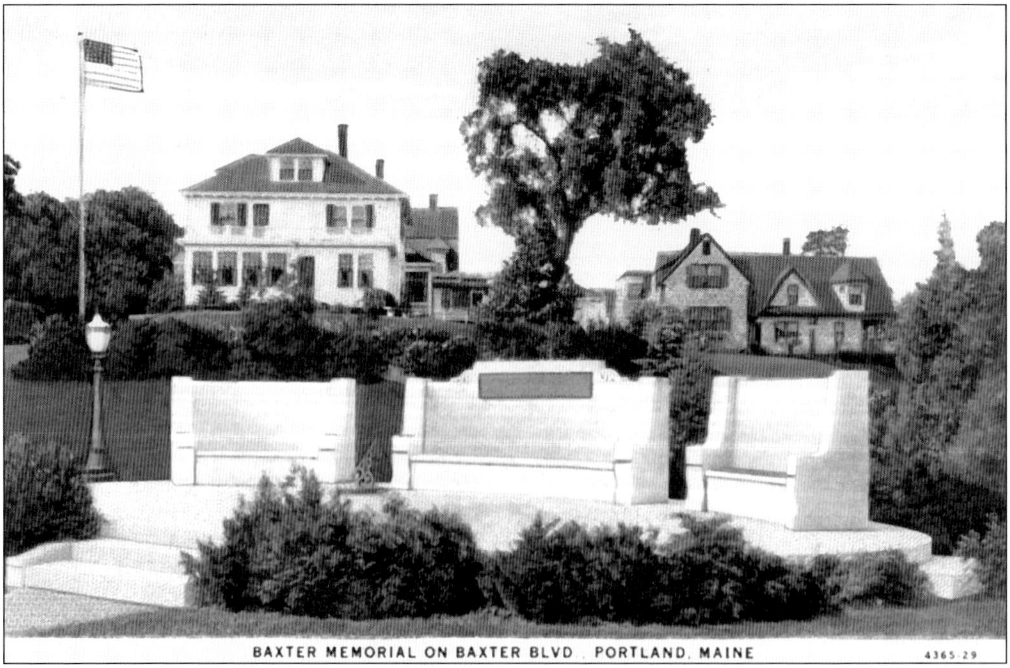


During his six terms as mayor, Portland businessman, historian, and philanthropist James P. Baxter worked tirelessly for improvements to the city's parks as well as for creation of the boulevard that bears his name. In 1925, four years after his death, Baxter was honored with this granite memorial at the corner of "his" boulevard and Vannah Avenue.

## Seven

# TRANSPORTATION

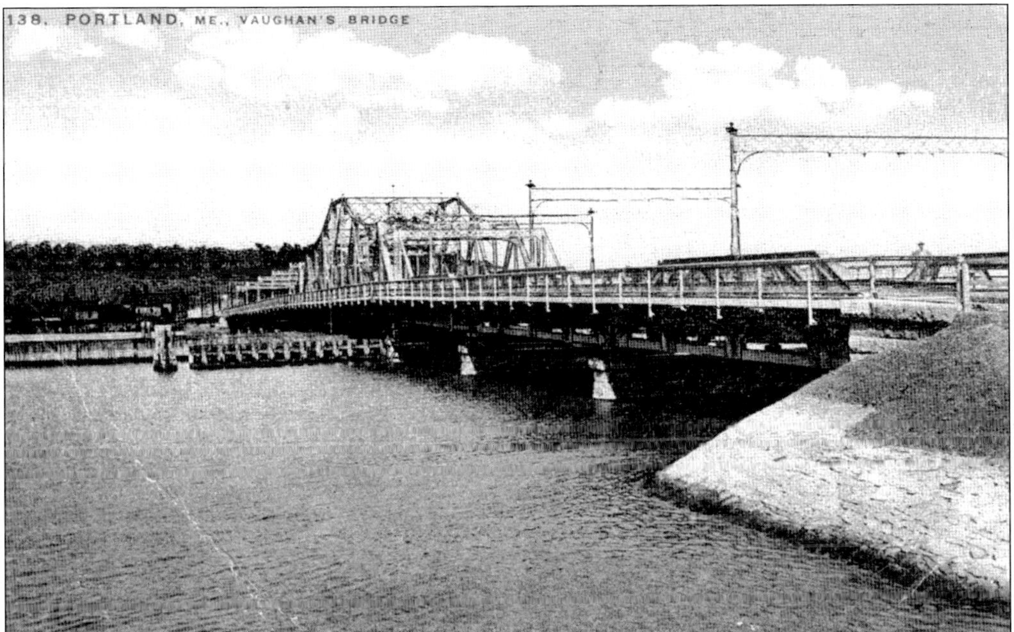


By the 1880s, the basics of the peninsula's transportation systems were in place. Most streets had been laid out, if not entirely built up, including Commercial Street, on filled land at the edge of the harbor, and others on fill at the head of Back Cove. Bridges united the peninsula with neighboring areas. Indeed, fill had made some of them more causeways than bridges. Five different rail lines came into the city; and other rails had been laid for a system of horse-drawn streetcars. Pictured is Vaughan's Bridge, first built in 1800 and named for its major proponent, William Vaughan. It was rebuilt a few times, including in 1913—about when this card was made—and replaced in the early 1950s by the Veterans Memorial Bridge.

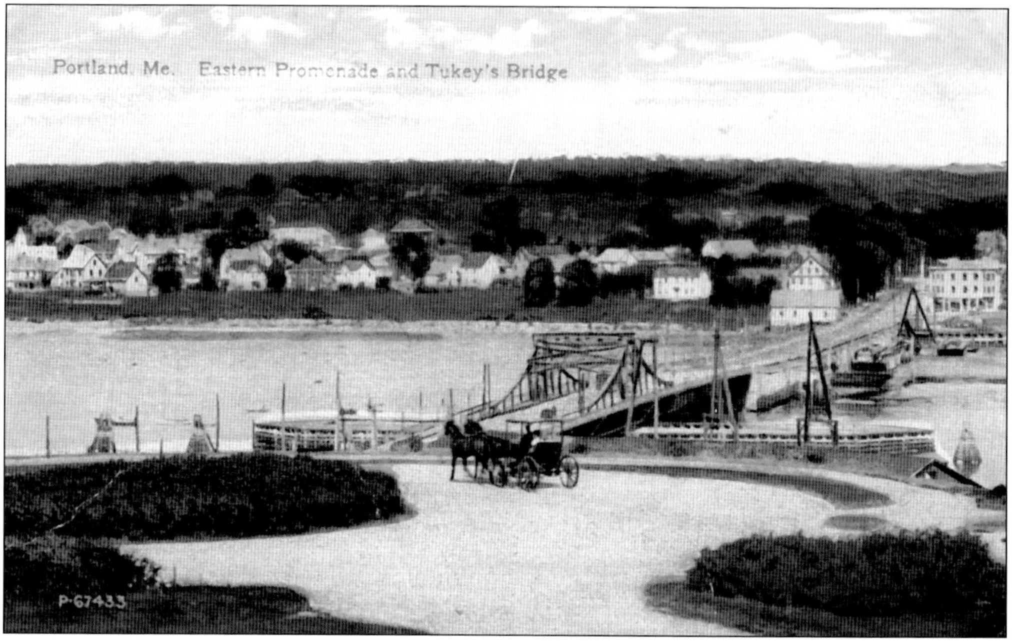


Tukey's Bridge crossed Back Cove between the peninsula and East Deering. First built in 1796 by private enterprise, it came to be known by the name of an early toll collector, Lemuel Tukey. Rebuilt in 1898, before this picture was taken, it would be replaced in 1960 by a higher structure for the interstate highway. The wagon is on the Eastern Promenade.

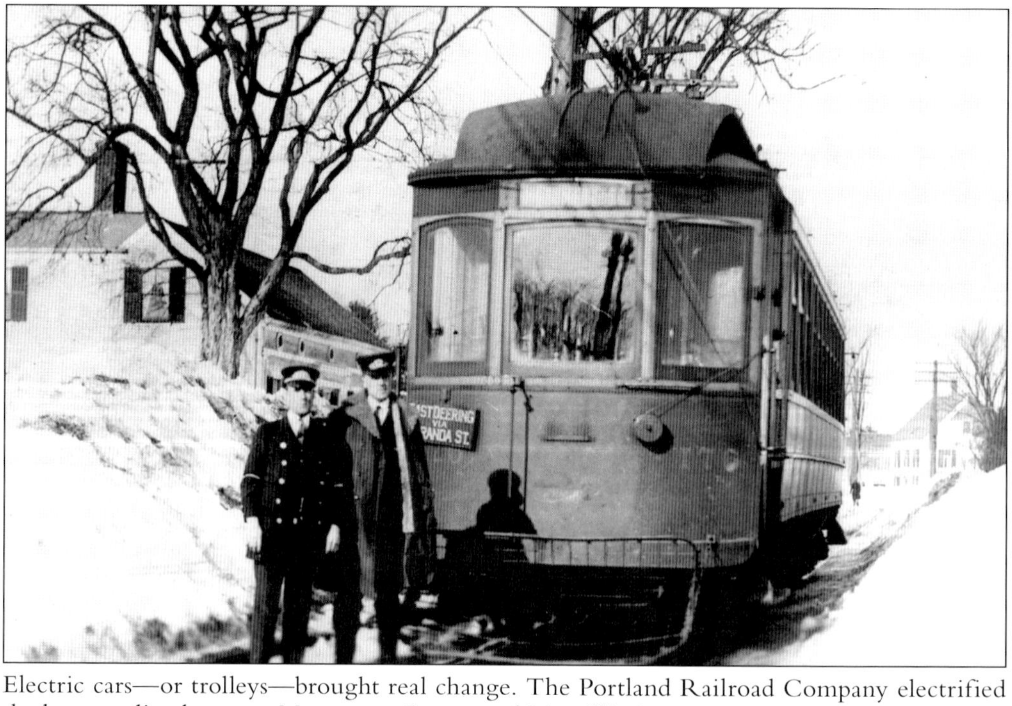


Electric cars—or trolleys—brought real change. The Portland Railroad Company electrified the horsecar line between Monument Square and Morrill's Corner, Deering, in 1891. Soon the company moved to electrify all lines. This car is on Veranda Street in East Deering; the house with wreaths on its entablature still stands. The company maintained special cars for plowing snow.

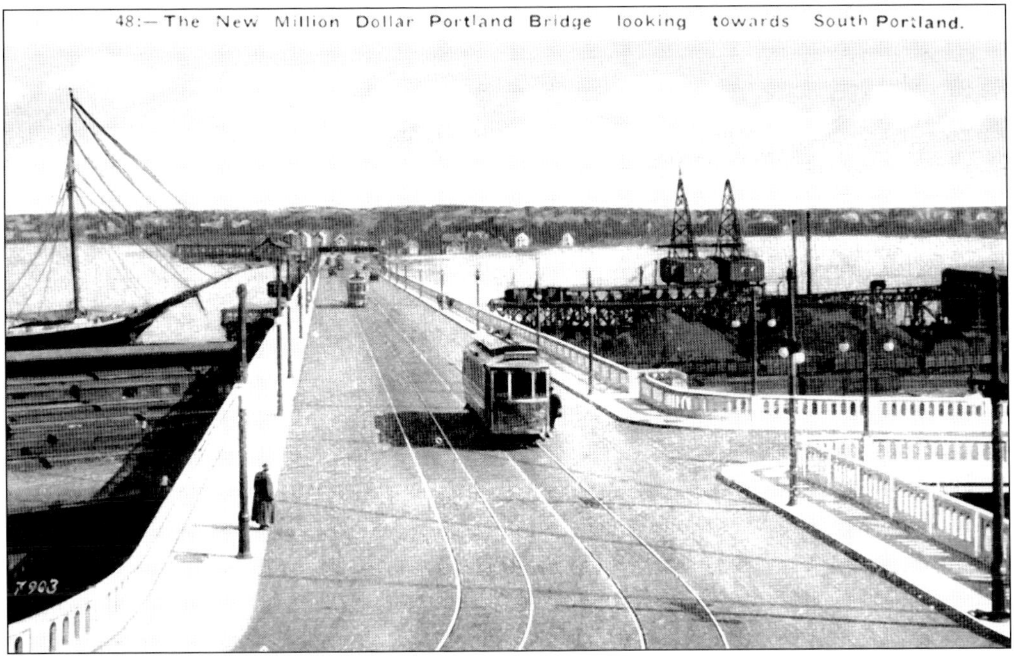


Trolleys became so much a part of city life that they—or their tracks—show up in numerous postcards. Here a car crosses the "Million Dollar Bridge" to South Portland, nicknamed for its price tag and completed in 1916. High enough on the Portland side to take traffic above Commercial Street and the parallel train tracks, it served until the 1990s.

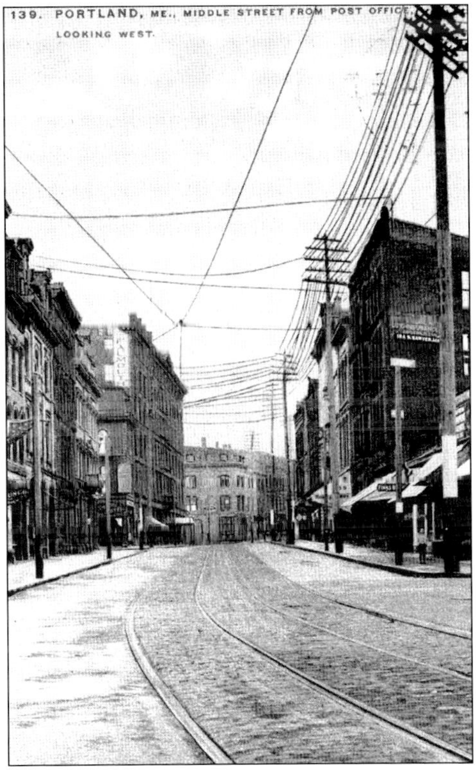


Another necessity for the "electrics" was the presence of overhead wires, which often were erased by those who printed photographs and cards. This view of Middle Street is something of an exception, although close examination shows that, even here, the wires fade out well before the trolley line does.

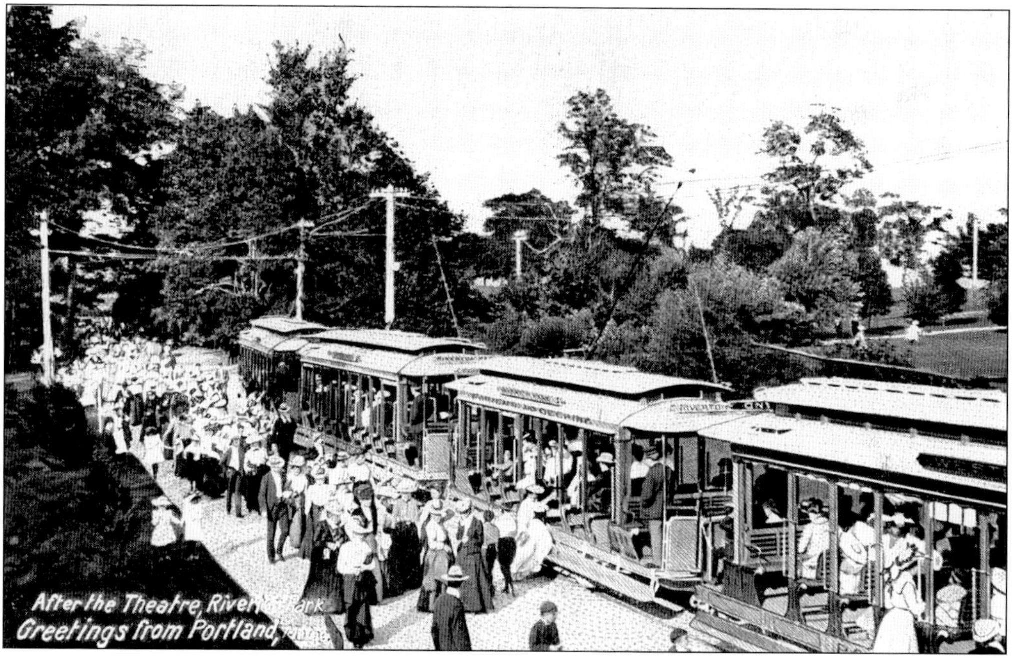

Trolley companies frequently built parks outside cities, partly to attract riders. The Portland Railroad Company built Cape Cottage Park in Cape Elizabeth, Underwood Park in Falmouth, and, in 1896, Riverton Park on the Presumpscot River (the far edge of Deering). Many cars were needed after a performance at Riverton's large open-air theater.

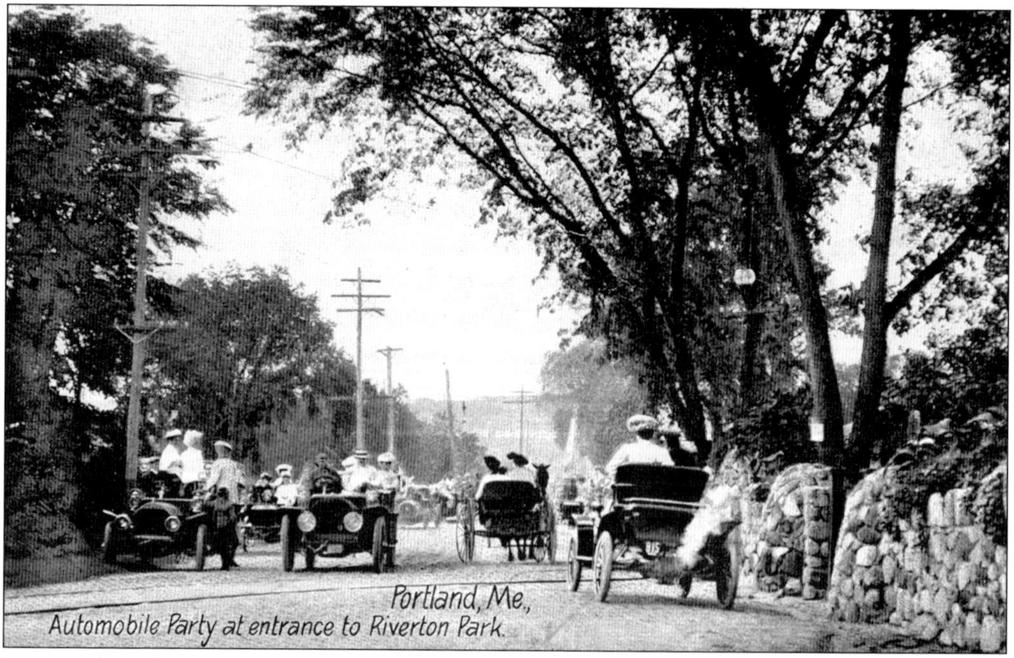

It might have been a trolley park, but Riverton's designers eventually provided an automobile entrance off Forest Avenue. Here cars, together with a horse and buggy, cross trolley tracks. The automobile, which allowed drivers to travel farther afield, is credited with helping cause the demise of such parks. The trolley company sold the park in 1920. (See also pages 112 and 113.)

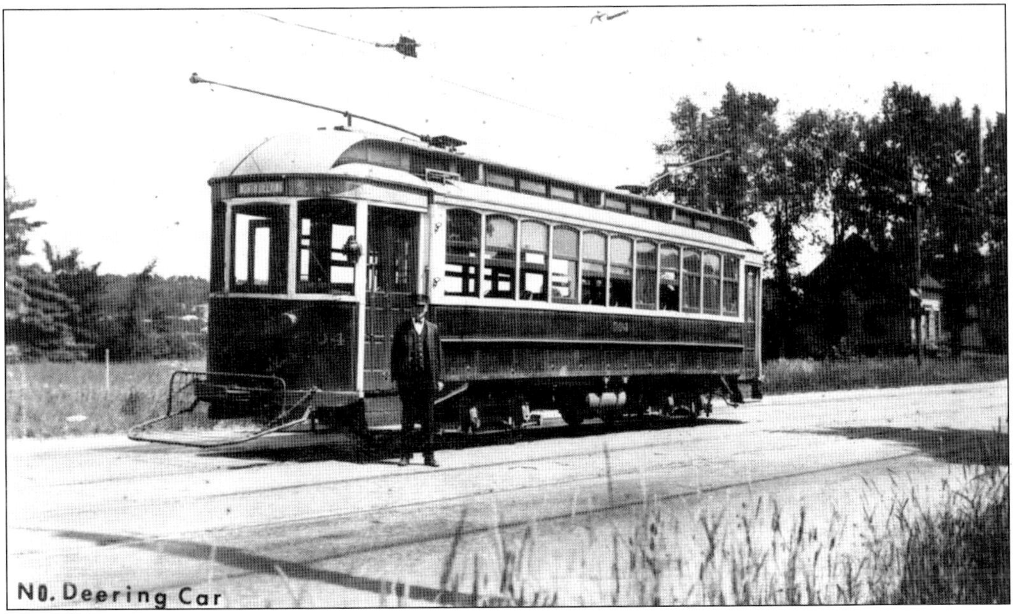


At its peak, the Portland Railroad Company not only covered the city and nearby towns but also reached Yarmouth, Gorham, and Windham to the northeast and west, and extended south to Saco. As revenues fell, the outer lines were abandoned one by one. This car made the final run in May 1941, on the Riverton and North Deering line.

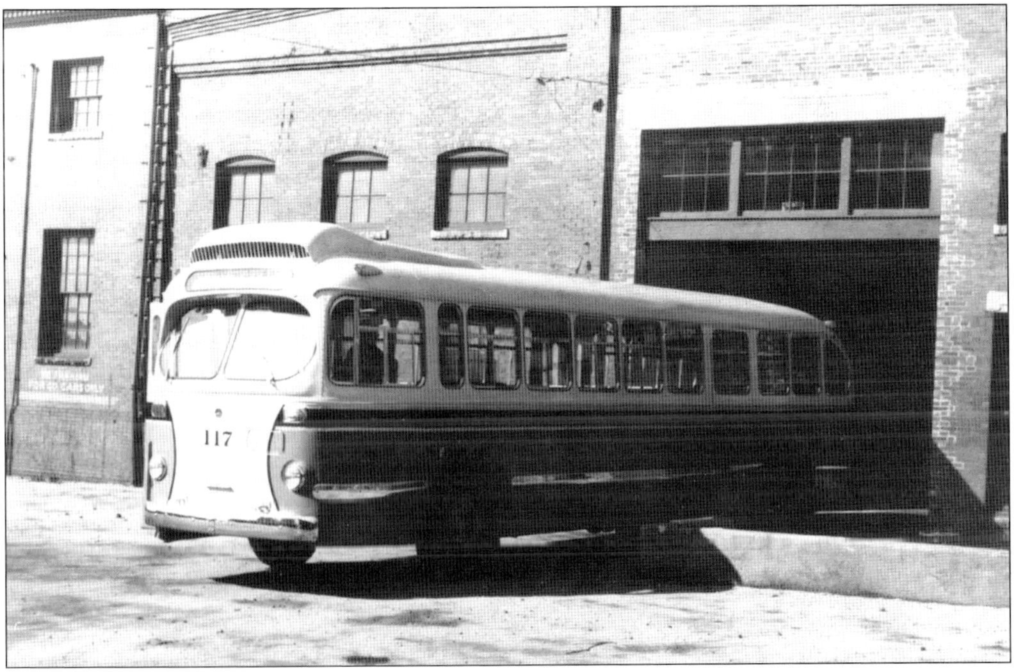


Portland saw its first automobile in 1899, but the numbers soon grew. In the early 20th century, more and more personal automobiles and larger vehicles were on the road. Traveling on state- or city-maintained roads, with neither wires nor tracks to keep up, buses competed with and increasingly replaced trolleys. The old trolley barn, shown here, came to house city buses.

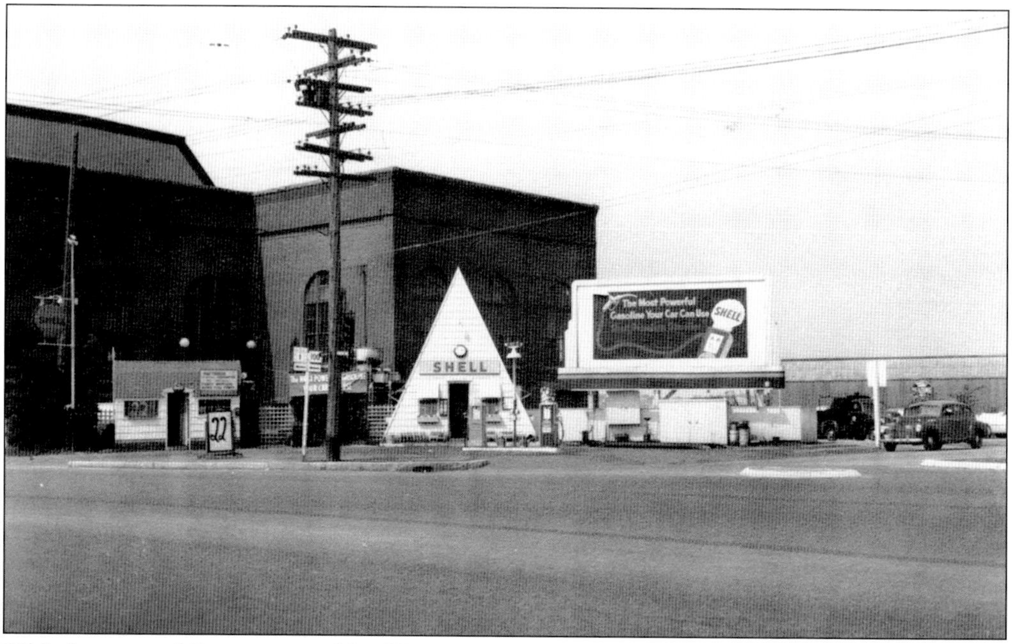


With the automobile came a need for filling stations. Older citizens will remember this imaginative tepee-like example, sited where Marginal Way meets Forest Avenue. The big building behind was the power station for the trolley system. How symbolic is it that the automobile, represented by the small building, conquered the trolley, supported by the bigger one?

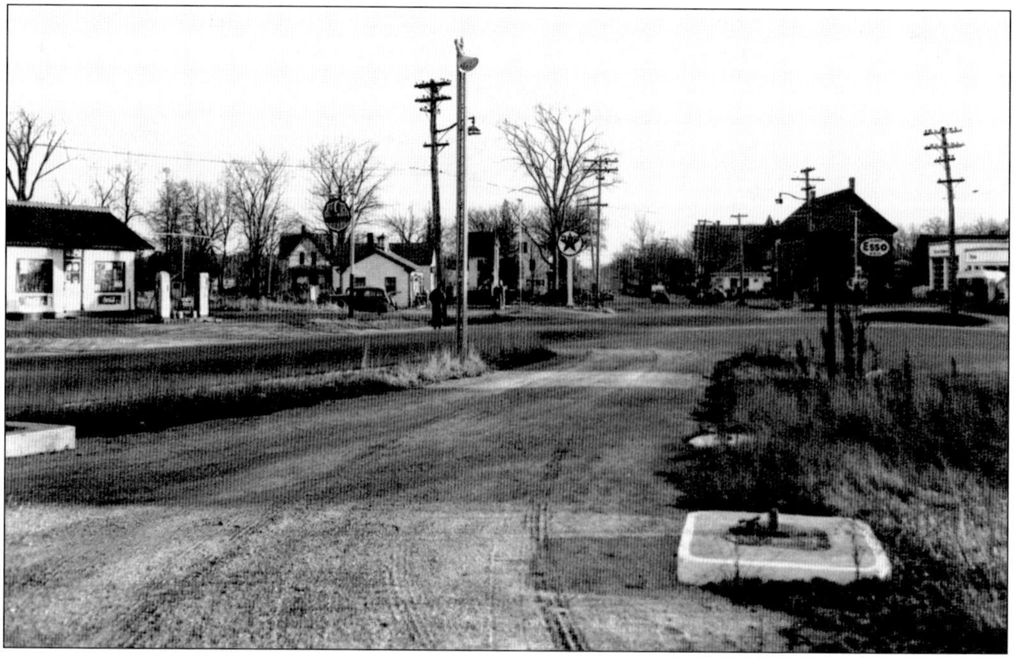


In time, gas stations appeared at nearly every major crossroads. At least three filling stations were at Allen's Corner, North Deering, with once-familiar brand names.

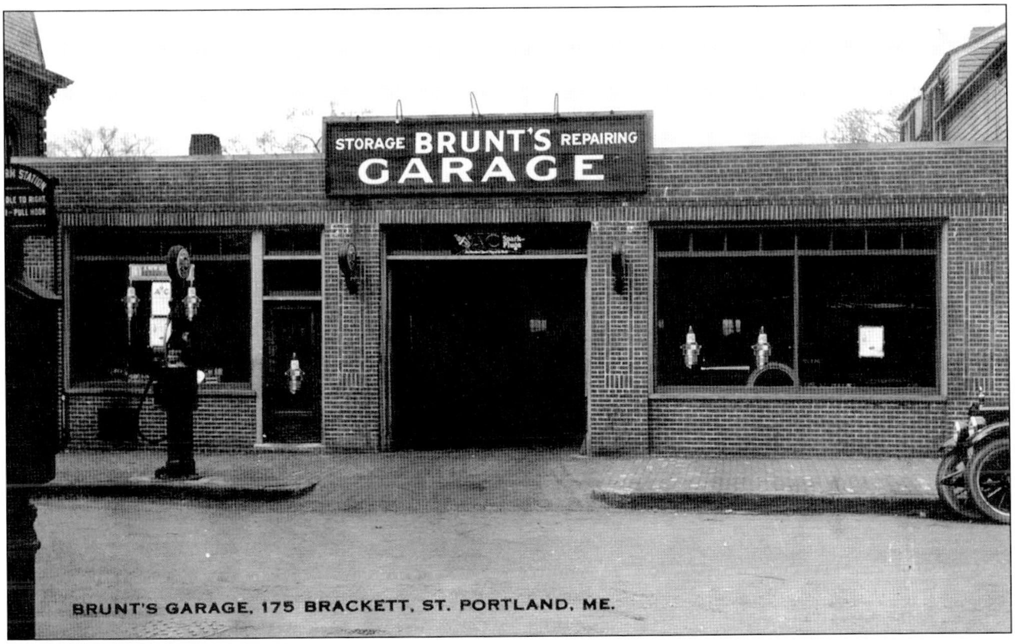


Another necessity, of course, was the repair shop. This small garage was built about 1922, tucked in between residences in the city's west end. Note that it too had a gas pump. The business changed names frequently. The building is still there but no longer holds a garage. Arthur Brunt, its proprietor in 1924, later owned a garage at Allen's Corner.

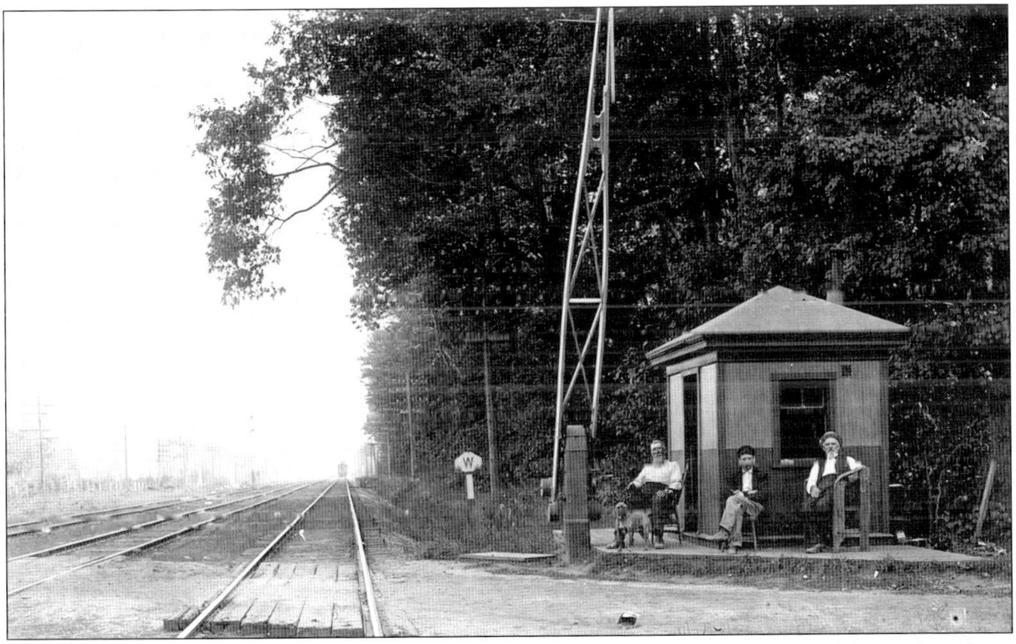

Because the automobile's noisy engines made it hard for a driver to hear approaching trains, there was more need for barriers at railroad crossings without clear views; and those barriers had to be hand-operated. Read Street crosses the Maine Central Railroad tracks about two-thirds of a mile north of the Woodfords station. Obviously the job was not especially demanding.

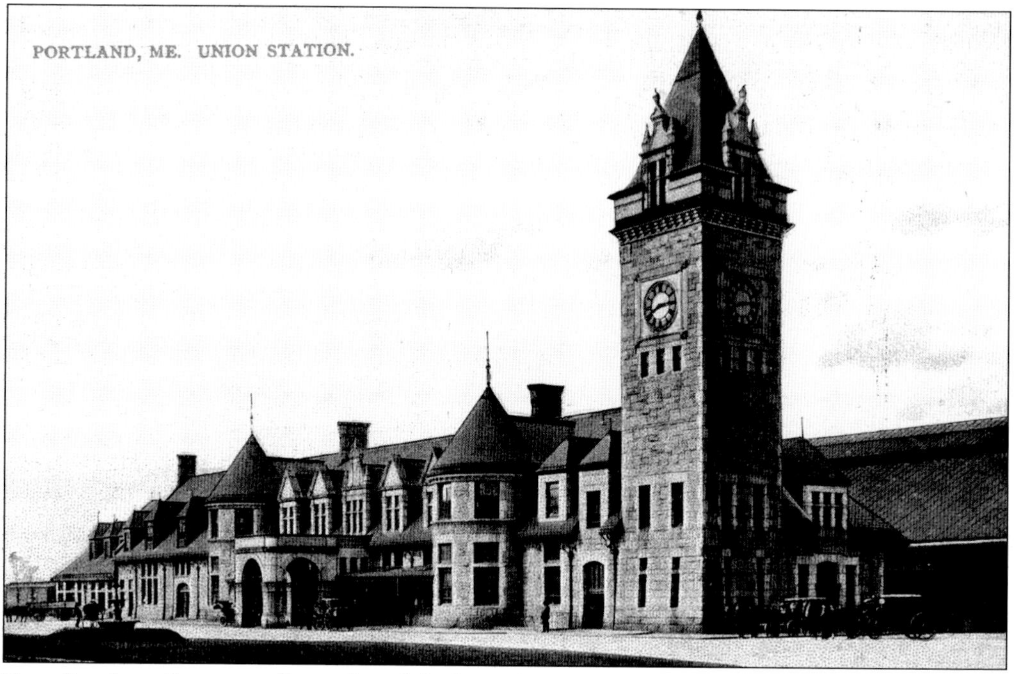


Traveling by rail was usually preferred for long trips, and the railroads attempted to make such travel appealing. In 1888, Union Station, designed by Bostonians Bradley, Winslow, and Witherell, was constructed to serve both the Boston and Maine and the Maine Central Railroads. A view with wagons in front shows the station soon after construction.

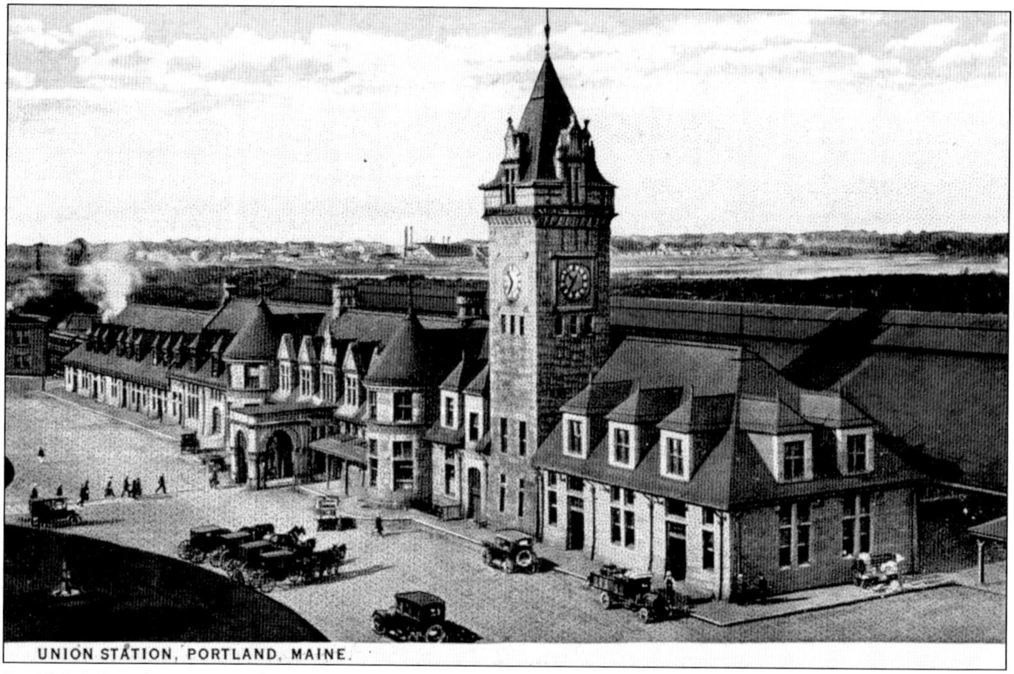


In 1906, by the time a few automobiles were taking up some of the parking, the station was lengthened. The St. John Street location took the depot away from the congestion of Commercial Street and made it easily accessible, off outer Congress Street.

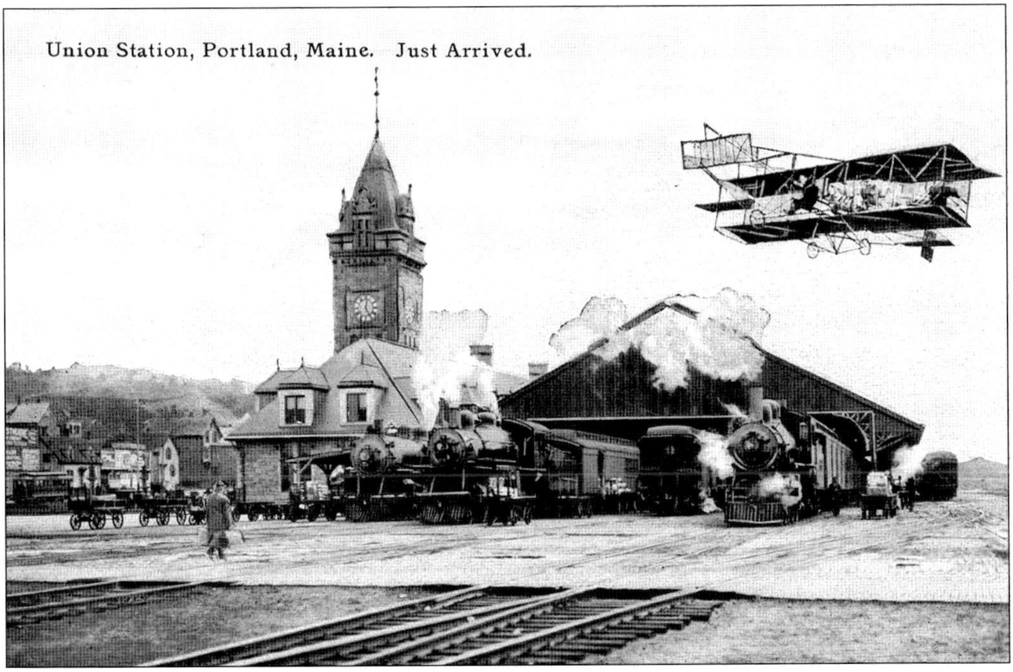


The train sheds (here seen from Congress Street) were extensive, but the airplane appears to have been inserted to illustrate a new and different mode of transportation, if not just to add interest to an expanse of sky. In the background is the much higher ground of the Western Promenade.

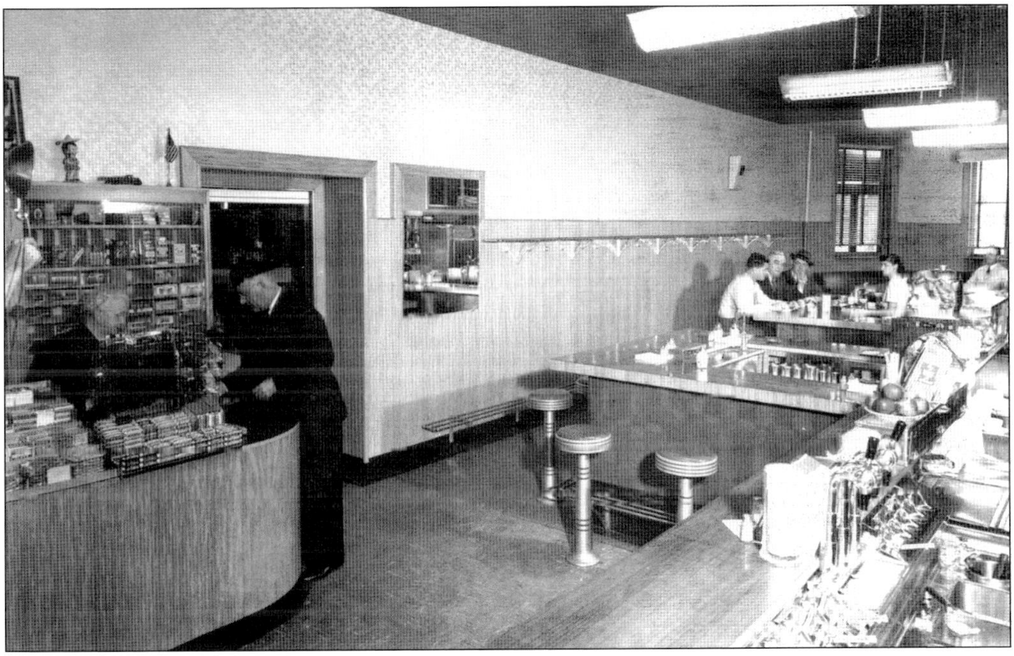

Within the station were the usual waiting rooms and an Armstrong Restaurant, with a café and a counter offering candies and other sundries—like postcards. Originally with some pretensions of elegance, the dining area is shown here as it looked in the mid-20th century.

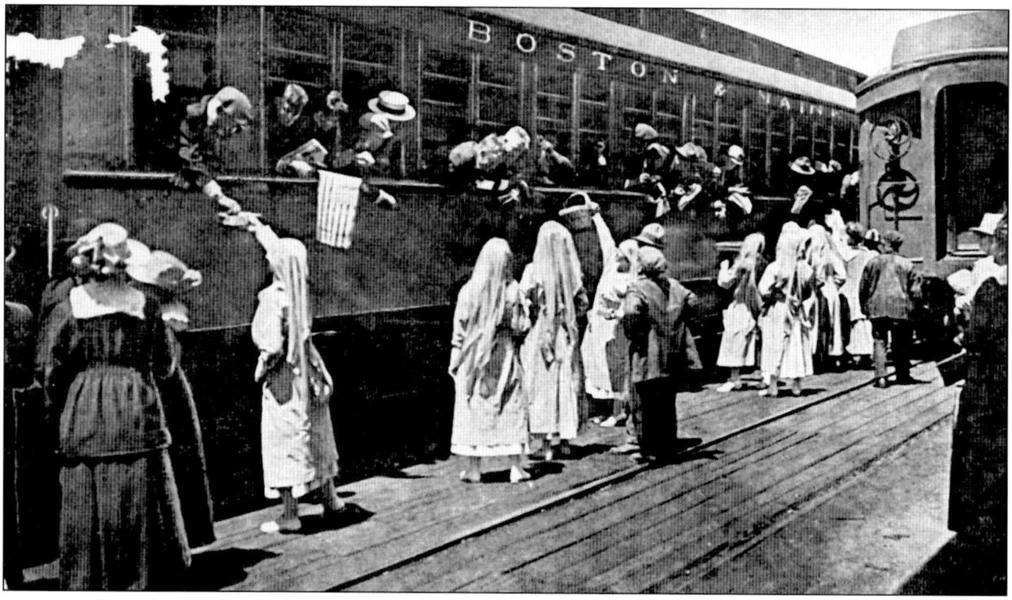


Inside Union Station's train sheds, Red Cross Canteen Service women distributed goodies to soldiers and recruits as a patriotic gesture during World War I.

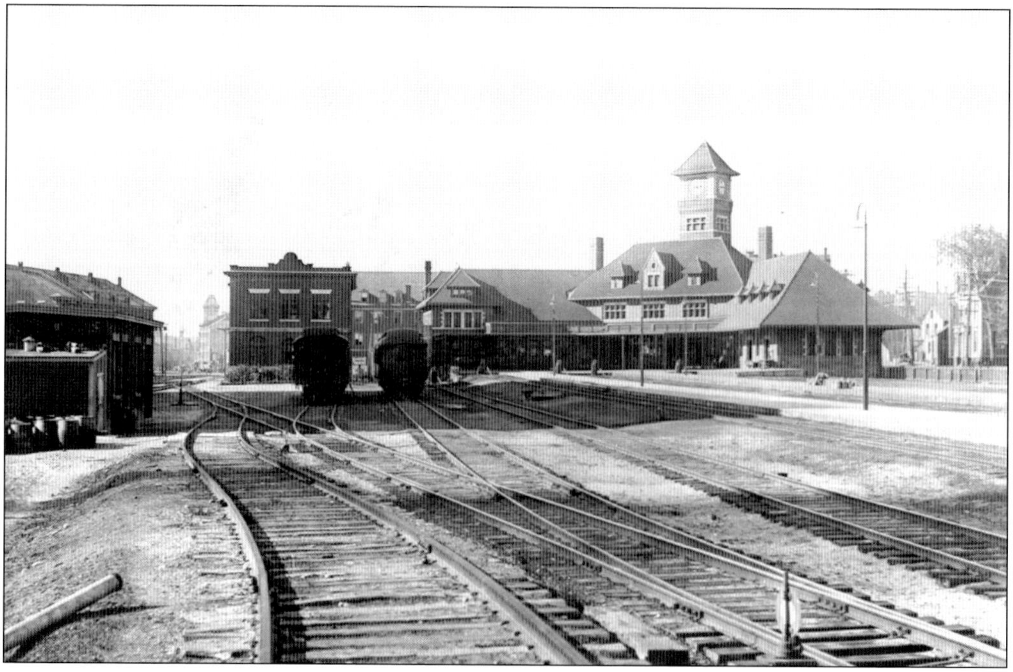

On the other end of the city, the Grand Trunk Railway, connecting Montreal with the port since 1853, followed suit in 1903 with its own new and imposing station and railroad office building, all designed by the Detroit firm of Spier and Rohr. The view from behind would have been familiar to individuals arriving by train for over half a century.

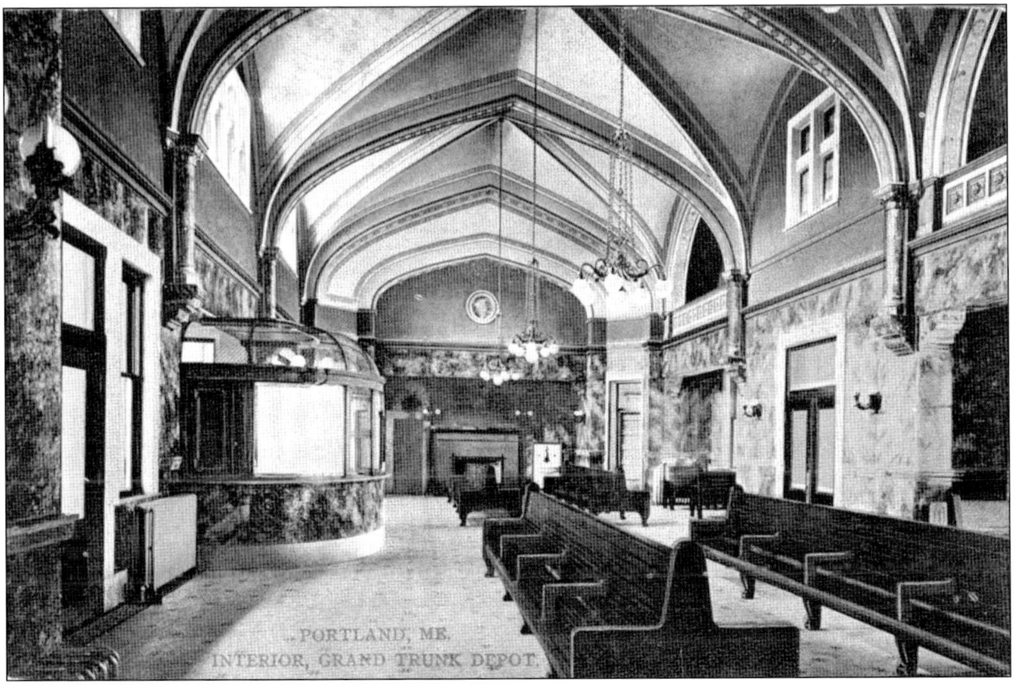


The waiting room was designed to impress. Many passengers arrived from Canada to spend summer months on Portland's islands or at other coastal resorts. Other visitors arrived at nearby docks, including winter passengers from Liverpool, who then took the train to Montreal.

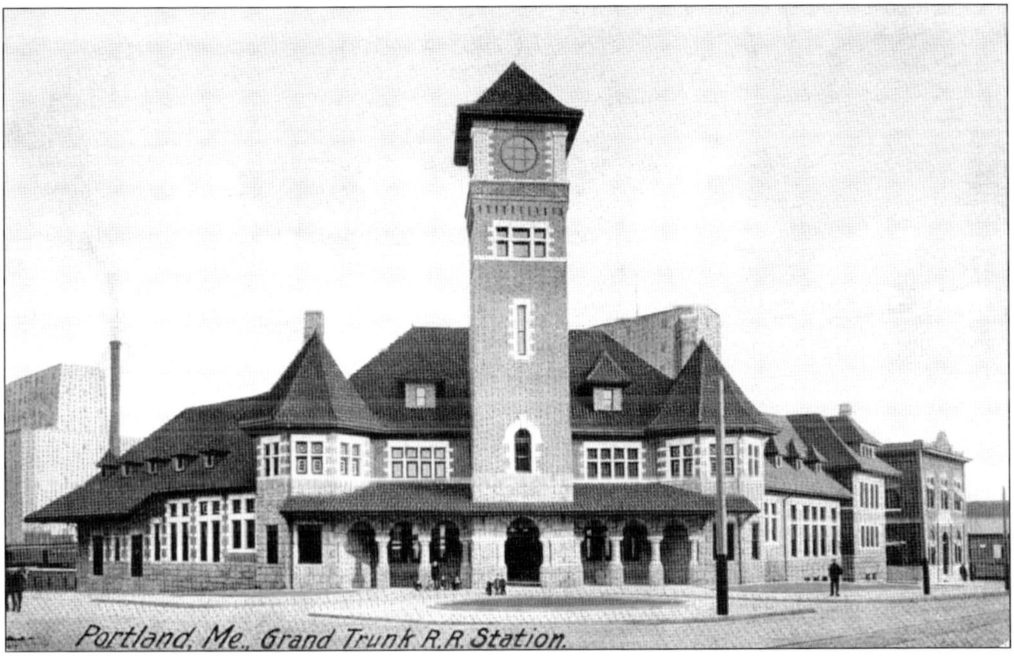


The front of the Grand Trunk Station was also impressive, but the 20th century was not kind to railroads. Union station was demolished in 1961. The Grand Trunk Station closed the next year and was razed in 1966. The docks and elevators also were destroyed, leaving only the office building at the far right to mark a once-imposing complex.

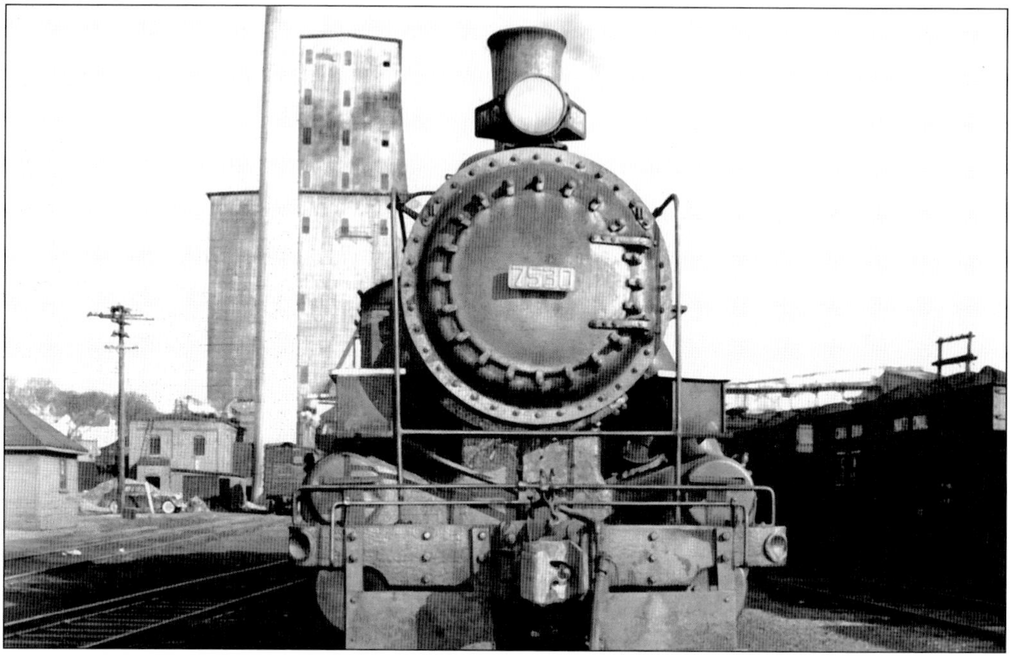


The Portland Company was formed in 1846, as construction began on the line to Canada; and it manufactured most of that railroad's early locomotives (but not this one), as well as engines for other lines. The company also made a range of other large iron goods, from iron staircases to elevators, from retorts for the canning industry to fire engines.

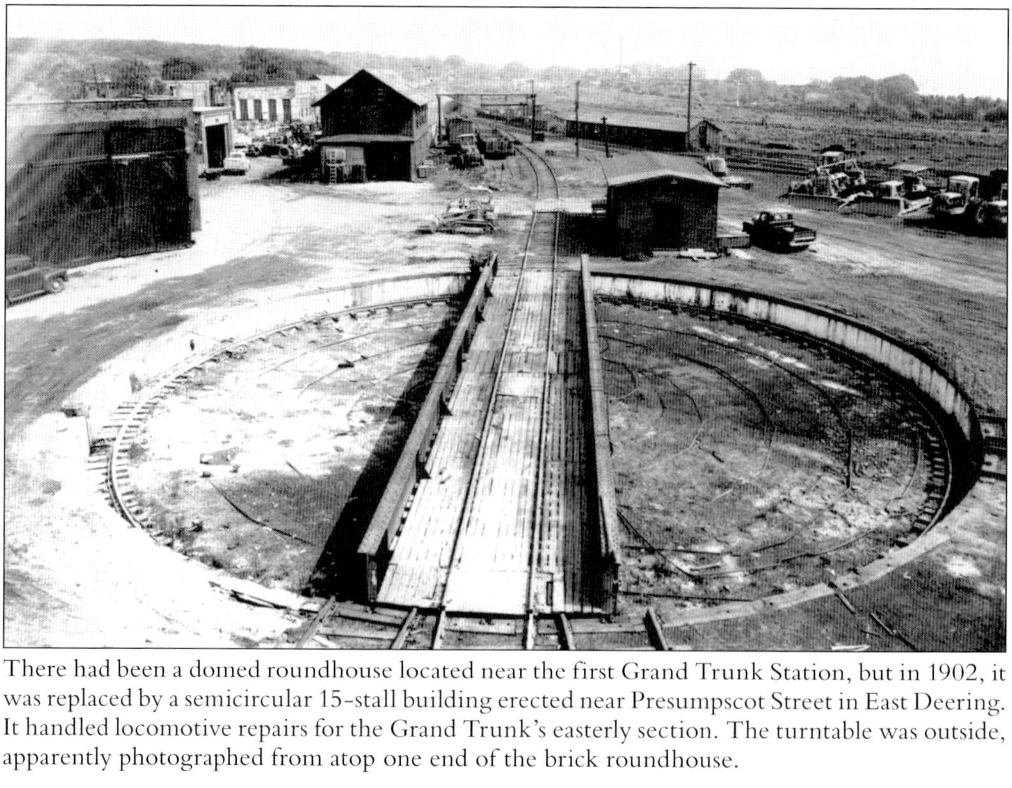

There had been a domed roundhouse located near the first Grand Trunk Station, but in 1902, it was replaced by a semicircular 15-stall building erected near Presumpscot Street in East Deering. It handled locomotive repairs for the Grand Trunk's easterly section. The turntable was outside, apparently photographed from atop one end of the brick roundhouse.

# *Eight*

# Deering

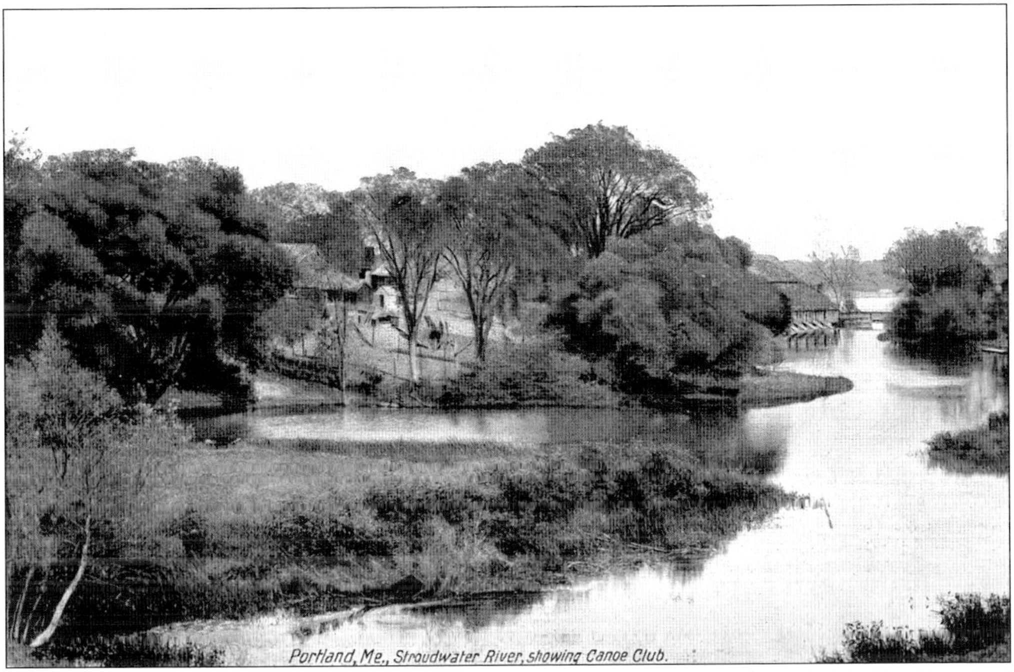


In 1899, Portland annexed the city of Deering, located to its west and north. Trolley lines had already formed ties, and many Deering residents worked in the bigger city; but the majority of its residents nevertheless voted to remain separate. The state legislature overrode their wishes; and Portland suddenly had almost eight times as much area as before, although population increase was proportionally much less. The southernmost part of the city of Deering was Stroudwater, with some of the oldest homes in the area. This particularly idyllic scene looks down the Stroudwater River toward Fore River and the peninsula, from downstream of the bridge carrying outer Congress Street. On the left would be the back yards of homes, such as the George Tate House (see page 13) and the Stevens home.

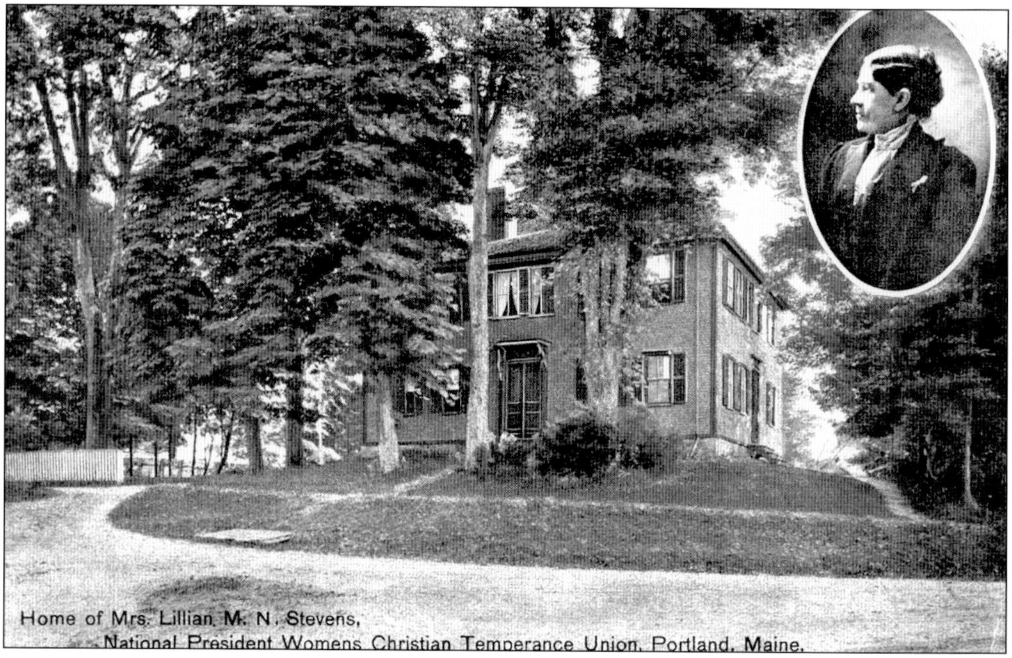


Brothers Tristram and Samuel Stevens built one large home (with two kitchens) for their two families in 1806. It was Tristram's daughter-in-law, Lillian M. N. Stevens, who made it well known. She worked to alleviate problems of poor women and children, in addition to opposing liquor, which she believed to be related. The picture shows the house as it was before Lillian's daughter had the front door made elaborate with a fanlight, sidelights, and an entry porch.

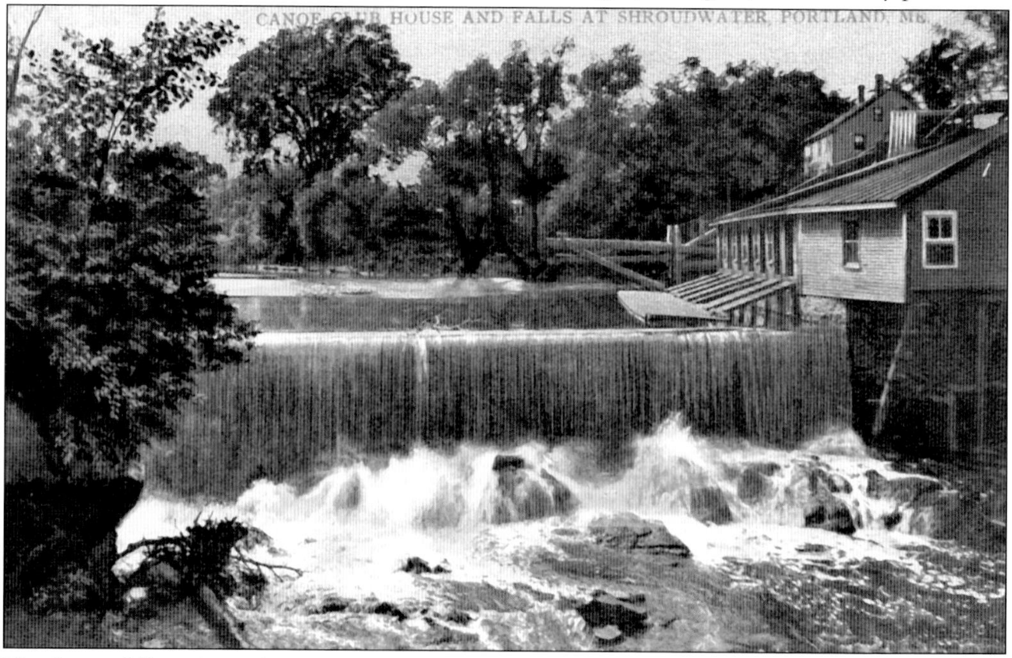


The lower falls at Stroudwater held a series of dams for sawmills, gristmills, and a fulling mill before the dam was raised to make a larger millpond for canoeing. The view is from the bridge on Westbrook Street.

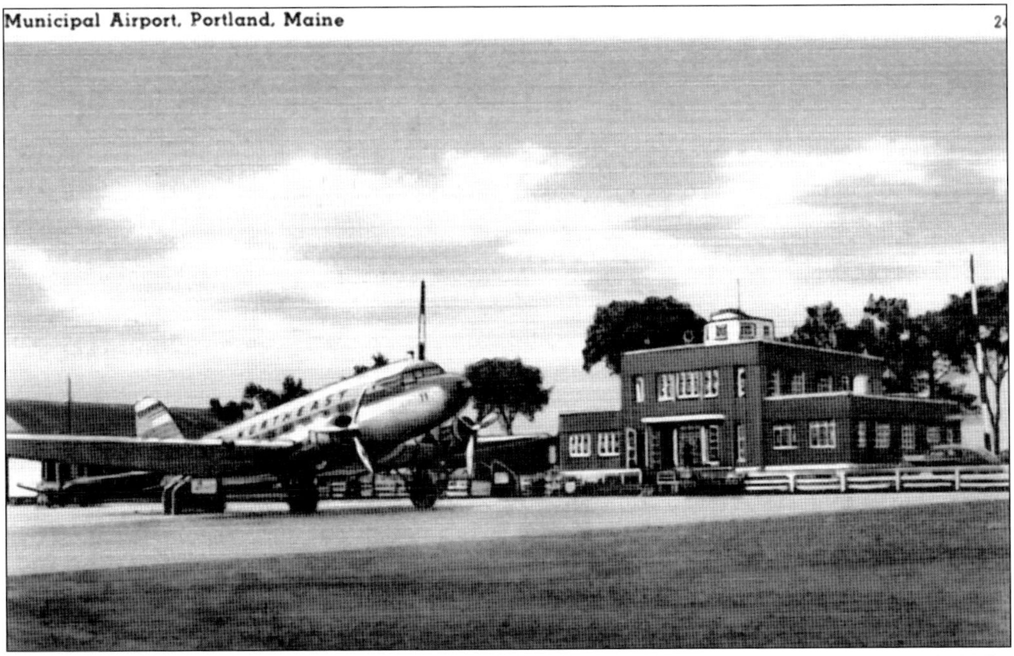


Modern Stroudwater is close to the International Jetport, which began as a private flying field for two local men before being first leased by the city and, in 1934, taken over as Portland Municipal Airport. The 1940 terminal was later enlarged and still later replaced by a modern facility. The airport itself also grew in size; it now extends into South Portland.

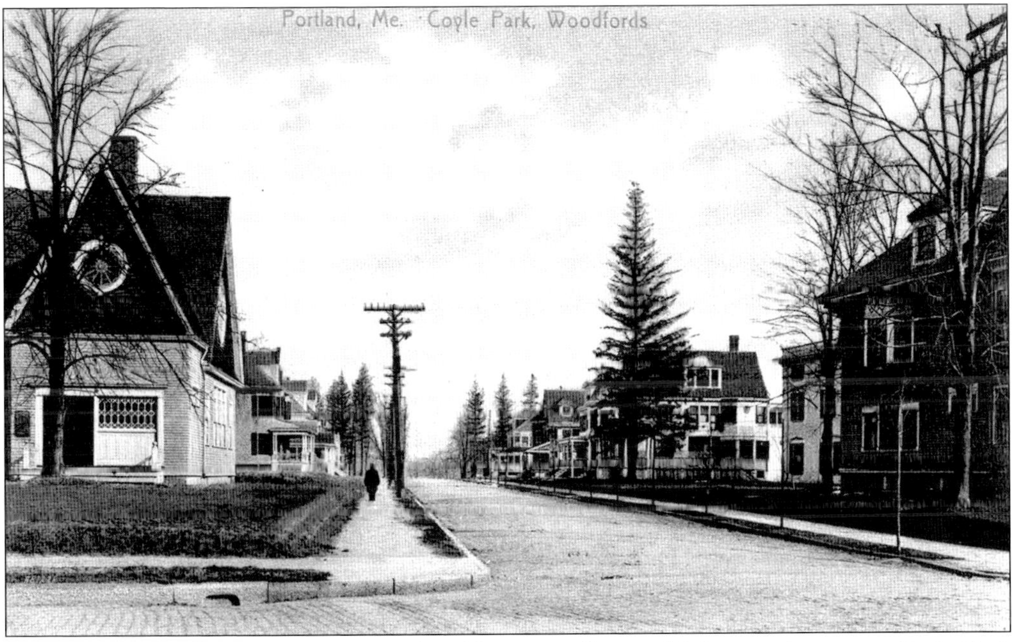


Deering had, before annexation, called itself "a city of homes." The area known as Coyle Park is between Forest Avenue and Back Cove, on what was once the estate of Capt. John B. Coyle, founder of the Portland Steam Packet Company in the early 1840s. Coyle had also urged the annexation. Development began in 1900.

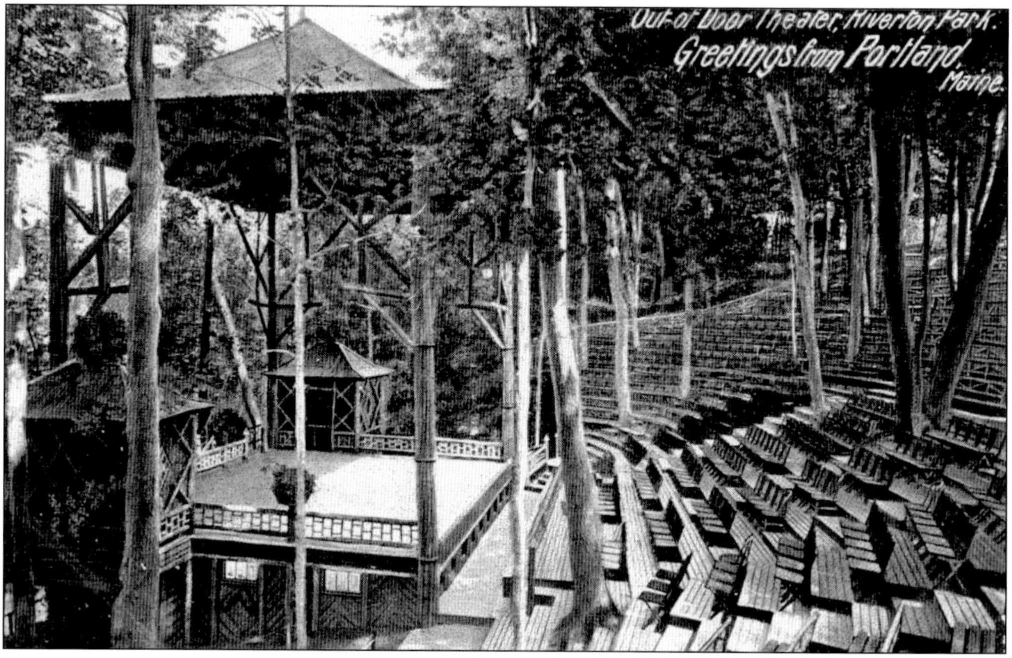


Deering included rural as well as residential areas. Riverton Park, set up on the banks of the Presumpscot River in 1896, provided a place where city dwellers could go by trolley to enjoy a country setting, even to lease boats to row on the river. Another early feature was the rustic theater, which could seat an audience of 2,200 for musical performances or vaudeville acts.

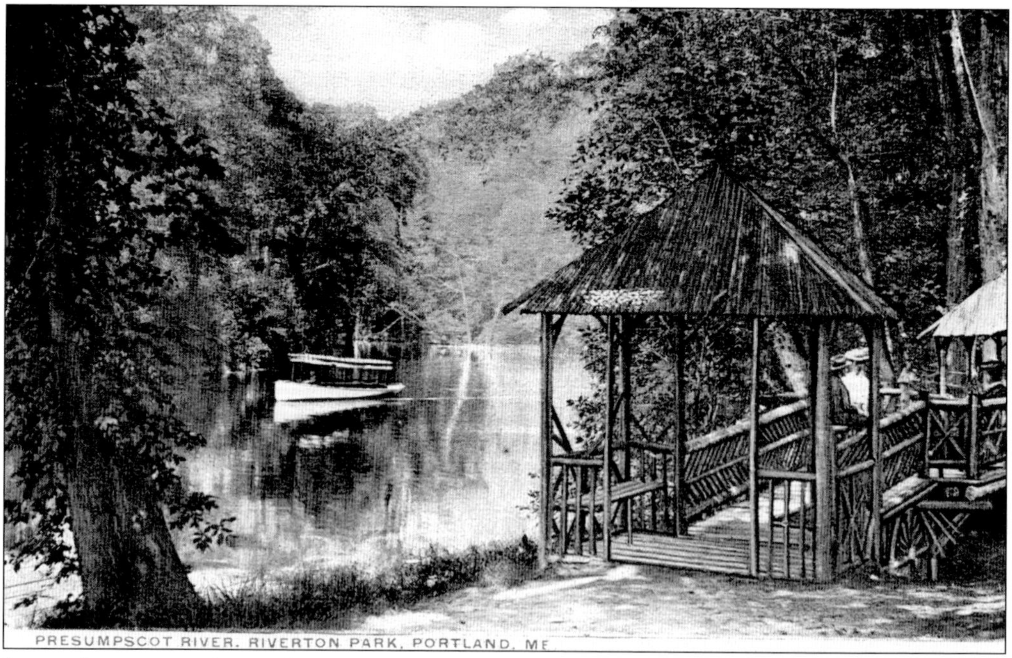


Suggesting a romantic spot for a chat, this particular scene of the park also appeared in a nighttime view, darkened and embellished with a moon in the sky and a reflection in the water below, but with the boat in the same position—as were the man and woman. Small steamboats navigated the Presumpscot River from its mouth to the Riverton location.

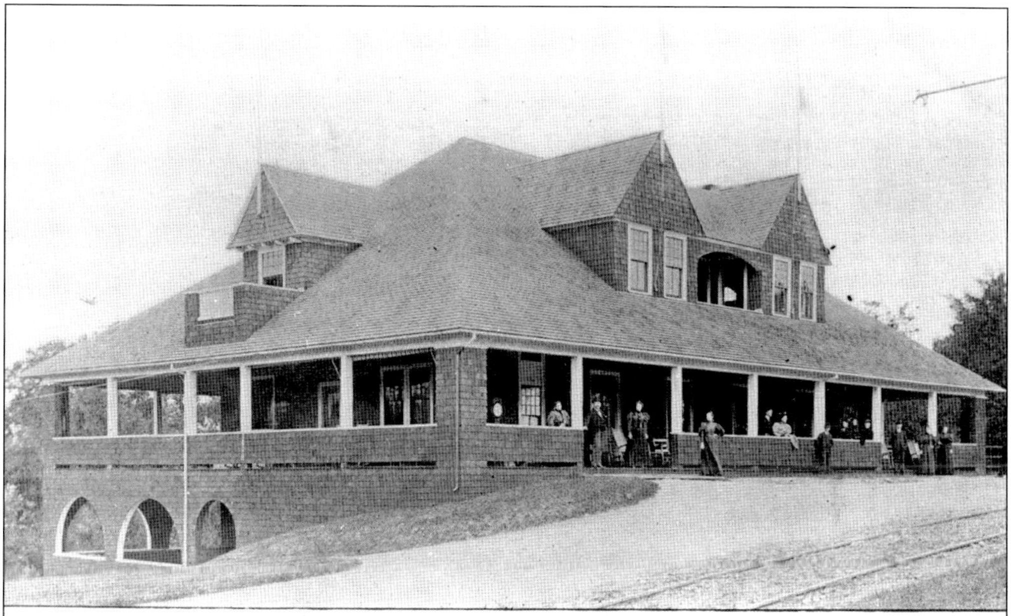

Casino and Restaurant, Riverton Park.

Like other parks established by trolley companies, Riverton had its casino with lounges and a dining room. This earlier version was designed by John Calvin Stevens, although the building would be enlarged within a few years by another firm.

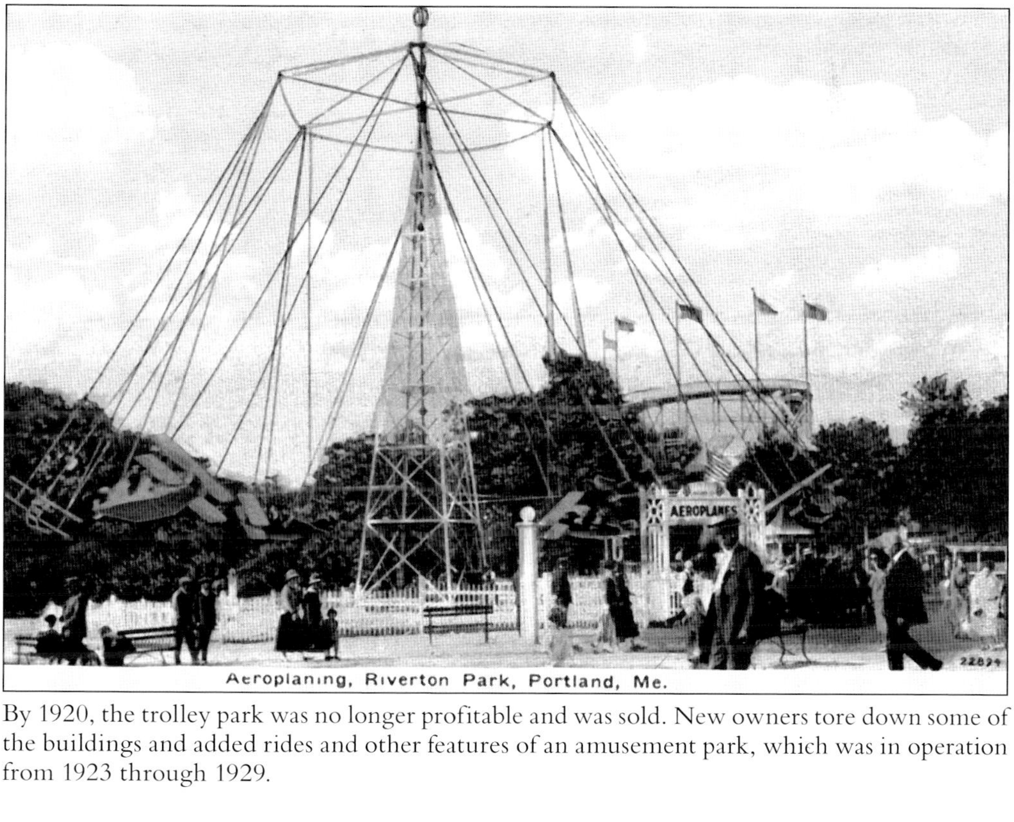


Aeroplaning, Riverton Park, Portland, Me.

By 1920, the trolley park was no longer profitable and was sold. New owners tore down some of the buildings and added rides and other features of an amusement park, which was in operation from 1923 through 1929.

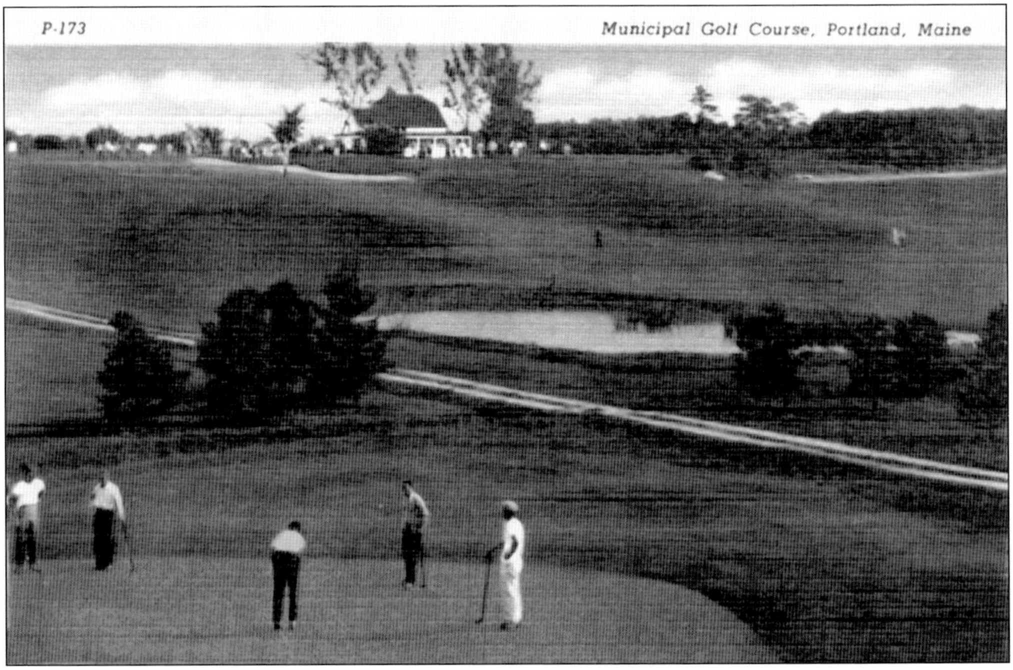


The city purchased a farm located to the north of Riverton, to be developed as a municipal golf facility known as Riverside Golf Course. It opened in 1932, with just nine holes, and was popular enough to be doubled in size four years later.

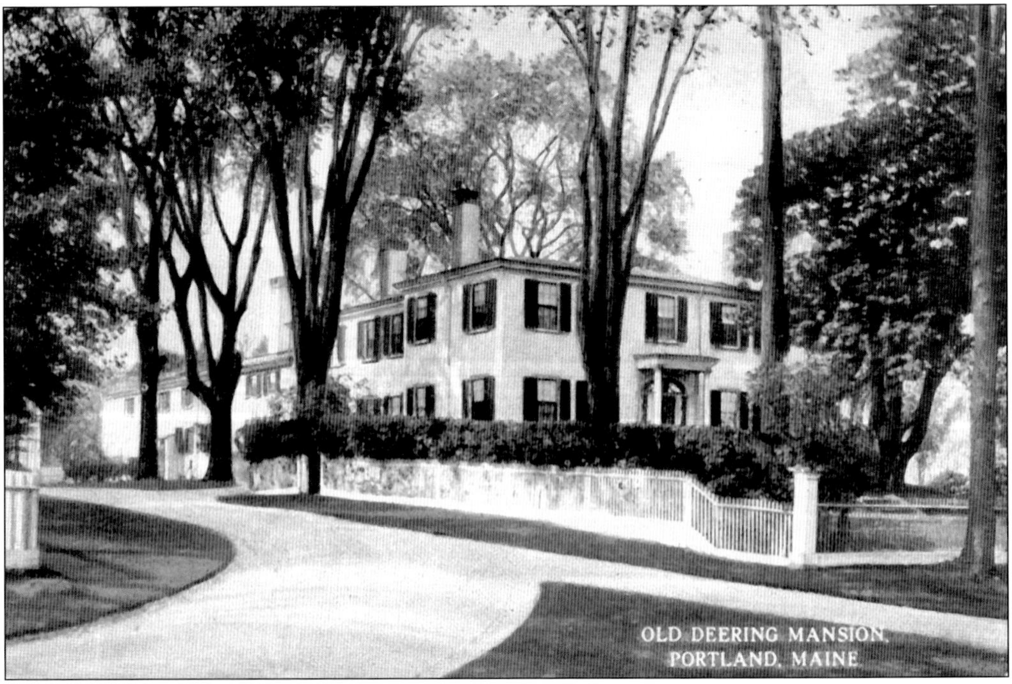


The area north of Deering Oaks combined industry with residences. The old Deering Mansion, home of the family who gave the park to the city, had been built in 1804 and stood until the 1950s. The land was then added to the campus of Portland Junior College.

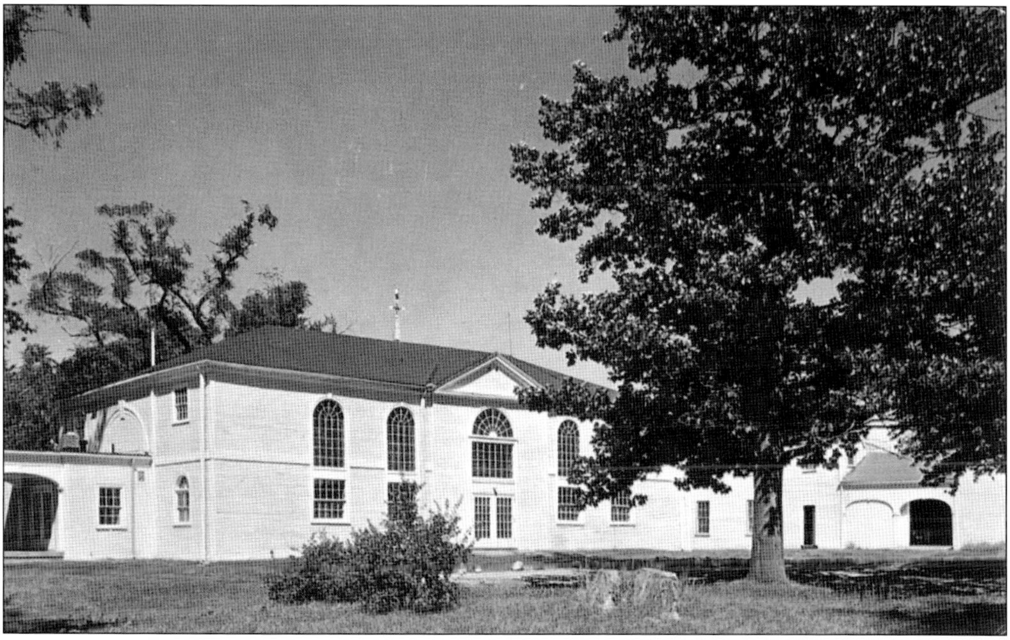

In 1946, Portland Junior College purchased part of the Deering property, including the 1805 barn designed by Alexander Parris, shown here after its conversion into a gymnasium and student center. In 1969, after the junior college had become a branch of the University of Maine, the building was razed. The campus is now a part of the University of Southern Maine.

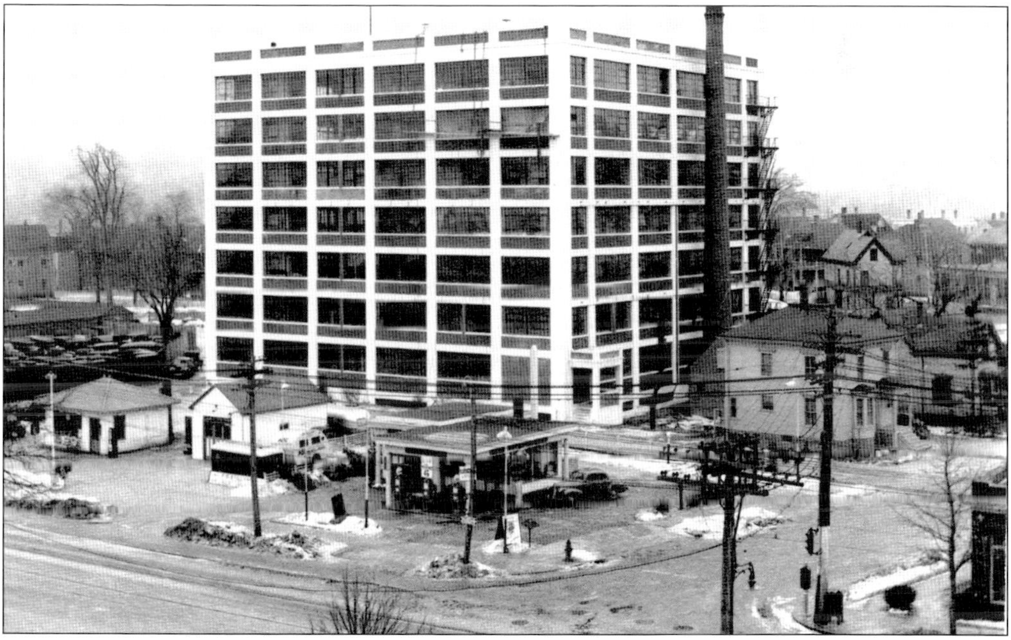

The Huston Biscuit Company, the "Baker of Better Biscuits since 1869," had a new bakery, designed by Webster and Libby, built near the Deering property in 1919–1920. After being used by the National Biscuit Company and still later serving as a warehouse, the building was remodeled to become, beginning in 1993, one of the libraries of the University of Southern Maine.

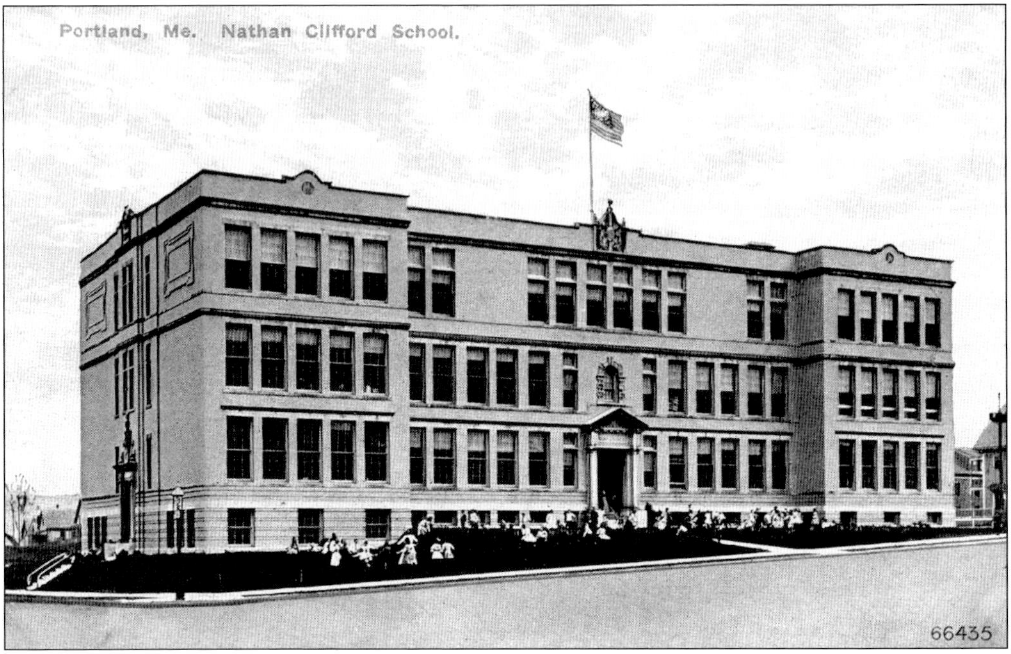


About a block west of the campus stands Clifford Elementary School, built in 1906 and named for Judge Nathan Clifford, of Portland, who served on the U.S. Supreme Court from 1858 to 1881. The architects were John Calvin Stevens and John Howard Stevens.

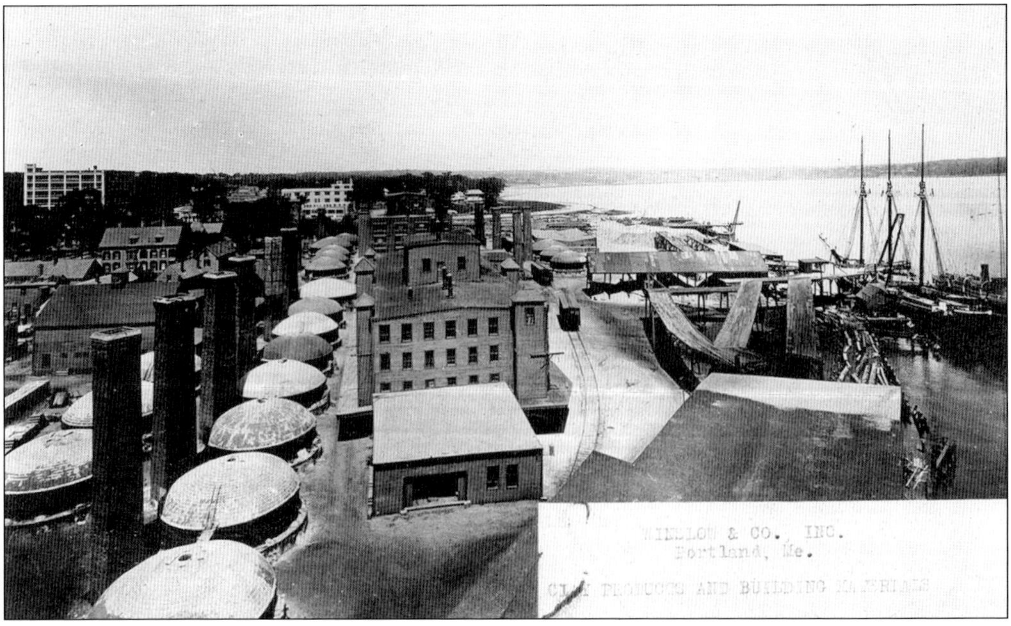


The firm of Winslow and Company was begun by John T. Winslow in 1846 to produce stoneware crocks and jars. It also made ornamental urns before turning, in 1870, to tile pipes, flues, and so on. The domed features are kilns. Note that the firm was located where it could ship by rail or by water. The site is now a small shopping mall.

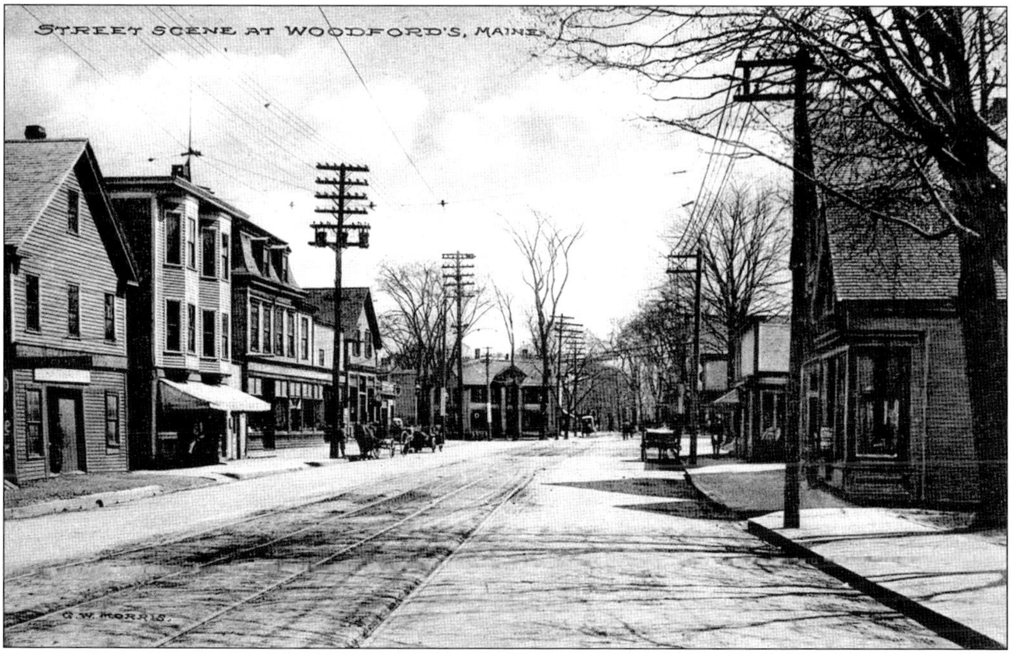


An early view of the Woodfords Corner area shows the house that once stood on the triangular plot of land where Deering Avenue joins Forest Avenue. Even in the 1890s, the area was clearly becoming a commercial center, but only the farther gabled building on the left is recognizable today.

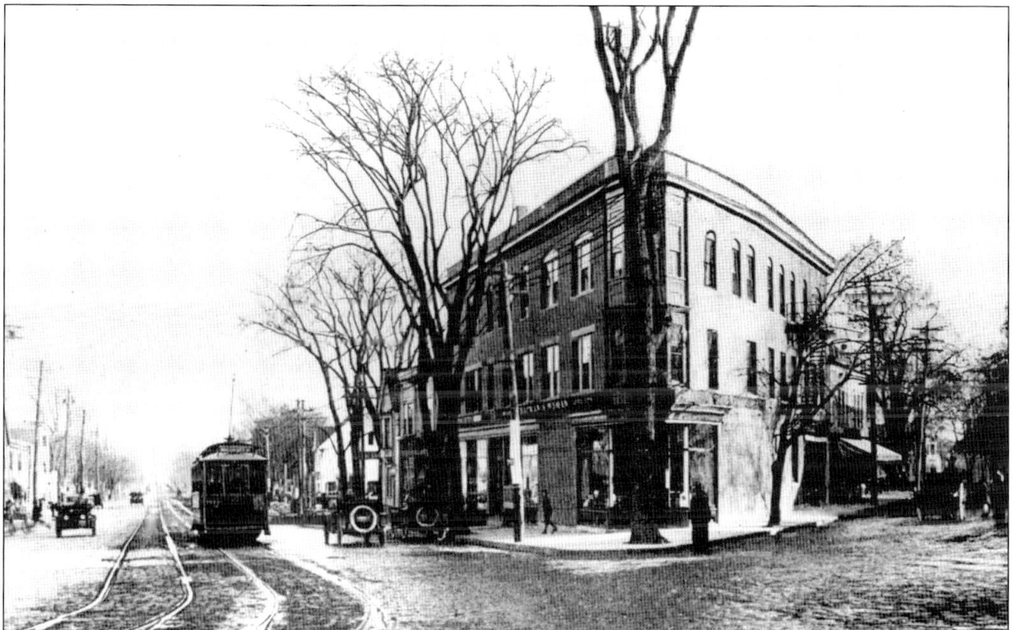

The Chapman Building was built on the wedge-shaped lot about 1922, giving the crossroads a few more small stores, as well as office space for individuals like dentists, realtors, and music teachers, all of whom were represented there a few years later. The trolley is on Forest Avenue, running along what had been the earliest horsecar line to be electrified.

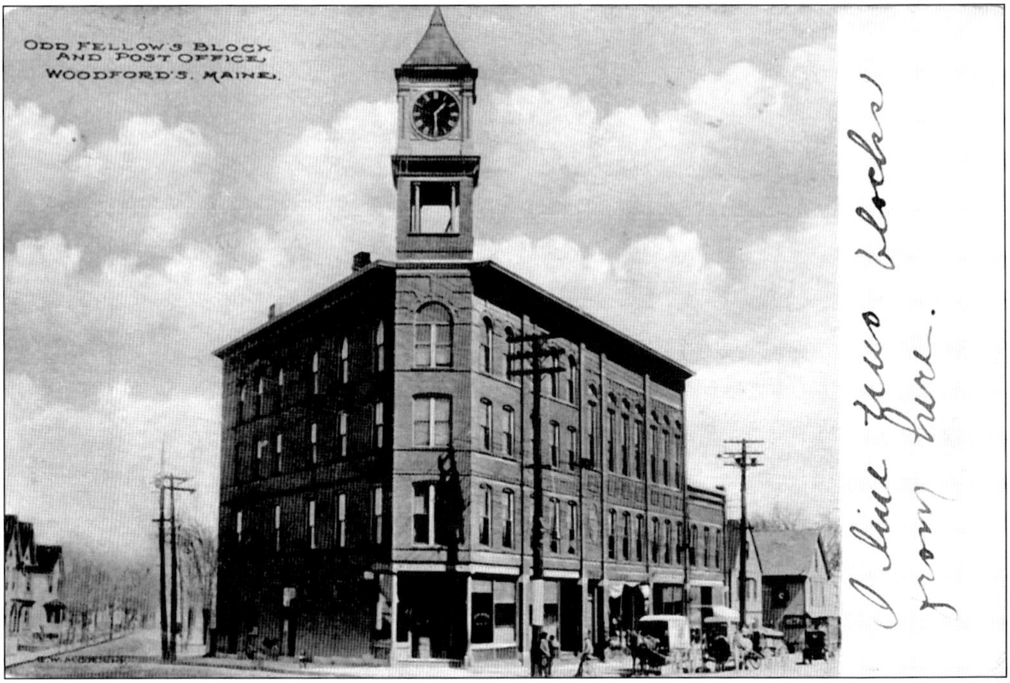


Across Forest Avenue, at the corner of Woodfords Street, the Independent Order of Odd Fellows erected a brick block in 1897. The meeting hall takes up the third and fourth floors on the far end, while offices fill other space, and various shops have been located at street level. Francis H. Fassett and Edward F. Fassett were the architects of this Deering landmark.

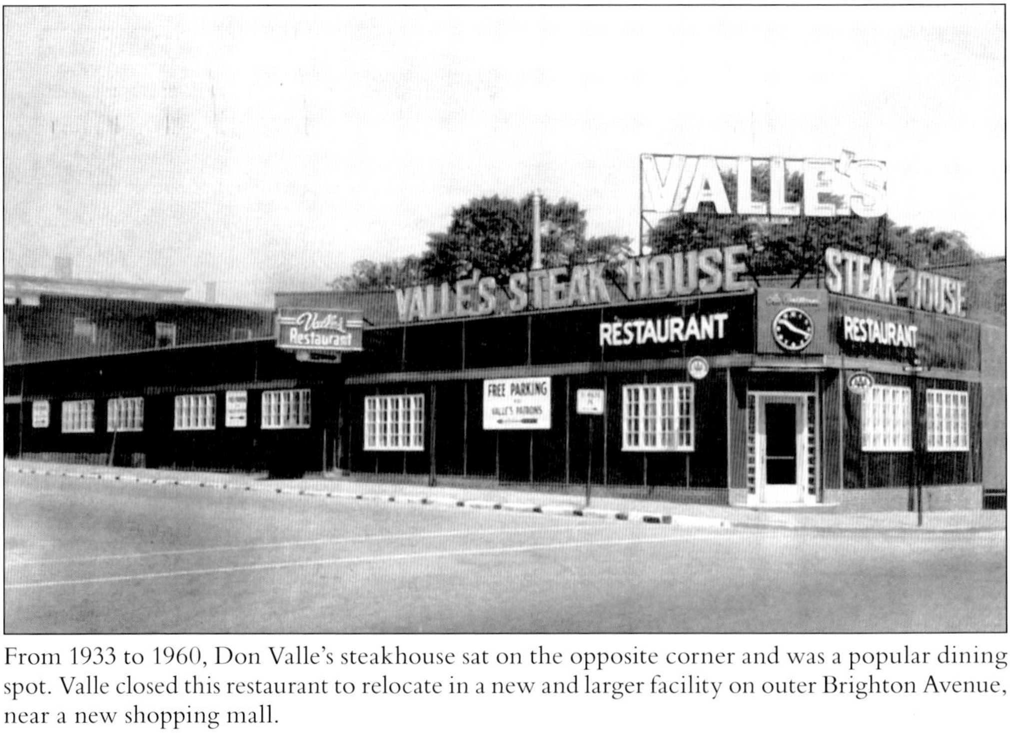


From 1933 to 1960, Don Valle's steakhouse sat on the opposite corner and was a popular dining spot. Valle closed this restaurant to relocate in a new and larger facility on outer Brighton Avenue, near a new shopping mall.

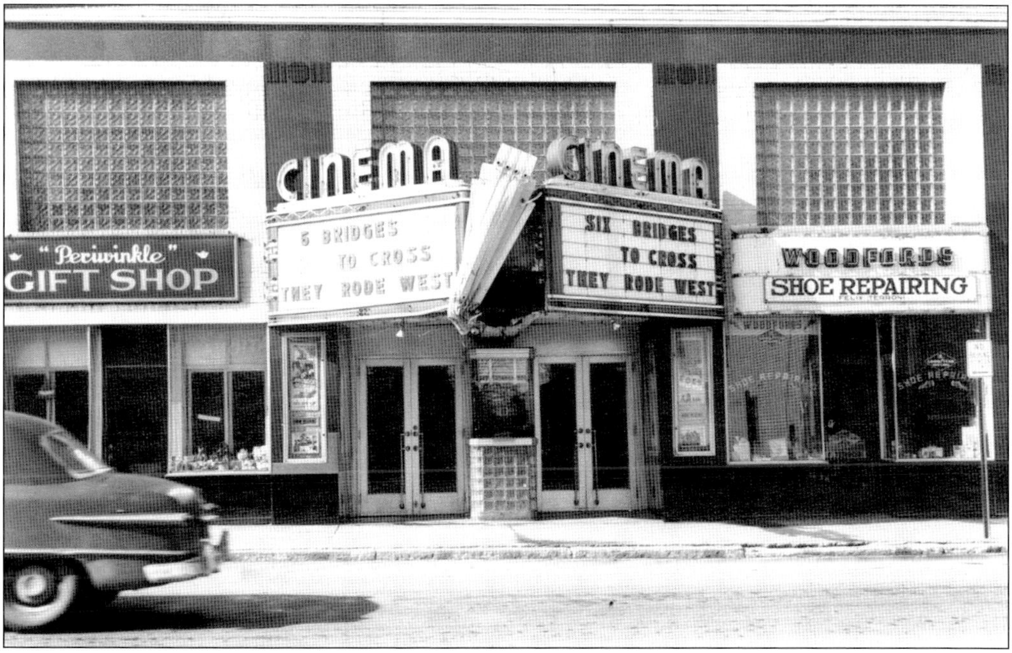


For decades after its 1941 opening, the small Cinema Theater nearby offered feature films, shown a little later than in downtown theaters. Nevertheless, the lower prices made many people willing to wait.

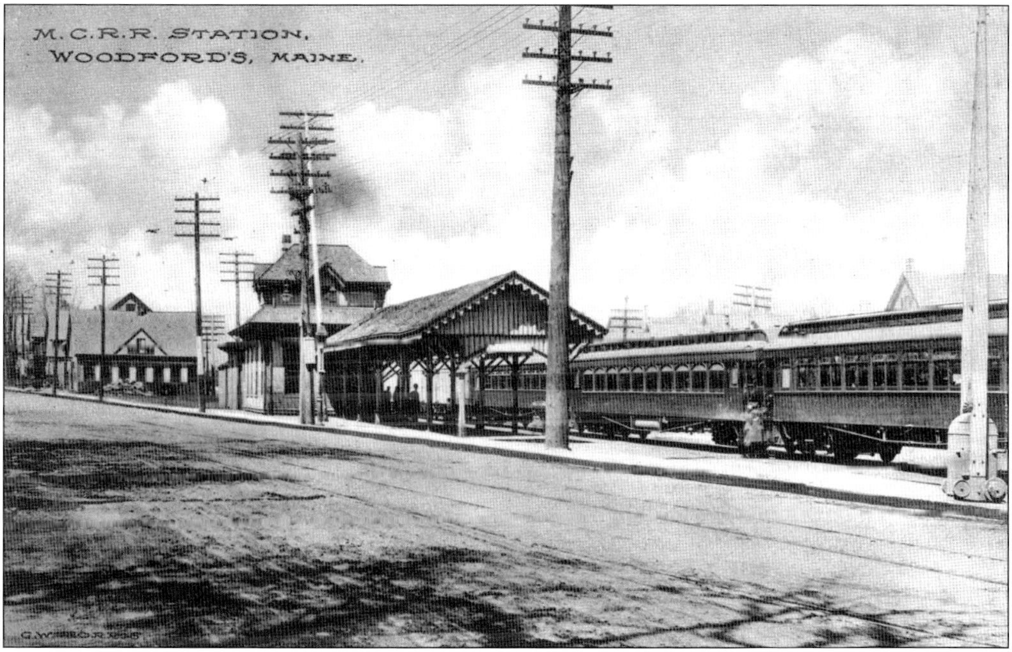


Woodfords Corner had its own railroad station, located on the Maine Central Railroad's line, at a spot where the train tracks ran close to Forest Avenue. Trolley tracks indicate that the "electrics" also traveled there. (They turned up Pleasant Street, across from the station.) Another early rail station, serving the Portland and Rochester line, was at Morrill's Corner, a mile to the north.

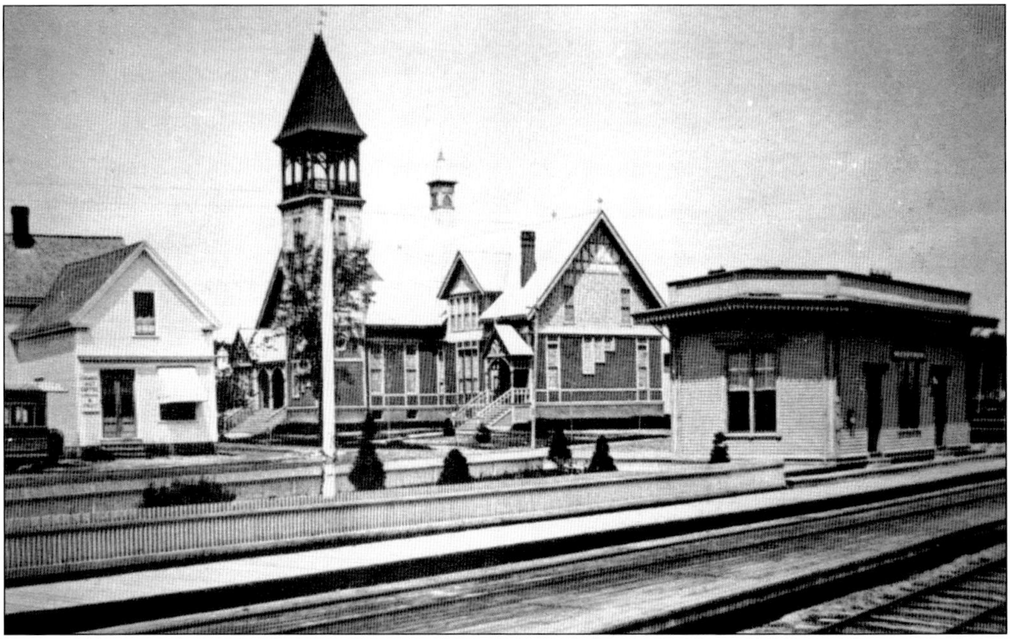

Across Forest Avenue was the attractive Stick-style Clark Memorial Church (Methodist, built in 1881–1882), named for Dr. Eliphalet Clark, who had been active with Wesleyan affairs as well as in medicine and in local transportation companies. The station is gone, but the church remains, although it lost much of its charm after being painted all white.

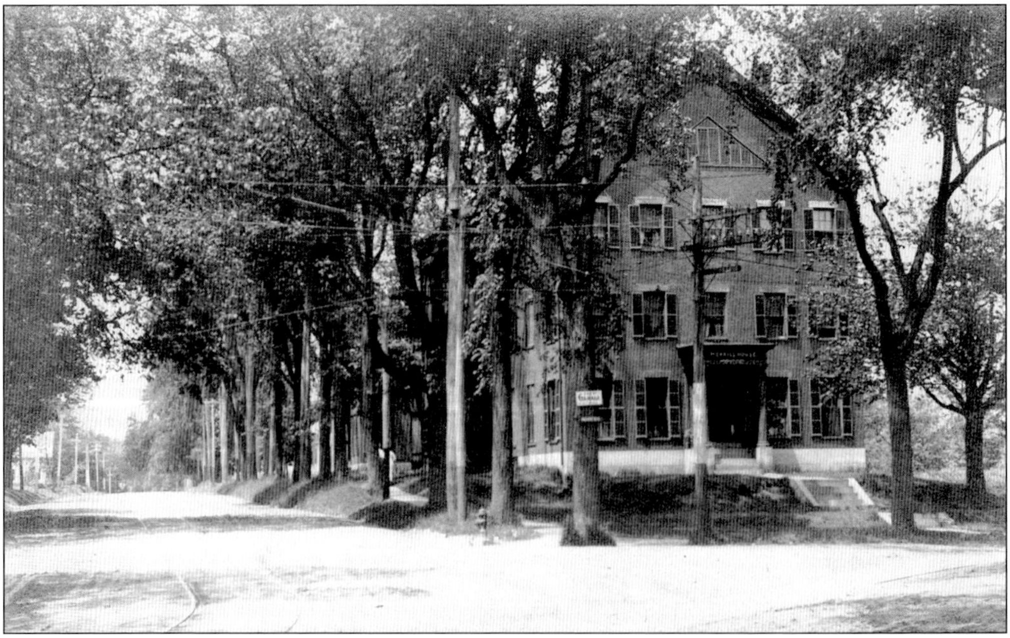

The 32-room Morrill House, at the junction of Forest and Allen Avenues, was seven or eight decades old when photographed around 1912. Morrills had earlier manufactured machinery for shoe binding and linings on the property. (A tannery was nearby.) A daughter, Mary, went as a missionary to China and became a victim of the Boxer Rebellion.

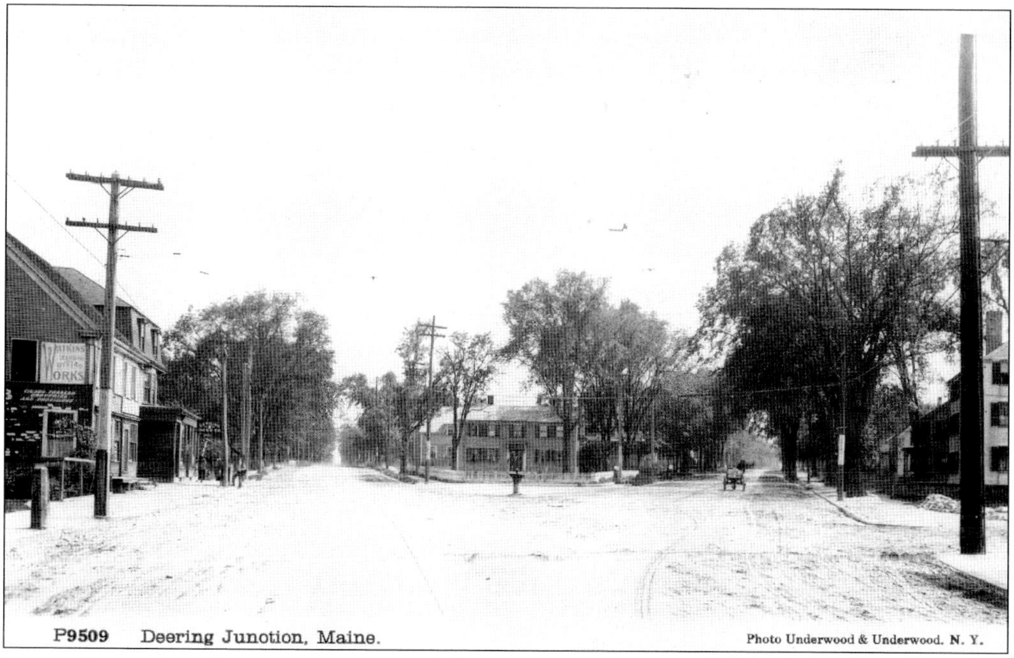


Just to the south, where Forest Avenue (left) was joined by Stevens Avenue, were more homes and small businesses. The wagon marks the approximate northern end of the earlier horsecar line. The photographer stood approximately where the Portland and Rochester Railroad crossed the street.

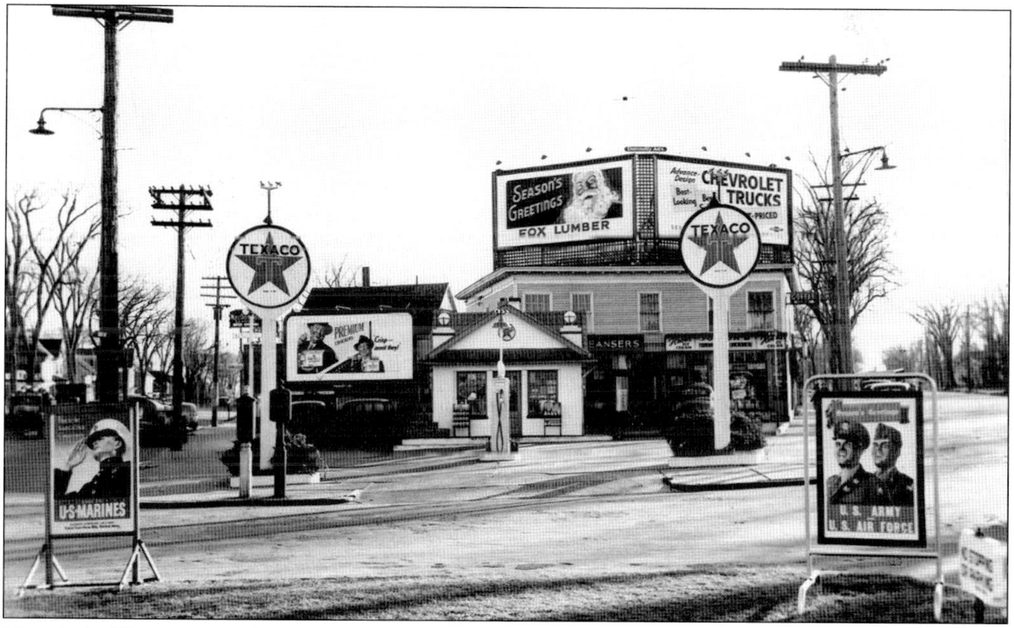


Nearly half a century later, much had changed, as homes had been razed to make way for more businesses, including the usual corner gas station. Both it and the store behind have since been replaced.

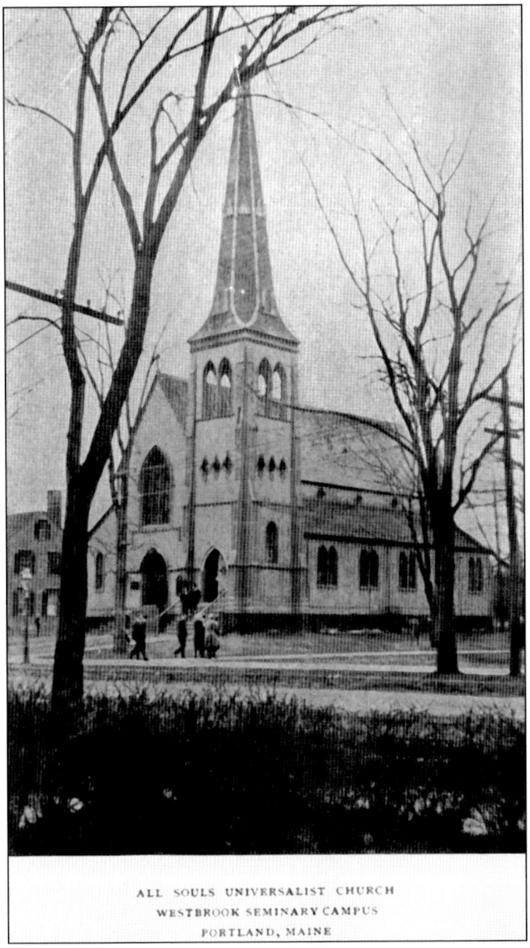


Stevens Avenue holds a variety of educational institutions. The earliest was Westbrook Seminary, begun as a coeducational academy in 1831, when the area was a part of the town of Westbrook, under the auspices of the Universalist Church. This 1867 Francis H. Fassett–designed church building still sits on a corner of the campus and now serves as an auditorium.

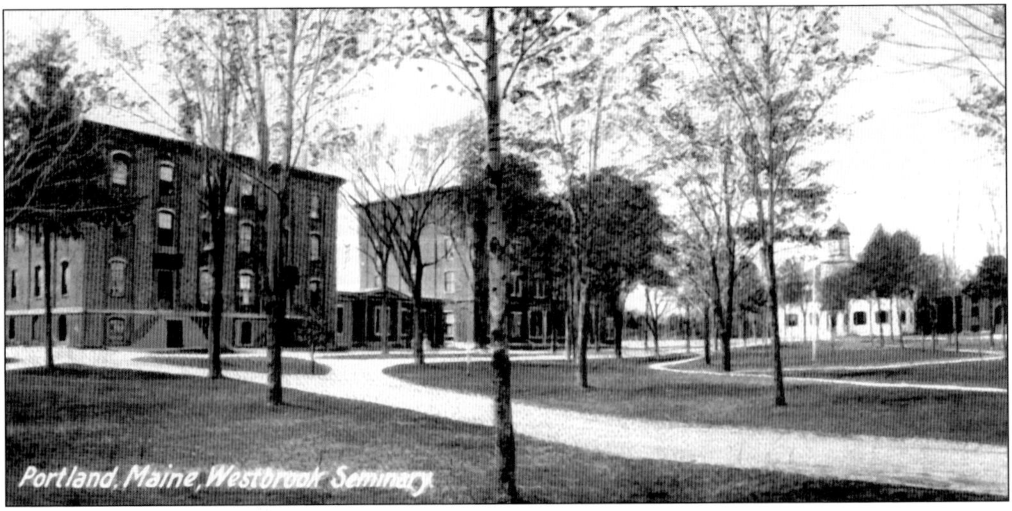


The seminary's first two dormitories, Goddard and Hersey Halls (erected in 1859 and 1869, respectively), were connected by a low dining room. Beyond are the first classroom building, now called Alumni Hall, and the old gymnasium.

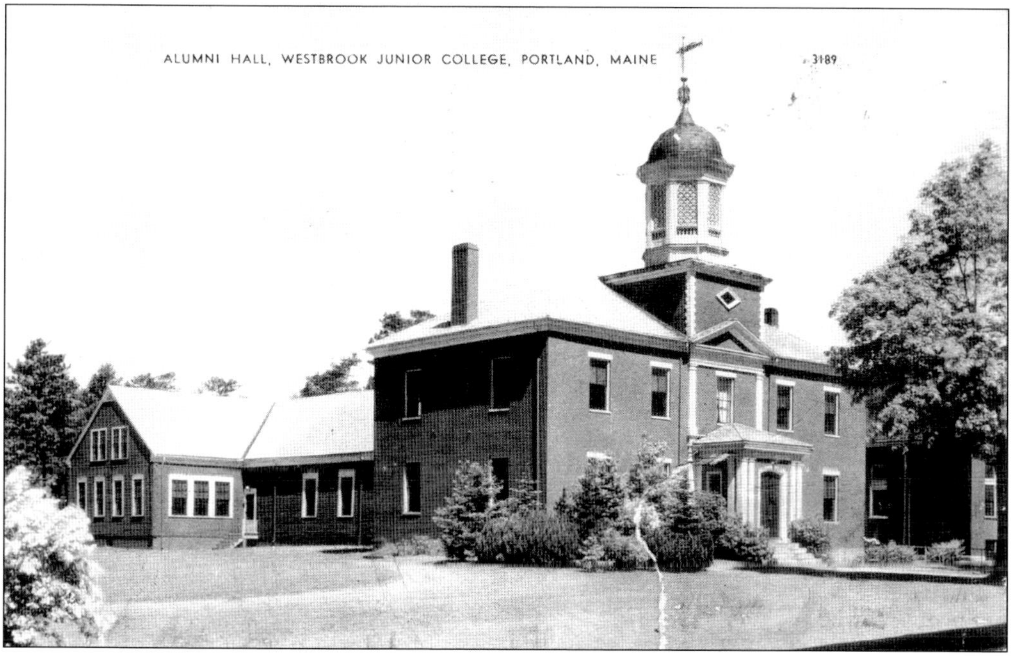


Alumni Hall was built in 1834 and adorned by what had been the tower of Portland's market house, removed when that structure was remodeled into a city hall in 1832. In 1931, the school, all-female since 1925, became Westbrook Junior College. The classrooms added to the rear have been replaced, but the main building is still in use.

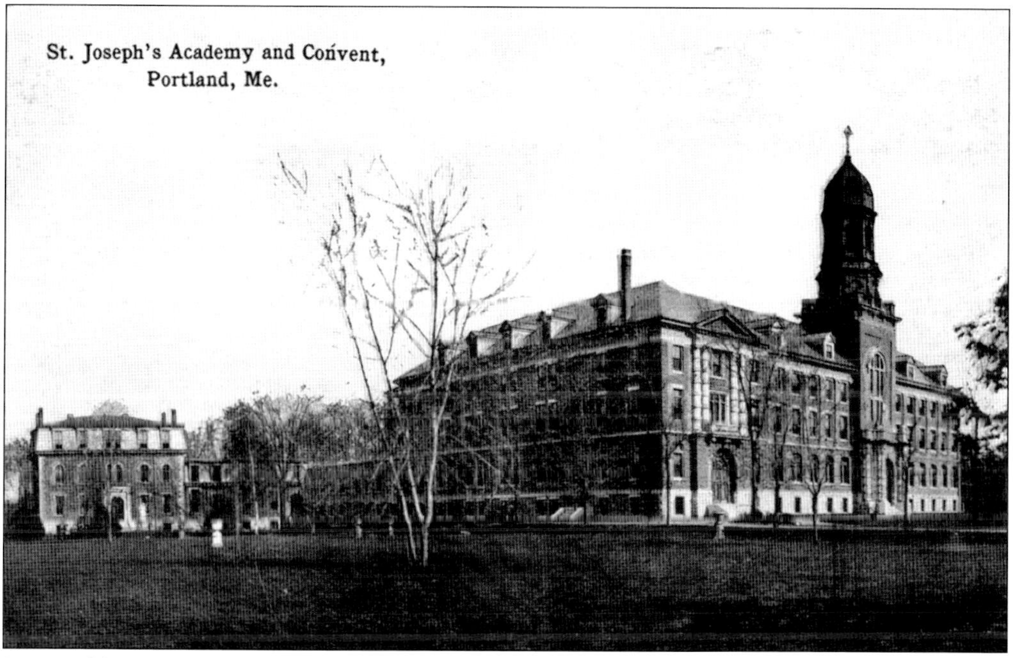


St. Joseph's Academy for girls, a few blocks away, was taught by the Sisters of Mercy. All had moved from the downtown sector to Stevens Avenue, where in 1915 they also established St. Joseph's College for young women. Catherine McAuley High School replaced the academy and now occupies the open area in the foreground of this picture. The college has relocated.

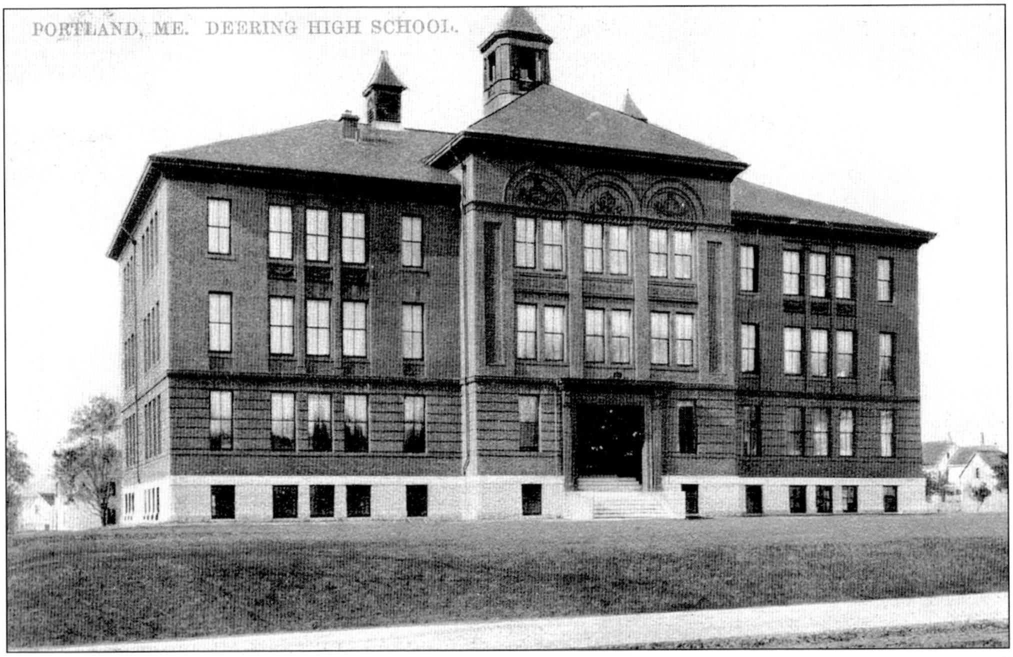


Deering High School originally stood less than half a mile to the south. Erected in 1899 and enlarged in 1913, it was soon too small again—an indication of the area's rapid growth. When the high school students moved to a new building in 1924, the older structure became Lincoln Junior High School.

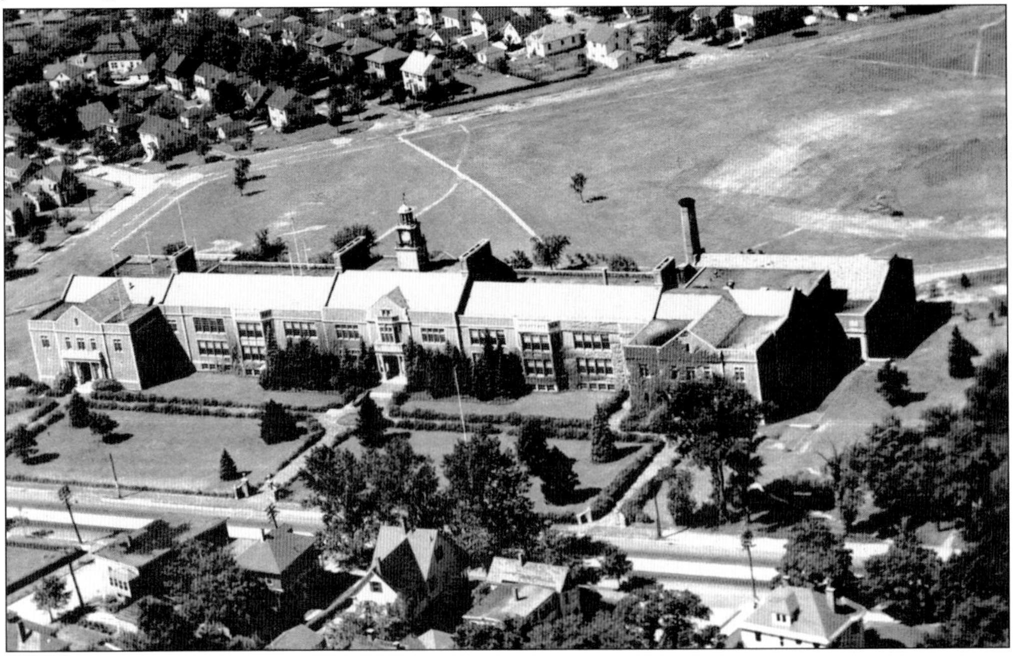

The new Deering High School, also on Stevens Avenue, was designed by Portland native John P. Thomas, who turned to English Tudor buildings for inspiration. Its sprawling character can be seen in this aerial view, which also shows residential areas developed nearby and the open reaches of Presumpscot Park behind the building.

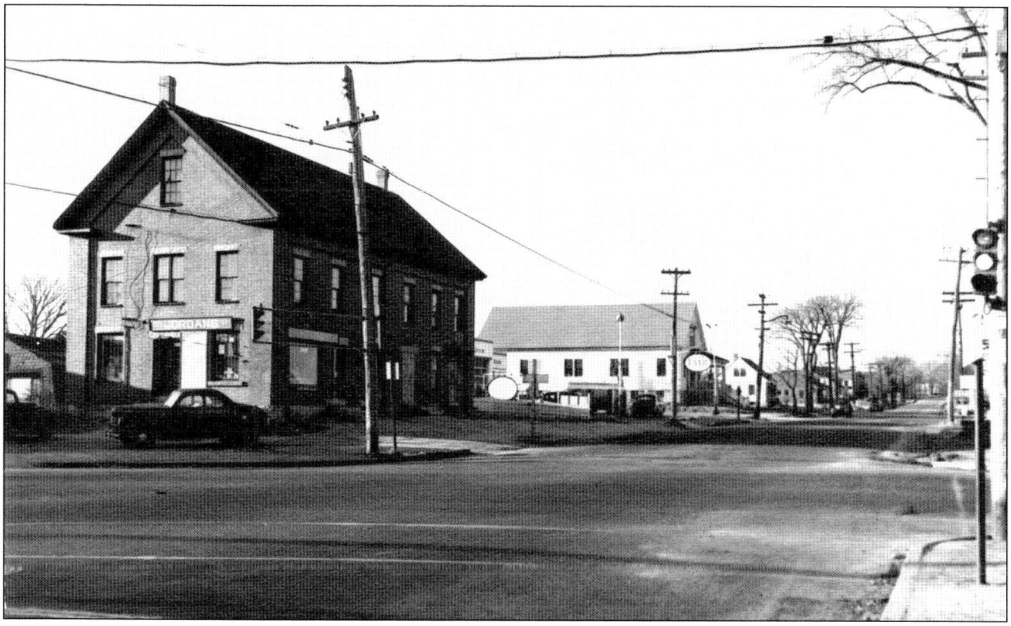

Allen's Corner has changed considerably in recent decades. The brick corner store is long gone, although the North Deering Grange Hall, seen beyond it, is still in use. Its location, now across the Gray Road from a large shopping mall and surrounded by suburban housing, belies the Grange's purpose, to serve farmers, although the area was once rural.

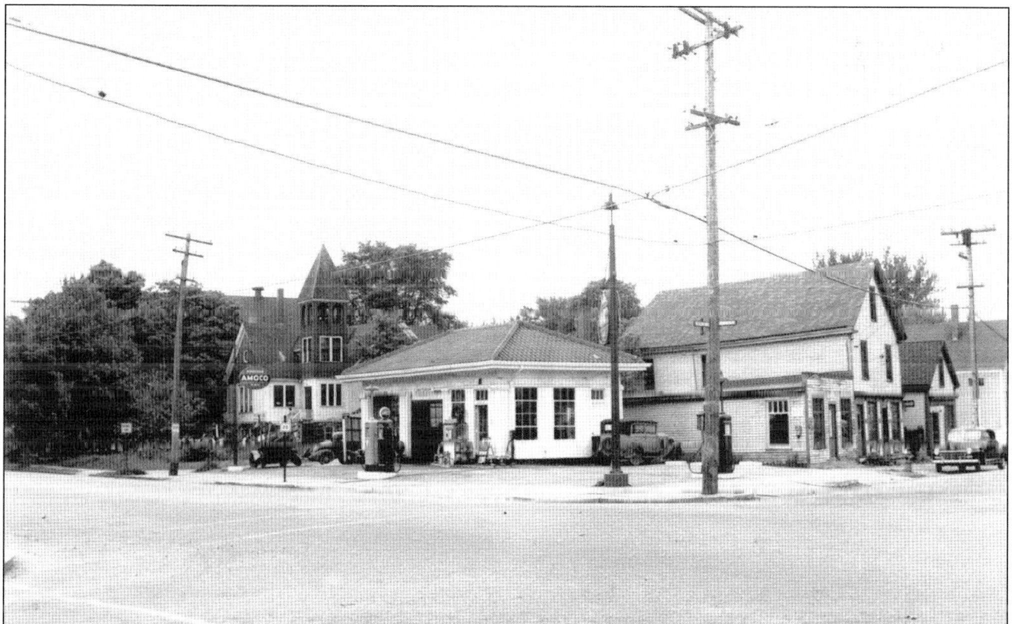


Another view of Allen's Corner, looking south on Washington Avenue at about the same time, also includes buildings no longer there. Only the North Deering Congregational Church remains, and it has been greatly enlarged.

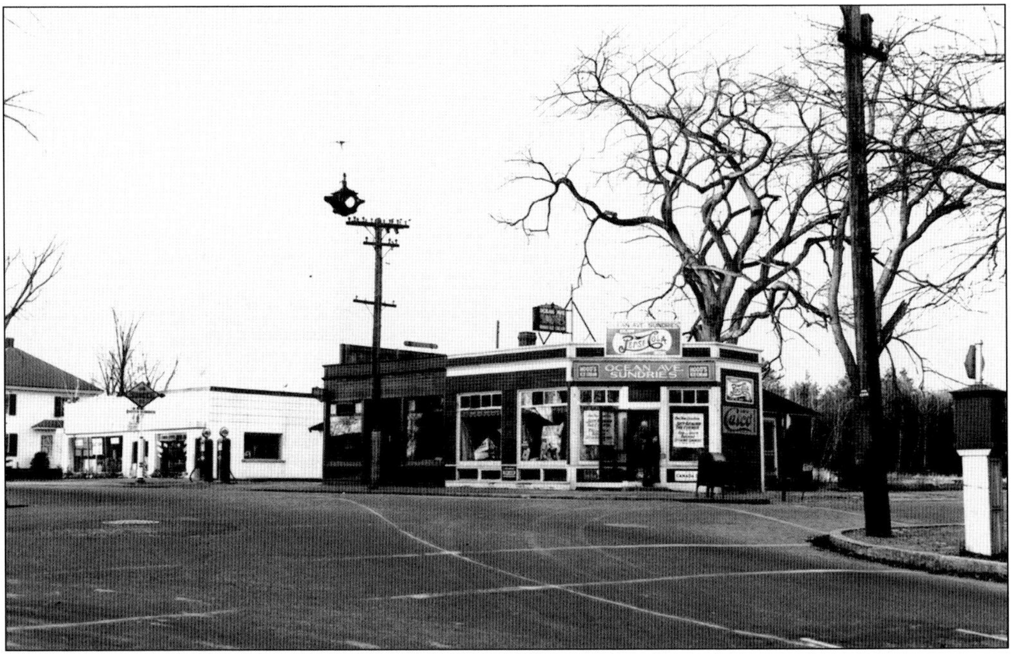


Farther south on Washington Avenue, where it crosses Ocean Avenue, is Lunt's Corner, named for the family who once occupied the location shown. The corner store and the small gas station have given way to a larger filling station/convenience store, but the fire alarm box on the right is still in place.

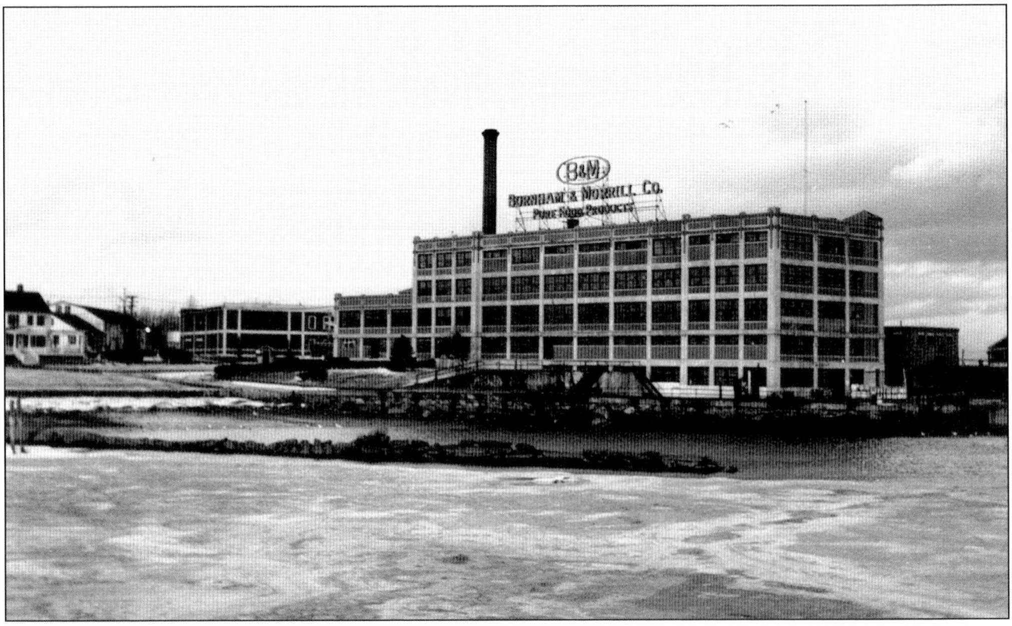


Since 1915, a major landmark of East Deering has been the Burnham and Morrill cannery, where the air is frequently redolent from baking beans. George Burnham was an early entrant into the canned foods industry, starting in the 1860s with sardines. The firm was on Franklin Street before the new plant, designed by a later George Burnham, was erected near the entry to Back Cove.

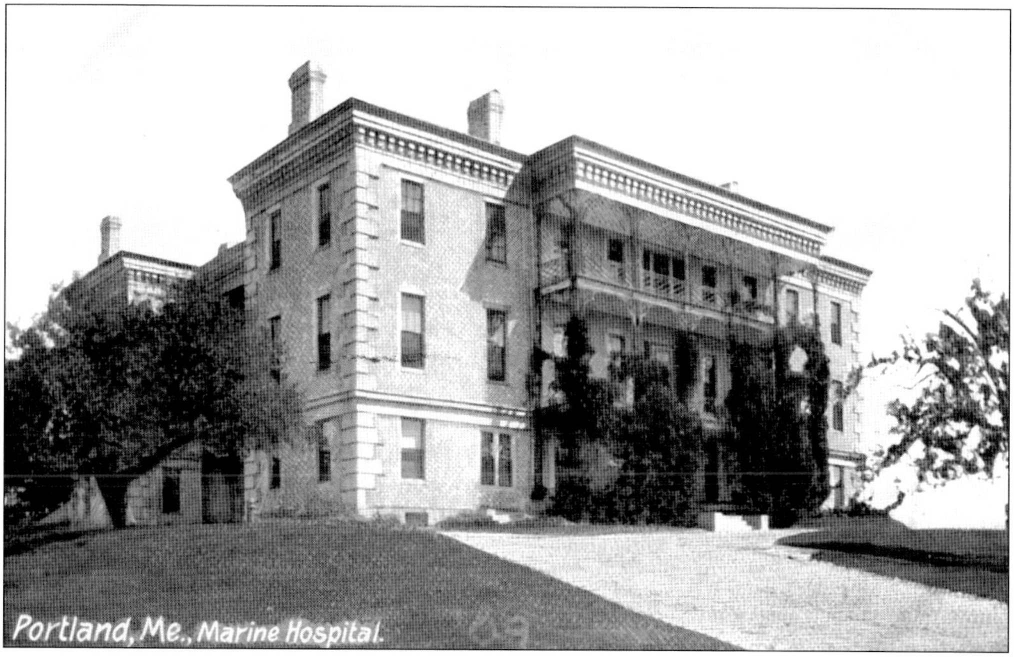


Also in East Deering, the attractive United States Marine Hospital, designed by Ammi Young, was built in 1859 on Martin's Point beside the mouth of the Presumpscot River. Set in extensive grounds, the facility provided care for ailing merchant sailors, both coastal and deepwater, until their numbers so declined that it was not needed. It now houses a modern health care facility.

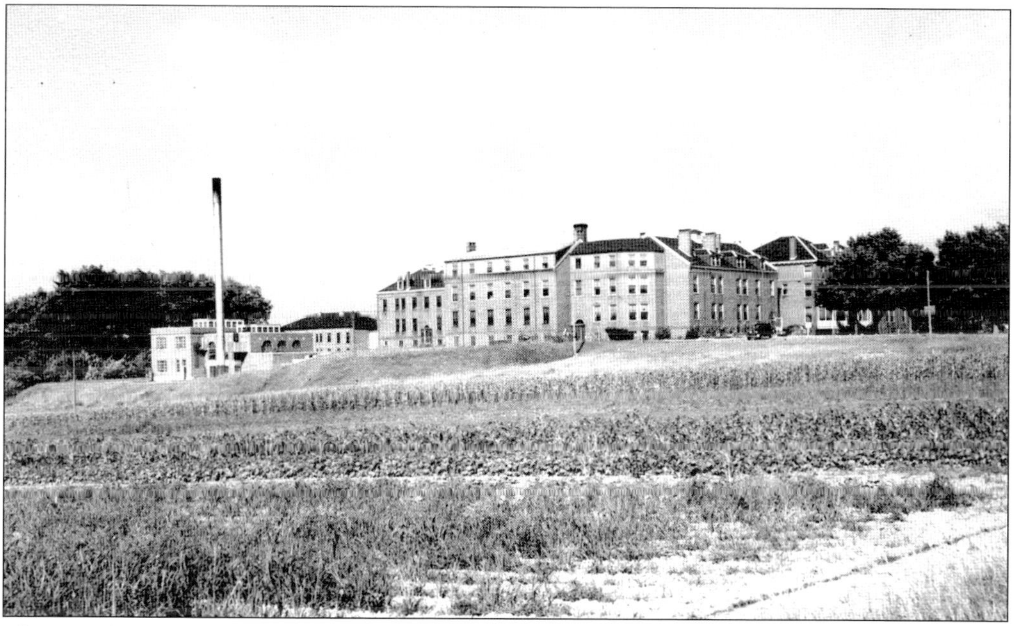

The city almshouse, designed by Francis H. Fassett and Edward F. Fassett and built in 1902–1904, became City Hospital by 1926, caring for those who could not afford private treatment. On the western outskirts of the city when built, the complex is now elderly housing, with a superhighway running through the field in the foreground and a shopping center across Brighton Avenue.